HOW eBay REALLY WORKS

HOW eBay REALLY WORKS

Brad & Debra Schepp

Sterling Publishing Co., Inc.
New York

Cover and interior design: Oxygen Design

Library of Congress Cataloging-in-Publication Data

Schepp, Brad.
How eBay really works / Brad & Debra Schepp.
p. cm.
Includes index.
ISBN-13: 978-1-4027-3769-5
ISBN-10: 1-4027-3769-6
1. eBay (Firm) 2. Internet auctions. 3. Selling—Computer network resources. 4. Internet marketing. I. Schepp, Debra. II. Title.

HF5478.S337 2006
381'.177—dc22

2006027384

10 9 8 7 6 5 4 3 2 1

Published by Sterling Publishing Co., Inc.
387 Park Avenue South, New York, NY 10016

Distributed in Canada by Sterling Publishing
c/o Canadian Manda Group, 165 Dufferin Street
Toronto, Ontario, Canada M6K 3H6

Manufactured in the United States of America

Sterling ISBN-13: 978-1-4027-3769-5
ISBN-10: 1-4027-3769-6

For information about custom editions, special sales, premium and corporate purchases, please contact Sterling Special Sales Department at 800-805-5489 or specialsales@sterlingpub.com.

To the staff of the Children's Department of the C. Burr Artz Public Library, for the joy you bring to children, for the way you care for each other, and for providing me with a place to be at home, even when I'm at work.

—Deb

To my mother, Arlene Lois Schepp, who has always encouraged me and made me laugh.

—Brad

CONTENTS

Part II: Selling

Acknowledgments

Nobody writes a book alone. The romantic notion of writing is to sit alone, typing out brilliance word by word, as you're hungry and cold in an attic somewhere. The reality is more than a little different. We never miss a meal. We definitely have climate control, and as for alone? Well, the cats who sit on the desks, laps, or backs of the chairs aren't much for conversation, but they make for great company. The only one who thinks anything we do is brilliant is the dog, and what does he know?

There is quite a long list of humans who deserve our thanks and have earned our eternal gratitude and respect. Let's start with the agent who first thought this was a good idea. Marilyn Allen is positive, patient, efficient, and right about most things. Thanks for everything, and we'll look forward to the next project. Meredith Peters Hale of Sterling Publishing has been a pleasure to work with, and we're very grateful for all her contributions to this project. Diana Drew was a wonderful copyeditor; detailed, precise, and so good at cleaning up our manuscript. She was kind but firm, the perfect combination for a copyeditor. The fact that this book looks so good is due to Oxygen Design, and we appreciate every bit of the work they did.

The eBay PowerSellers who helped us deserve special thanks. They were available at the drop of an e-mail. No matter how many times we asked for help, they never told us to go away and stop bothering them, even if they wanted to. We're going to introduce you to them by name and eBay member ID so, if you're curious, you can take a look at their businesses for yourself to see what successful sellers do to become successful: Kevin Boyd, preferreddiscounts; Nick Boyd, tradernick; Bob Buchanan and Greg Scheuer, avforsale; Christina Carr, wiccanwell; Marcia Cooper and Harvey Levine, generalent; Sarah Davis, fashionphile; Paul Fletcher and Gary Heath, dealtree-auctions; Drew Friedman, whitemountaintrading; Stephen Ganus, eagleauctionsUSA; Adam Hersh, adamhershauctions; Stephanie Inge, stephintexas; Michael Kolman, parrothead88; Phil Leahy, entertainmenthouse; Mike Martyka, solidcolornecties; Jennifer Riojas Mogan, eauctiongurus; Andy and Deb Mowery, debnroo; Carlos Paris, elvibora; Randall Pinson, rocket-auctions; Gary Richardson, harleyglasses; Jody Rogers and Asad Bangash, beachcombers!; Robert Sachs, rosachs; Hendrik Sharples, hendrik; Jim and Kelli Shaw, dream-adventures; Marguerite Swope, mhswope; John Wade, john_wade; Jack Walters, bids4u-2; David and Debbie Yaskulka, blueberryboutique; and Catherine Yeats, 4-a-little-lady.

Those who follow may not be PowerSellers, but they were still quite helpful to us as we researched and wrote this book. We'd like to thank David Frey and Dave Popowich of Terapeak; Rachel Gelhaus, eBay lover, buyer, and seller; Edward Klink and Stephen Klink, authors of *Dawn of the eBay Deadbeats;* Debbie Levitt of As Was Incorporated; and Sharon Tendler, granddaughter of the great boxer, Lew Tendler. Ina Steiner of AuctionBytes has been a devoted friend and supporter through all our eBay work. She, along with her husband David, do such great work that we are honored that she considers us worthy of her help.

The staff of the Children's Department of the C. Burr Artz Public Library, in Frederick, Maryland, helped see Deb through this project. They are creative, supportive, inventive, and so dedicated to the children of our community that it is a privilege to be counted among them. So, a special thanks goes out to them for delighting children every day, and Deb, too.

Dr. Lisa Houck and Tim McCallum of the Middletown Sport and Spine Clinic deserve a medal. They straightened Deb's back and listened to lots of whining over the course of our association. Never once did they lose their patience or good humor, even though we wouldn't have blamed them one bit if they did.

Finally, thanks to our family, both here at home and scattered around the globe. We hope you missed us as much as we've missed you. If not, please let on as if you did, so as not to further dent our self-esteem. We've had to make do with phone calls, when visits would have been so much better. We've started so many conversations about the progress of this book. We've been more than just a little distracted. Believe us when we say, we do think you also have lives. It's not just all about us!

Brad and Debra Schepp

www.bradanddeb.com

Introduction

WITH SCORES OF EBAY BOOKS already published, does the world really need another beginner's guide? Who are we to think we could provide something so new and different that it would be worth chopping down the trees needed to produce it? As we weighed the opportunity to write this book, we looked over many of the books "out there." We thought about it for a good, long time. We talked about it endlessly. Then we came to a fascinating realization.

If our goal were to produce another step-by-step guide to using eBay, we'd rather leave the trees standing. There are several fine primers that do a perfectly adequate job of teaching newcomers how to navigate eBay. Plus, eBay itself has worked hard over the years to make its site ever more manageable and easy to use. So if we were going to write a new eBay guide for beginners, we'd have to find a compelling reason to do so. We wouldn't be satisfied just telling people which links to click and which screens to read. And that's when our kids turned on the lights.

Within the last several years, we taught our kids Stephanie and Ethan how to drive. Now today's cars make driving fairly simple. Transmissions are automatic. Lights can be set to turn on when they should. Power steering and power brakes are the norm. Global Positioning Systems can even tell you which road to take and which turn to make, so you never have to get lost again. Yes, driving is easy. But, driving well is a challenge. As we prepared to let our kids go, we realized that teaching them to drive and teaching them to drive well were two very different things.

So we thought about creating a book that wouldn't just teach our readers how to navigate and enjoy eBay, but that would actually teach them how to do those things *skillfully*. We decided that if we could write a book that featured insider tips and strategies from those who have stood in our readers' shoes, we'd be onto something. And if we could provide information that was truly helpful, regardless of whether it towed the eBay line, then we'd really have something different and valuable to share. The book you hold in your hands is the result of that decision.

As you work through this book, you'll learn, for example, that the extra features eBay encourages you to purchase to make your listings stand out—from bold text to highlighting to special placement—are not all equal. Some may help, but many will do nothing more than cost you money. We'll help you to see which ones are which. We'll help you decide when you shouldn't allow certain buyers to bid on the items you're trying to sell. We'll even tell you when eBay isn't your best shopping destination. Certain purchases really are better made in other places.

What we can offer you is the voice of experience, as eBay experts and professional communicators. We've bought and sold on eBay ourselves since 1999, given many seminars on eBay selling, and have even sold things for others. We've also written books and articles for advanced eBay members, interviewing hundreds of successful buyers and sellers in the process. Your intellect, together with our experience, will make learning how eBay really works simple and enjoyable. As you read through this book, you'll find that we have a great deal of respect for you, our reader. We begin with the premise that you're smart. We don't for a minute think of you as a "dummy." You may not be educated or experienced in the ways of eBay, but you are curious about how to use the site, and, therefore, we're confident that you can become a savvy eBay buyer and seller. This smart person's guide to using eBay is for you.

The chapters ahead outline some basics, such as how to get started as a buyer and a seller. More than that, however, you'll find advice about which choices to make and how you can confidently and wisely buy and sell on eBay, with the experience of old pros guiding you as you go. We've been part of this community for most of the past decade. Plus, we've talked with hundreds of people who not only love eBay as a forum for shopping, but who also earn their livings there by selling.

That's why this book has two sections. You'll start by learning techniques for smart buying, and then you'll move on to discover how best to sell. (While almost everyone starts out by buying stuff on eBay, we think most people who like shopping will want to try selling, too.) Because we respect your abilities, we've included a Quick Start Guide for each section of the book. These brief outlines tell you just what you need to do if you want to jump in and start buying or selling without too much fanfare. We understand your enthusiasm, and we'll be waiting right here for you if you get there and decide you need some help.

For those of you who want to start more slowly, join us as we take you through every aspect of using eBay. You'll find explanations, insider advice, and anecdotes throughout the book that cover what you need to know and show you how to avoid some common beginners' mistakes. Each chapter ends with a story about My Best eBay Buy or My Best eBay Sale, because everyone who has used eBay for any length of time has some wonderful stories to share, and who doesn't love a good story? We leave you with two appendices: One gives you a glimpse into selling vehicles on eBay; the other includes a list of some of our favorite resources. Finally, the glossary provides a handy, quick reference guide to eBay terms you'll need to know.

So, settle back and get yourself ready for a wild ride. eBay is fun, exciting, challenging, and ever changing. We're delighted you've decided to join us as we explore this corner of the galaxy. We suspect that, once you learn your way around, you're going to love it here!

Brad and Debra Schepp

www.bradanddeb.com

Part I

BUYING

Quick Start Guide—

eBay Buying in 5 Steps

Ready to join in the fun and buy something on eBay? We understand. Just follow these steps, but remember to start with an inexpensive item until you get your sea legs. You'll learn more about checking out sellers and items in the chapters that follow, but for now stick with sellers who have as close to a 100 percent positive feedback rating as possible.

1. Register!

- Click the Register hyperlink on eBay's homepage at www.eBay.com.
- Enter your personal information in the form.
- Choose an eBay user ID and password.
- Read and accept eBay's User Agreement and Privacy Policy.

2. Explore!

- Click the BUY button at the top of any page.
- Enter some keywords for your item in the search box, OR
- Browse through eBay's categories.
- Shop 'til you've found something you'd like to buy.
- Be sure to read the entire item description carefully.
- If you're not sure about something, ask the seller a question.

3. Bid!

- Auction? Enter the amount you're willing to pay for the item.
- Buy It Now (BIN) item? Click the Buy It Now Button.
- Confirm in the next step.
- Wait for the auction to end to pay, or if BIN, continue on.

4. Pay!

- Find and follow the seller's payment instructions.
- Include any shipping and handling charges.
- Pay by check or money order (or you can sign up for PayPal*)
- Send payment to the address the seller or eBay e-mails to you.

5. Review Your Shipment and Leave Feedback

- Open your item carefully and save any packing slips.
- Inspect your item to ensure that everything is OK.
- Leave feedback for the seller by clicking on the link.
- If something went wrong with your transaction, see chapter 8.

*This service will allow you to pay sellers by credit card without revealing your credit card number. It's optional but highly recommended.

What's All This Fuss About eBay?

LET'S GO SHOPPING! Many of us hear those words, and our propellers start to spin. We grab our credit cards, put on our shopping shoes, and we're out the door. Some say it's baseball, but we think shopping is the Great American Pastime. It's a hobby all of us can enjoy, and we do. So is it any surprise that eBay is a worldwide phenomenon?

Not only does eBay let you shop any time of the day or night, but you can also look for anything that exists anywhere in the world. You can even browse for things you may remember from your childhood, but haven't seen in decades. Look long and hard enough, and they're bound to show up on eBay. Plus, once you fall in love with eBay shopping, you can become an eBay seller as well. Then you can actually turn stuff you no longer want into more cash for buying more things you do want. And you never have to struggle for a parking place or deal with crowded checkout lines again.

That's not to say eBay isn't a crowded marketplace. You'll find more than 200 million of your neighbors are already shopping there. But that's good news. It means eBay is easy and fun to use. Otherwise, so many people wouldn't be using it. It also means there's a thriving marketplace to explore. The more customers there are looking to buy on eBay, the more sellers there will be actively pushing their wares. That makes the shopping experience rewarding for everyone!

All this came from a simple idea. A simple, brilliant, remarkable idea. We've all heard the legend of Pierre Omidyar and his Pez dispensers. You know, the story of how this ordinary computer programmer created a Web site over one Labor Day weekend to make it possible for his girlfriend to trade and expand her Pez dispenser collection. But, although Pierre had a great idea and we wish it had been ours, the whole Pez dispenser tale is more legend than reality. The idea behind Pierre's Web site was to create a marketplace where people could come to swap things they didn't want for things they did. The philosophy behind Pierre's idea was that most people are basically honest and good. If you give them a place to do business, they'll do it in a friendly way, with integrity, that will be contagious. He devised a simple feedback system so that trading partners could rate each other as a method of self-policing the site, and the rest of the story is eBay history.

WHERE DOES THE MONEY GO?

According to a May 2006 presentation that eBay gave for stock analysts, in 2005 there were eight categories that accounted for at least $2 billion in sales each.

CATEGORY	BILLIONS OF DOLLARS SPENT
Motors	13.6
Consumer Electronics	3.5
Clothing & Accessories	3.4
Computers	3.1
Books/Music/Movies	2.6
Home and Garden	2.5
Collectibles	2.2
Sports	2.1

In fewer than ten years, Pierre's idea has grown into a gigantic, worldwide bazaar unlike anything that's ever existed. By the end of 2005, eBay had 180 million registered users. More than 1.9 billion items were listed that year, and the total value of all successfully closed listings was $44.3 billion. The sidebar above shows you where much of the money goes on eBay. You may be surprised how much the categories have expanded far beyond the realm of collectibles.

More Than Anything, eBay Is Fun!

To keep things in perspective, let's take a look at just a few of the fun and interesting things we've bought on eBay over the years. You see, we've been collectors of all sorts of odd things for more years than we'd like to admit to, and eBay gave us a whole new way to add to our collections. Figures 1-1 to 1-3 show several of our favorites. The Schepp's coconut label (Figure 1-3) is a real winner! The family who owned this company is probably no relation of ours, but the monkey is great, and it certainly starts some interesting conversations in our kitchen.

Figure 1-1: *An original lobby card from the 1960 movie* The Apartment.

Whether you go to eBay to search for fun and frivolous things or whether you're looking for car parts, computer equipment, razor blades, or baby clothes, the item you're seeking is out there. We're here to help you find it quickly, assess the seller who's offering it, and manage your purchase from start to finish. eBay is simple to use, but it's not so simple to use *well.* That's where we come in. We're here to show you how to be a smart eBay user from the very beginning. We want you to have fun and feel you got the best deal possible (these things tend to go together).Once you make eBay shopping a part of your life, you'll never look at a toaster, a computer, a pair of shoes, or any other "commodity" in the same way again. When you need to buy something—anything—your thoughts will turn first to eBay. A young woman we know needed to buy a wedding dress. She was putting her wedding together on a shoestring budget, and the dress really had her stumped. She finally chose three different dresses and bought them all on eBay. She then had plenty of time to weigh her decision. She tried them all on, lived with the idea of each one for a while, and finally chose to wear only one of them on her big day. Of course, after the wedding, she listed the other two back on eBay and earned back the cost of her indecisiveness! This is not an option with most brick-and-mortar bridal salons. (Not to mention that no salon on earth can boast the kind of selection eBay does. As we write this, more than five thousand wedding

Figure 1-2: *A Golden-Age Superman comic book from 1946.*

Figure: 1-3: *A label from a can of Schepp's coconut. Before eBay, we didn't even know we had been in the coconut business!*

dresses are available for sale on the site.) Oh, by the way, we've seen the pictures. The bride looked lovely.

eBay delivers right to your computer screen any kind of shopping experience your beating heart desires. It incorporates the thrill of the chase. It's a different type of chase than the usual one at the mall, but the idea of scooping up a great find at a bargain price is integral to eBay shopping. There's also a competitiveness to it that makes eBay shopping a little like a horse race. Only one person is going to end up with the auctioned item, and that person is known as the winner! And who doesn't like to feel like a winner? Now you can enjoy the thrill that comes with tracking down that doll or comic book you had as a kid, or experience the competitiveness of shopping for an item in limited supply that everyone wants, just by turning on your computer and going to eBay.com. Yes, the Internet has finally allowed computers to fulfill their promise as an indispensable information and shopping appliance. Those magic little boxes became far more important in our lives once they allowed us to connect to each other. Well, just as the Internet changed the home computer, eBay has changed the Internet. Now, not only can we connect with each other, we can buy and sell things from each other, anytime and from any location. Throughout this book, you'll see how this reality has changed life for countless individuals.

Before we start, here's a word of caution. That way, you can't say we didn't warn you! eBay is habit forming. It's so much fun that you can actually get caught up in it and lose all sense of reason. That's one reason why we're here. We'll show you how to be smart in your eBay shopping. We'll show you how to determine if something really is a good buy by describing the research you can do right on the eBay site.

Mostly Everyone Loves eBay

Today's teenagers will not remember life without eBay any more than they'll remember life without a notebook computer or a cell phone. As for the rest of us, eBay has become so much a part of our culture that it's almost impossible to find someone who hasn't at least heard of the site. That's not to say everyone except you is active on eBay. We still meet plenty of people who claim never to have visited eBay. But they say it with a tinge of regret and a suggestion that they should definitely check it out.

Through our writing, as well as our work as eBay sellers and trainers, we've met Adam Hersh, one of the largest and most successful sellers on eBay. Adam began his eBay life as a college student in 1996. He'd read about the site and was a little curious about how it worked. Once he explored it a bit, he started to look around his dorm room for things he could sell. He liked turning unwanted stuff into cash so much, he told his friends all about it. Since they were his friends, he offered to list their things for them at no charge. He was just a college kid helping out his buddies. Then he noticed he'd begun to acquire more and more friends. They all wanted him to sell stuff for them. What college kid doesn't need extra money? When a perfect stranger asked Adam to sell four tires for him, Adam asked to keep a percentage of the profit as a commission. Thus began Adam's life as a Trading Assistant, or someone with the background and credentials to help others sell on eBay. (In chapter 20 we'll discuss Trading Assistants in some detail.) Now he manages dozens of employees across two states and hosts more than 100,000 eBay auctions a month. He's even served as a consultant to the South Korean government, because they wanted to sell on eBay, too. Oh, we forgot to mention that Adam is now all of twenty-seven years old!

A fascinating eBay couple we've come to know is Harvey Levine and Marcia Cooper. They are now both in their sixties. They were downsized several years ago and left without an income at an age when most people are starting to think about retirement. With nearly seventy years of corporate experience between them, they found themselves smart and full of information, but practically unemployable.

They had never been on eBay before, when Marcia's son asked them to help him out with some of his sales. Today they are not only eBay PowerSellers (sellers who maintain a high level of sales and positive feedback), but they are also educational consultants teaching dozens of eBay courses every month. Considering that until five years ago, neither had even visited the eBay site, they found a pretty remarkable way to remake their retirement years. Marcia and Harvey are planning to write a book specifically for people over fifty who want to explore life as eBay sellers. You'll find that demographic is a thriving market for eBay buyers, too!

The eBay Craze Knows No Boundaries

Not too long ago, we traveled to the island of Jamaica. There, amid the mountains, touring a beautiful jungle retreat, we had the chance to talk to some of the local artisans. They asked about our livelihood, and when we told them about our work, they said, "Oh, yes, of course, we know about eBay, Mon." That's when we came to see how ubiquitous eBay has become.

The numbers for international sales back up our anecdotal experience. According to eBay, the site has users from over 150 countries. Of eBay's total revenue, 25 percent is generated outside the United States. A laptop computer sells every three minutes in Korea. If you want to sell jewelry, consider Australia, where someone buys a piece of jewelry on eBay every twenty-three seconds. If the Internet has tied the world together into one communications network, eBay has turned the world into one big marketplace. Pierre's little idea has swept the world!

eBay Explained

eBay gives you the "place" to buy and sell, essentially setting up the empty stalls in the marketplace. How a seller decorates his stall, how and when you visit other people's stalls, and how you shop is left entirely to eBay's members. The people at eBay pride themselves on providing what they call a "level playing field." That means that no matter who you are or how much you spend, you'll receive the same treatment from eBay. If you spend $10 a year or $100,000 a year, there's no difference. If you sell one item a month on the site or if, like Adam, you sell thousands, you're not going to be treated differently by eBay.

This virtual marketplace consists of millions of listings of all types—traditional auctions where buyers bid up the price of an item until the auction's conclusion, and others where items are sold at fixed prices (which aren't really "auctions" at all). In a traditional auction, the most familiar and popular type of eBay listing, a seller sets an opening price and lets bidders determine what the item sells for. Like a traditional, offline auction, an eBay auction is your opportunity to compete in a bidding war for that rare collectible or low-priced MP3 player you've been coveting. As you peruse eBay's offerings, you'll also find other types of listings, such as Fixed Price listings. We discuss all the various listing types later in this book. In all scenarios, once you purchase your item, you pay the seller directly, using whatever payment methods she accepts, and she's then responsible for shipping the item to your door.

eBay deliberately stays out of transactions between buyers and sellers, and makes that position very clear in the Terms of Service Agreement that you must sign to become a member. So does that mean that eBay won't step in if you have a problem? Well, maybe yes and maybe no. If the person you're buying from is selling something that is banned from the site—such as bootleg recordings, lock-picking devices, narcotics and steroids, or items that have been recalled—you can report it and it's likely eBay will take down those listings and notify the seller that they've done so. And, if sellers are stealing each other's listing descriptions and photos, eBay will end those auctions. But if your seller never sends the item you purchased, you'll have to report him and hope that a few more disgruntled buyers report him as well. With three strikes against him, eBay will close his account and end his business, but unless you're careful, you will lose your money. Since eBay never handles the money exchanged between buyers and sellers, you will only get your purchase price back from eBay under certain conditions, and even then you're only eligible to receive up to $175. (The conditions under which eBay will reimburse you are spelled out in its Standard Purchase Protection Program, described in detail in chapter 8. PayPal, eBay's "preferred payment method," also offers some buyer protection. Chapter 6 describes PayPal in detail, while chapter 8 discusses how to work with PayPal in the event of a dispute.)

As you make your way through this book, we'll teach you how to shop carefully and protect yourself from fraud. However, surprising as you might find it, Pierre actually was right. Most people who come to eBay do so to buy and trade with honesty and integrity. It's part of the philosophy and spirit of eBay. Where else is a buyer expected to compliment the seller who completes the sale competently? Did you thank CVS the last time the checkout clerk successfully sold you a greeting card or the pharmacist filled your prescription correctly? Remarkably, thousands of buyers deliberately visit the site every day with the express purpose of rewarding their sellers with positive feedback. It's a remarkably effective yet simple system.

At the same time, Pierre's little experiment has grown beyond anything he could have imagined. Whole industries have cropped up offering tools to help buyers and sellers operate more effectively on the site. You'll find electronic newsletters devoted to eBay selling. Visit any Wal-Mart or Target, and you'll see expanded home office departments filled with packing supplies and materials. Even the U.S. Postal Service is offering eBay seminars to help the thousands of people who want to sell on the site and ship their items more efficiently.

eBay itself has grown more complicated, even as it has remained true to its roots. As always, you can set your maximum bid on an item and eBay's software will automatically increase your bid for you throughout the life of the auction. The system will even send you an e-mail notice when you've been outbid so that you

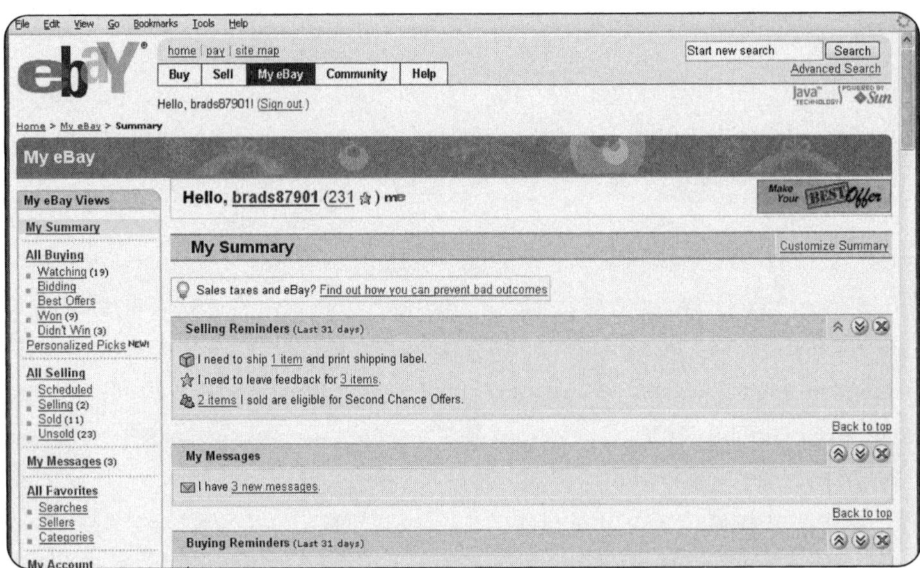

Figure 1-4: *Your My eBay page provides a snapshot of all your eBay buying and selling activities.*

have a chance to change your mind and offer more. Enhancements like your own My eBay page, shown in Figure 1-4, make it easy to see what you're thinking about buying, what you've bought, what still needs to be paid for, and everything that you're selling, too. You can even track all your messages to and from other eBay members through this one simple dashboard.

In addition, eBay offers help pages, live assistance, a site map, tutorials, and seminars to help you learn to become a more efficient user of the site. Through its online payment company, PayPal, you can register your credit card and banking information so that you can shop without worrying that your private information will be hijacked by unscrupulous sellers. They never see it. Don't be overwhelmed by all these details. By the time you're finished reading this book, they'll seem as simple as turning on your computer.

eBay Is a Community

eBay has come a long way from the simple idea imagined on that not-so-long-ago Labor Day weekend. Yet it remains, at its core, what it's always been: a community. Yes, it's international. It's huge. But while it may seem impersonal, eBay is really just another gathering of human beings. When you sign on to eBay, you're joining a community, and how involved you wish to become in that community is up to you. We encourage you to become part of it.

You'll find message boards and groups to join on the site, where you'll have the chance to discuss issues concerning buying and selling, such as bidding techniques, creating auction listings, taking high-quality photos, proper packing and shipping, and feedback. In eBay's category-specific boards, collectors chat with their fellow hobbyists about everything from art to vehicles. You'll discover people who are happy to spend their time making your life on eBay more fun and enjoyable. Who knows? You may even meet your next best friend through eBay, because eBay is really about people.

Now, just as in any other community of people, you'll come across the good, the bad, and the somewhat bizarre. Unfortunately, the ones who get the most attention fall into the last two categories. It doesn't make for interesting news to focus on all the millions of transactions that run smoothly on eBay each month, with the seller receiving a good price for his product and the buyer receiving a good product for his price. Where's the fun in that? Rather, it's much more exciting to cast a spotlight on the bizarre and downright evil members of the community.

Let's start with the bizarre, because at least those examples are amusing. Have you heard about the divorced man who sold his ex-wife's wedding dress on eBay by posing for the listing photo while wearing it? It was pretty clear that he still harbored a lot of hostility toward his ex, because the description he wrote was a hilarious but insulting diatribe against his unfaithful wife, who, according to the spurned husband, would never have been able to fit into the wedding dress by the time she left him anyway. With his gift for irony and his ridiculous photo, his listing attracted more than a million viewers. He sold the dress for thousands of dollars, and he even received multiple proposals to remarry, which, happily, he turned down. His little episode on eBay even won him a spot on the David Letterman Show! Take a look at the box below for even more absurd items listed for sale on eBay.

CRAZY THINGS LISTED ON eBAY

At one time or another just about everything has been for sale on eBay. While eBay did shut down some of the auctions for the items listed here, most resulted in a sale.

- Jack Nicholson's teeth
- John Kennedy Garden Gnome
- French fry resembling Abraham Lincoln
- Real stuffed piranha
- Flying pig hat with working wings
- Arnold Schwarzenegger's discarded cough drop
- Used breast implant
- Baby-naming rights
- Prom date
- Real shrunken head
- Used penis enlarger
- Ghost in a jar
- Human casket
- Advertising space on a living room wall
- The pope's used car
- Human soul (This last item received five bids and sold for $483.05! Its condition was described as "used.")

Far less entertaining, but at least as newsworthy, is the criminal element that preys on the world of eBay commerce. As with any gathering of human beings, some have joined the crowd for the purpose of picking pockets and committing crimes. Identity theft, e-mail fraud, buyer scams, seller scams—these are but a few of the dangers that await you when you venture onto eBay. We wouldn't be reliable tour guides if we weren't willing to be honest about the realities of the e-commerce world. But just as we don't think you should avoid a trip to New York City because there may be muggers in Central Park, we don't think you should swear off eBay because you might meet a criminal there. Instead, we advise you to be educated and smart as you roam around eBay and learn how to protect yourself. Of course, we've got lots of good ways for you to become a sophisticated eBay user quickly. That's why we wrote this book.

What You'll Need to Get Started

If you already use the Internet from a home computer, you've got all you need technologically to get started buying on eBay. If you decide that you want to venture into eBay as a seller, in Part II of the book we'll give you a list of some tools you'll need to add to your computer system and home office to make your life easier and your work more productive. However, buying on eBay requires very little in the way of computer equipment. If you live in a location where high-speed Internet service is available, we highly recommend it. You can certainly navigate eBay with dial-up service, but everything on the Internet is more fun with a faster connection. Plus, if you find yourself in the middle of a furious bidding war for an item and you have a slow dial-up connection, you may lose out to someone with cable or another type of broadband service.

One more thing you'll need to do is to register as an eBay user. We're not going to walk you through that process because eBay has made it so simple that we know you can do it for yourselves. (Remember: This is a smart guide to eBay, not a guide for dummies!) Just click on the Register hyperlink at the top of virtually any eBay page, and you're on your way. We do want to offer you a little advice about choosing an eBay username. Your username becomes your eBay identity, so choose it with care. Note that eBay won't allow you to use your e-mail address. That's to protect you from spammers who use usernames from sites like eBay to harvest a list of potential victims for their junk e-mails. Beyond that, choose something that will please you, but not give away too much information. For example, for privacy and safety we use our first names and nicknames, but we'd never use our full names. (There have been instances where a disgruntled trading partner showed up at someone's door!) If you think you might be a seller one day, why not choose a name that's in keeping with the types of things you'll be offering, such as debsvintageclothing.

Now, that you have your username at the ready, use that computer with the fast connection to navigate to eBay's homepage, shown in Figure 1-5. From this welcoming page, you'll find options for just about anything you'd like to do on the site, from browsing to buying to selling to chatting with friends. Oh, and in case you haven't noticed, there's also a bit of advertising to enjoy! As you can see, the tabs along the top of the page give you quick access to various areas of eBay, including Buy, Sell, My eBay, Community, and Help. You can also skip directly to searching both in the simple and advanced mode. These buttons appear at the top of almost any eBay page you visit, so you'll always have the same choices.

In our view, one of these buttons is especially valuable for times when you feel

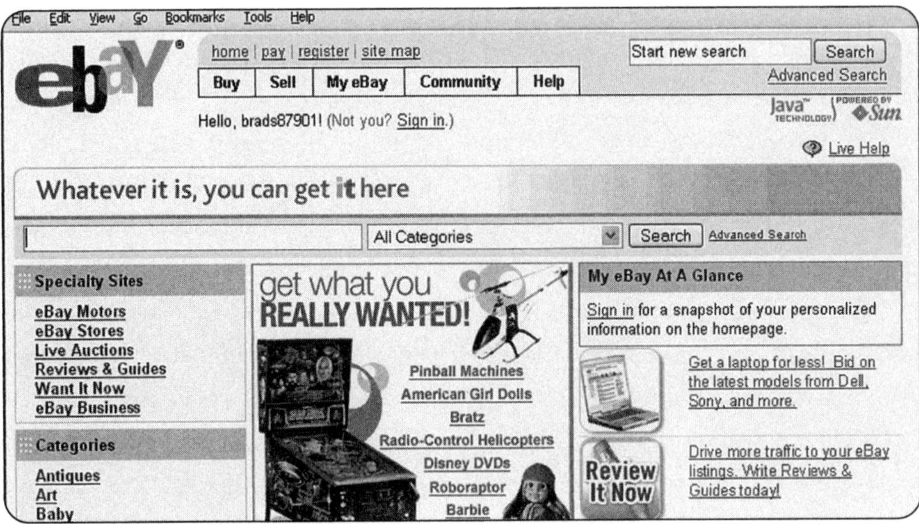

Figure 1-5: *eBay's Homepage.*

stuck and need a little help. Surprisingly, it's not the Help button. eBay's Help pages are notoriously frustrating. Here's an example. We wanted to learn more about the eBay Pulse feature, a daily take on what's hot on the site. So we went to the Help page and searched for the term. We got 199 responses that included things like Shipping Concerns and Understanding Feedback. We didn't even begin to scroll through the more than ten pages of results to see if there was anything relevant to eBay Pulse. Instead we went to the top of the page and clicked the little hyperlink for the Site Map, shown in Figure 1-6.

The Site Map is one of our favorite places on eBay. It's as good as eBay's Help pages are frustrating. It's organized by topic, such as Buying Resources, Selling Tools, and News. It takes you directly to the part of eBay you're trying to learn about. Time and time again, we've found just what we're looking for through the Site Map, and yet many long-time eBay users have never bothered to click that little link and discover what a valuable tool it is. So as you start exploring the neighborhood, keep the Site Map in mind. It makes navigating this new territory as simple as clicking a mouse.

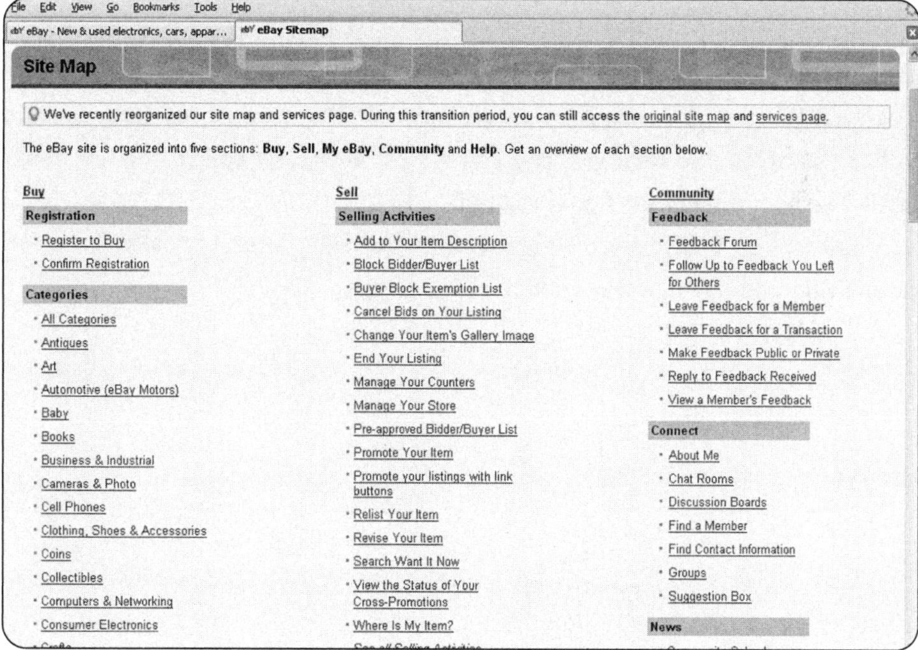

Figure 1-6: *eBay's Site Map provides easy access to eBay's many nooks and crannies.*

Beyond a computer, Internet access, and a little navigational advice, you'll also need to find additional time to devote to eBay—perhaps more than you were planning on. That's certainly true if you decide to sell. Few people in the world work harder than those who pursue eBay selling as a full-time career. But even if you're only interested in buying, you're going to devote many more hours to eBay than you thought you were. That's because you should never make any move on eBay that hasn't been researched and considered carefully. We'll walk you through the process and explain how you handle each step, but to buy successfully on eBay you need to understand exactly what you're getting, exactly how much you're actually paying for the item (don't forget the shipping), and exactly how honorable and trustworthy your trading partner is. The good news is that all this work is really fun, and the reward is finding just what you're looking for at a great price.

The last item you'll need for your eBay shopping experience is a realistic budget beyond which you simply will not go. You will soon discover that it's very easy to get caught up in an eBay buying frenzy. Why? Well, you can find virtually anything you can think of to buy there, and you actually get to compete and beat someone else out for the treasure. These factors, taken together, amount to a potentially dangerous combination of shopping, gambling, and fun that makes it easy for you to get in over your head. We actually had a friend exclaim, "I have no idea what I'm getting from eBay this week alone!" That's not a position you want to find yourself in. So we'll give you some great advice for controlling the frenzy just as we help you get the frenzy started.

Now let's go find you some great stuff to buy and introduce you to some fun people who occupy the world of eBay!

SEVERAL YEARS AGO, eBay member Robert Sachs wanted to surprise his wife with a birthday gift of a Chatty Cathy doll she remembered from her childhood. Unfortunately, he knew very little about the doll. So how could he tell a "good" one from a "bad" one? He did a lot of research on eBay and had a little help from his mom, who knew much more about dolls than he did. "It came down to asking a lot of sellers a lot of questions to educate myself as quickly as possible," Bob told us. He finally found a wonderful doll in the best condition he could afford. She was complete and working, meaning she still talked! She was even still dressed in Chatty Cathy's original outfit. What a way to say Happy Birthday!

How Do I Find the Good Stuff?

IN 2005, HUNDREDS OF THOUSANDS OF PEOPLE, many of them just like you, listed close to two billion items on eBay. Let's let that sink in for a minute. Nearly two billion items! Of course, all those items were not available at the same time. The average number of items available for sale on eBay at one time is a more modest sixty million or so.

We're belaboring this point a bit to emphasize the challenge awaiting you as a new eBay shopper. Faced with so many choices, how do you keep from becoming overwhelmed and intimidated? How do you keep from taking one look at eBay's homepage and deciding to head back to the mall? You start by not letting the sheer volume of eBay's choices overwhelm you. As Martha Stewart would say, "It's a good thing"!

Of course, you're going to need to know what's available and how to find your way around the neighborhood, but that's one reason why you're reading this book. There are two basic ways to find what you want on eBay: browsing and searching. For most of your eBay life, you'll choose searching. Once you know your way around eBay, searching is much faster. You'll get better at searching as you gain experience in using eBay. You'll learn how to choose keywords that will bring you the items you're looking for, and you'll learn which categories are most likely to house your favorite things. But just to get you started we're going to ask you to spend some time browsing. Trust us, it's fun!

Browsing eBay's Categories

Browsing eBay is a lot like perusing the directory kiosk at a mall you're visiting for the first time. You won't know how to plan your shopping trip and make sure you visit all your favorites if you don't know what choices you have. So to get acquainted with eBay's categories, spend some time browsing through them just to learn what's there. The categories run the gamut from antiques to video games, and in between there's a lot of territory to cover. Browsing allows you to get familiar with the way sellers categorize their items. For example, eBay has an Antiques category, as well as one for Collectibles. What will you find in each? If you're into Art Deco clocks, for example, which category should you turn to? (If you guessed Collectibles, you're right, since many people don't consider Art Deco items old enough to qualify as antiques.) The lines separating some of the other categories are also blurry, such as those for Computers, Consumer Electronics, Cell Phones, and Cameras. And then there's that "Everything Else" category! So try to figure out in which categories sellers are likely to offer the items you are looking for.

When you finally get to the actual item listings, pay close attention to their titles. That way you can get a feel for the keywords sellers use to describe the things you like to shop for. A keyword may be a word or an acronym used to describe or elaborate on a given item. *Certified* may be an appropriate keyword to use in searches for coins, for example. Then there's a whole glossary of colorful acronyms that appear all over eBay; these can be very effective in helping you limit your search to what you really want. For example, if you're looking for an advertising display, you might want to include *NOS* as a keyword for New Old Stock. That way, you're limiting your search to old items that are in seemingly new condition, such as old warehouse finds. Don't worry about these arcane acronyms right now. We'll cover them in more detail later in this chapter. Keep in mind that if you don't know how to choose the most effective keywords, your searching experiences can be frustrating and disappointing.

Browsing may not be the most efficient way to shop on eBay, but it's as simple as clicking your mouse. Let's do a sample browse together, and you'll see just what we mean. Suppose today we're going to shop for an ABC book for a toddler we know. Let's start on the Buy page shown in Figure 2-1. (To reach this page, we

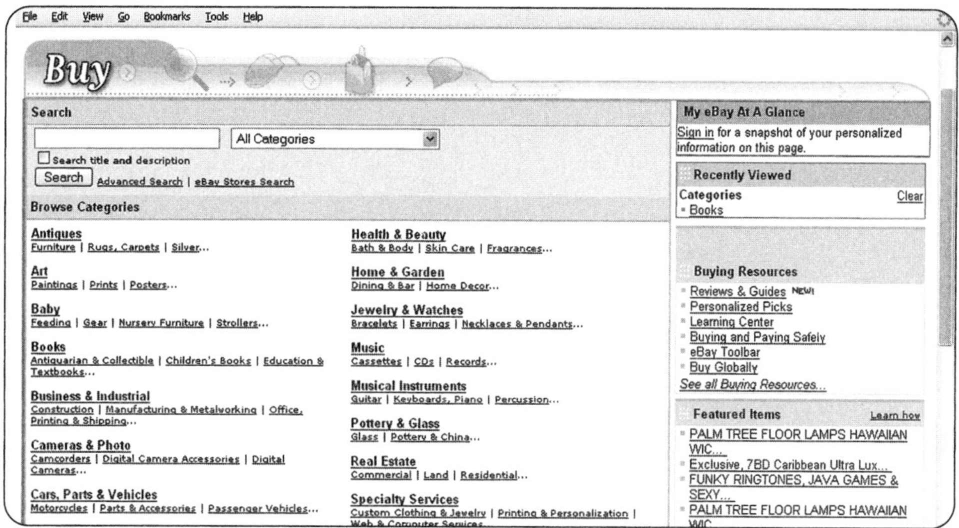

***Figure 2-1:** eBay's Buy page shows the many categories of items available for purchase.*

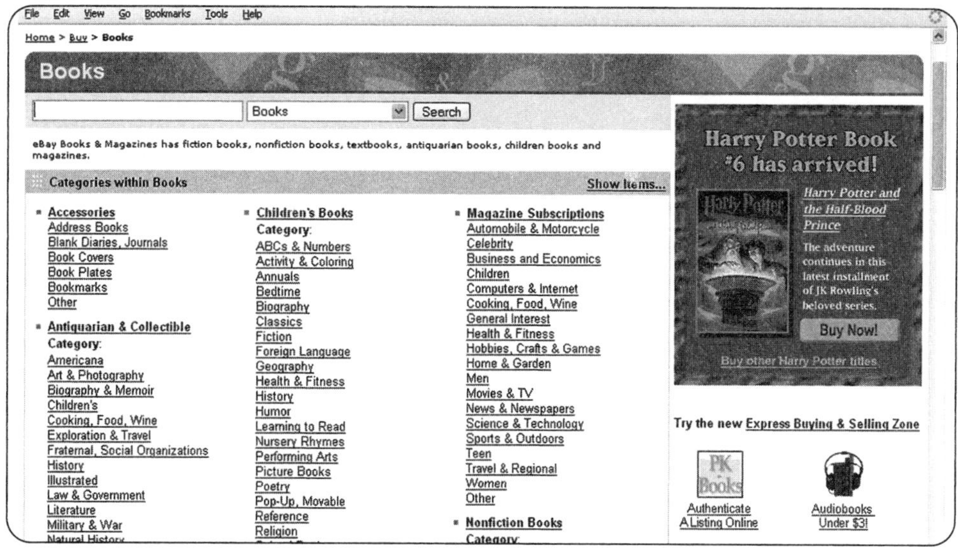

***Figure 2-2:** The screen that appears when you click on Books from eBay's Buy page.*

just clicked Buy at the top of eBay's homepage at www.ebay.com.) Here you'll see the topmost list of eBay categories.

We're going to click on Books. From the Books screen that appears next (Figure 2-2), we'll click on the link for Children's Books at the top of the middle column. We could have clicked directly on the subcategory right below it for ABCs &

Numbers, but remember, this is a learning exercise. So we're now in the Children's Books category, which lists more than 41,000 items. That's way too many for us to browse. But we didn't want to view all the books anyway, just the ABC books.

Now, if you're online and following along with us, hit the back button on your browser to return to the Books category page (otherwise, just refer back to Figure 2-2), and you'll see the link for ABCs & Numbers again right under Children's Books. If you were to click on that ABCs & Numbers link, you'd see the variety of ABC books broken down further by categories, such as Board Books, Hardcover, and Softcover. Of the choices we have, we're going to choose Board Books. They're sturdy and washable, and perfect for a toddler.

We clicked on the Board Book choice and found over one hundred items. Scrolling down the page allowed us to begin evaluating our choices. We decided to check out the auction for the Discovery Toys board book set, the first item listed in Figure 2-3. It seemed to be what we were looking for. Some of the other books listed were used, and since we wanted this to be a present, we realized pretty quickly that used wasn't our first choice. Others seemed fairly ordinary, featuring characters that are common to the toddler world. We also know and like Discovery Toys. Having been out of the toddler toy market for a few years, we didn't know that Discovery Toys offers such a product.

File Edit View Go Bookmarks Tools Help

Item	Bids	Price	Shipping	Ends	Distance
BRAND NEW Discovery Toys ABC Box 26 Board Books NIB Feedback: (266) 100%	1	$0.99	$4.00	Jan-07 08:48	245 mi New York
Little Golden Book NUMBERS 1955 1st Ed letter A Feedback: (990) 99.9%	-	$2.99	$2.00	Jan-07 06:29	275 mi North Carolina
LITTLE GOLDEN ABC illus by Cornelius DeWitt 1951 T Feedback: (990) 99.9%	-	$2.50	$2.00	Jan-07 06:23	275 mi North Carolina
"CLICK THE MOUSE" Early Learners (1-3) Book - NEW! Feedback: (1401) 100%	-	$4.25	Calculate	Jan-07 06:05	415 mi Indiana
NEW - TEDDY BEAR, TEDDY BEAR, COUNT TO TEN BOOK Feedback: (666) 99.9%	Buy It Now	AU $4.50	Not specified Australia	Jan-07 05:24	Australia
FUN TO LEARN FIRST DICTIONARY& FIRST NUMBERS Feedback: (19) 95.2%	-	GBP 0.01	Not specified United Kingdom	Jan-07 05:20	United Kingdom
SPACE PRECINCT book Feedback: (316) 99.7%	-	GBP 0.99	Not specified United Kingdom	Jan-07 03:29	United Kingdom
Sesame Street-Lot Of 12 Board Books-Elmo,Gro ver,kids,NR Feedback: (44691) 99.2%	-	$1.99	Calculate	Jan-06 19:00	United States

Figure 2-3: *The search results screen showing the Children's ABC board books available.*

In theory, we could have searched for *Discovery Toys ABCs* in the Children's Book category. But since we didn't know this product existed, that didn't occur to us. We ultimately learned more about what we actually wanted by browsing than we would have by searching. We also learned how many different choices there were for a product as simple as an ABC book for children. If we wanted to buy more of these items, we'd know a lot more about looking for them on eBay, and we'd be better educated when it came time for searching.

There are other ways you can browse—you don't have to start with categories. You can also browse with a little help from eBay. If you were online and at the main Buy page, you'd see the Other Ways to Browse area, under the main categories box. Here you can still browse rather than search, but you'll be browsing based on different suggestions. Options include eBay Marketplace Research, eBay Keywords, Popular Searches, eBay Pulse, Store Index, and Category Index. eBay Marketplace Research and eBay Keywords are actually links to areas that will help you learn more about what's selling on eBay and for how much, as well as ways to refine your search terms to create effective searches. Popular Searches will help you see how other eBayers are searching for items, and eBay Pulse will show you what is currently hotly sought after on the site and which stores are the most popular. The Store Index is a great way to get to know eBay stores, where sellers can list stock at a reduced price. (We'll discuss eBay stores at length in chapter 19.) Finally, the Category Index allows you to drill down through a *highly* detailed list of eBay categories and subcategories and work your way to a group of items you'd like to check out. You can also get there through the same browsing exercise we've already completed, but this is a way to see all the categories available in areas that interest you.

Searching

Once you've learned your way around the neighborhood, for the most part you'll use keywords to search for the things you want. When you search using keywords, you are trying to match the product you're looking for with the words the seller chose when titling his item listing (a keyword search is really a title search). Keyword searching requires you to put on your seller's cap for a moment, and think about the words a seller might use to describe the item you are looking for.

Don't be intimidated by this exercise. When the seller chose his keywords, he was wearing his buyer's hat, trying to think of the words *you'd* use if you were looking for the item.

Basic Search

Using keywords, you can choose between a *Basic Search* or an *Advanced Search.* Here we'll show you how to use Basic Search; we'll save the bulk of our Advanced Search discussion for chapter 9, where we cover PowerBuying. In the top right-hand corner of nearly every eBay page, you'll find a little Search button and a box in which to enter your search terms. If you're confident about your keywords, go ahead and pop them into this box and see what you get. Of course, you can move just slightly down the left-hand side of the page and designate to search only particular categories, but for the sake of this exercise, try your keywords across all of eBay's categories. Let's do one together so you can get the idea.

We'll start by using the Search button we just pointed out to you. Let's search for *Gone with the Wind.* Enter that term and click search. The day we did this, we got more than 1,900 search results. As you can see in Figure 2-4, you've got choices that will help you narrow down your options a bit. You've searched with eBay's default setting, which shows you all items—both auction listings and Buy It Now (BIN) items. (You can buy BIN items immediately for a designated price, without going through the auction process. They're great if you know what you want and are willing to settle on a given price, but they're not nearly as exciting as auction items.) You can press the tabs that run along the top left of the search results to see items grouped within either of these categories. When we clicked on Auctions we received more than 1,700 results, still too many. Buy It Now gives us more than 500—still unwieldy.

But wait, there's more. Further down the left side of the Results page shown in Figure 2-4, you'll see the Matching Categories where our *Gone with the Wind* items are further categorized. Refining your search through these categories is often the final step you need to take when searching with keywords. Now if we want to get a new DVD of the movie, we're all set, because DVDs & Movies is a prominent subcategory. But, what's that you say—you wanted a *Gone with the Wind* coffee mug? Okay, well let's go back and specify *mug* as one of our search

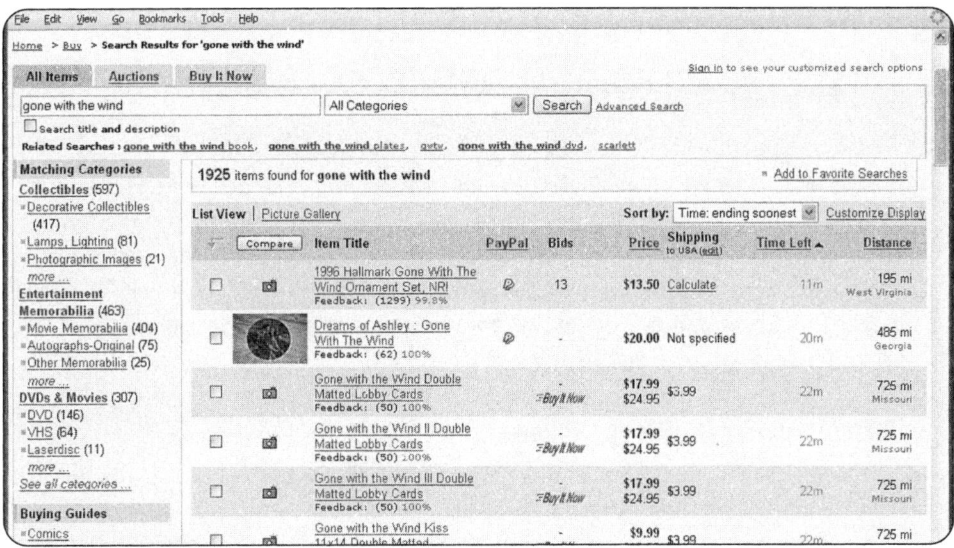

Figure 2-4: *The results of our "basic" search for* Gone with the Wind *items.*

terms. Enter *Gone with the Wind* mug and see what happens. We did this and got sixteen results, a perfect number for us to view and decide on.

So one of the first rules of searching is to choose keywords that are specific enough to get you to the item you really want to buy. There's a delicate balancing act involved here. When we searched for *Gone with the Wind* mug, we got sixteen results. If we add *coffee* to that search string, we only get nine results. *Coffee* doesn't add any valuable information to the search; rather, it eliminates almost half the results that could be on the mark. So you want your search terms to be specific enough to get you results, but not so specific that you eliminate good choices. Searching with keywords is like any other acquired skill: You get better as you practice.

Although the more you search the better you get at choosing keywords and retrieving a manageable number of listings, beginners are never really lost. eBay helps you if you want to retrace your steps. On your search results page, right above the All Items, Auctions, and Buy It Now tabs, you're shown the path you've taken to get to where you are. For example, if you are searching for old ads for American cars, your path may look like this:

Home >Buy >Collectibles >Advertising >Cars >American

If you wanted to retrace your steps to head down another alley, you could start from any point by clicking on a word somewhere along your path.

SEARCHING TIPS FROM EBAY

Here are some quick tips from eBay on how best to use keywords:

- Try a variety of search terms. Sellers can use whatever terms they want to describe an item. When titling their listings, some may not have used the terms you first thought to try when searching. For example, suppose you were in the market for a bookbag for your bright-eyed high school freshman. If you were to search for a *red bookbag* you'd get only a few hits (we got ten when we tried it). However, if you searched under *red backpack* instead, you'd get many more hits (our search yielded over six hundred). So if you're not finding what you want, think of some other terms to try (reviewing existing listings may help with this).
- Be specific! Obviously, it's not a good idea to plug *Elvis Presley* in the search box, all by its lonesome, when what you're really after are Elvis Presley recipes. The more words you can use to specifically describe what you're after, the more likely it is that the results will be what you're looking for (bringing you one step closer to those peanut butter and banana sandwiches)!
- Use quotes to specify that the terms must appear together. For example, if you were looking for collectibles from New York, type in *"New York Collectibles"* rather than *New York Collectibles.* By using the quotation marks you will exclude possibly extraneous items (in this case, those collectibles from York, Pennsylvania, that happen to be in new condition).
- Narrow your search by attributes, such as model number, color, date, brand, condition, and so on. The more delimiters you include, the better. So if you plug in *"Canon PowerShot A520"* instead of *"Canon Digital Camera,"* you'll save yourself a lot of browsing time. Do the necessary research ahead of time by checking sources such as *Consumer Reports* to determine how best to limit your search.
- Treat words like *or*, *the*, and *and* as search terms. This is because eBay's search engine regards them as such, and whether or not you include them will affect your results. So you should only use them if they are part of the item name. For example, if you search for *"Paul Revere and the Raiders,"* you will get different results than if you searched for *"Paul Revere Raiders."*
- Punctuation matters, too. If punctuation is part of the search term (as with *T-shirt)*, then use it. Otherwise, don't bother.
- Don't worry about whether to use upper- or lowercase letters. They're all the same to eBay's search engine. So *dell laptop* will yield the same results as *Dell laptop.*

Advanced Search

Just under the search box that appears on nearly every eBay page, you'll find a blue hyperlink to the Advanced Search page, shown in Figure 2-5. The Advanced Search page gives you several valuable options that are not available to you through Basic Search. On the left side of that page, you can choose to search by bidder, seller, or item number. You can also choose to search eBay stores or search eBay Motors. If you know a specific member's username, you can search for that member, and if you're involved in a transaction with a seller, you can get the seller's contact information (name, city, and telephone number) to speak with her directly. (That information will come to you via e-mail and, at the same time, an e-mail will be sent to your trading partner, notifying her that you requested her contact information.)

We'll discuss all these options and more in chapter 9. For now, we know you're eager to start shopping, so let's move ahead quickly.

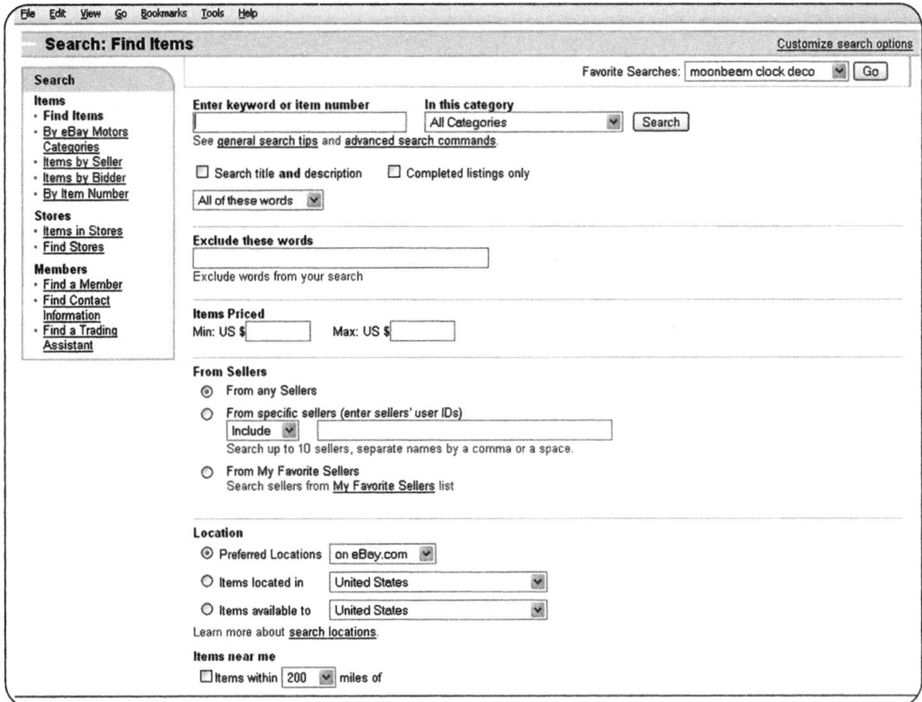

Figure 2-5: *The Advanced Search page gives you many options for narrowing down your eBay search.*

COMMONLY USED EBAY ACRONYMS

When you are searching or browsing for items, it's helpful to know the shortcuts many sellers take when titling their items. Sellers often use acronyms as keywords because they only have a limited number of characters to work with, and as a way to give savvy buyers shortcuts when searching. You'll find acronyms like these in use all over eBay—not just in auction listings themselves but on discussion boards, too. Here are some of the most popular ones—so you know what it means when an item title includes NBW!

BIN Buy It Now

COA Certificate of authenticity

COL Collection

GBP Great Britain Pounds

LTD Limited edition

MIB Mint in box

MIJ Made in Japan

MOC Mint on card

NBW Never been worn

NC No cover

NIB New in box

NM Near mint

NOS New old stock

NR No reserve

NWOT New without tags

NWT New with tags

OEM Original equipment manufacturer

OOAK One of a kind

PM Priority Mail

SH Shipping and handling

VHTF Very hard to find

Once you get deep into a category, you may find other acronyms commonly used. For example, you may find these acronyms when searching through auctions for books or manuscripts:

1st First edition

ANTH Anthology

AUTO Autographed

BOMC Book of the Month Club edition

EXLIB Ex-library book

HB Hardbound

HB/DJ Hardbound book with dust jacket

HIST Historical

NC No cover

OOP Out of print

PB Paperback

Other Shopping Options

In finding things to buy, you're not limited to just browsing or searching for stuff. eBay will also do a lot of the work for you, with the help of its zillion or so computers. You can use searches that have worked well for you in the past (Favorite Searches), or you can shop with sellers who sell the kinds of things you like at reasonable prices, and who ship your stuff to you on time and unbroken (Favorite Sellers). As with advanced searching, we're going to save our discussion of these things for a later chapter. But here we did want to mention a few other options you have for finding stuff on eBay.

Want It Now

Want It Now (http://pages.ebay.com/wantitnow/), a relatively new eBay service, lets you create and post a personalized Want Ad to let eBay's sellers know what you're looking to buy. This may be useful if you are seeking something that's *very* arcane. As you can see in Figure 2-6, your Want It Now posting consists of a heading and then a paragraph or so of description. eBay advises you not to include contact information in these ads (eBay will e-mail you when a seller responds), and to be as specific as possible. As we write this, Want It Now is still very new, and, in

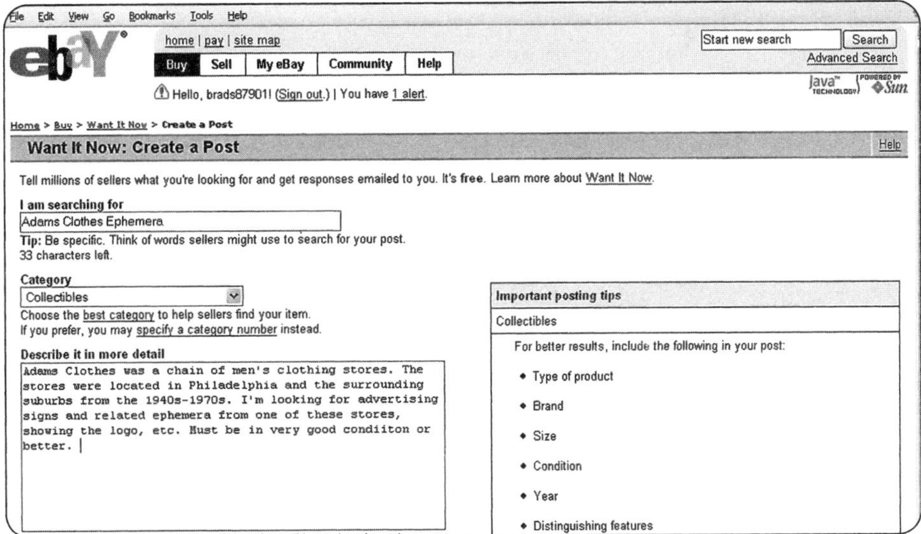

***Figure 2-6:** eBay's Want it Now feature lets you post an ad for that rare item not often found on eBay.*

our experience, of questionable usefulness. Sellers may interpret your ad very broadly and have eBay send item descriptions to you for products you're really not interested in. (If a mismatch like this occurs, you can notify eBay by clicking a hyperlink in the Want It Now response, and eBay then presumably wags a finger at the errant seller).

Personalized Picks

Here's some shopping help eBay offers to you without your ever asking for it. Once you've bought a few items on eBay, you'll receive suggestions for other things you might like to have. Yes, eBay makes assumptions about your tastes and habits, based on the things you buy and the searches you conduct. Your Personalized Picks appear on the right side of the eBay homepage (assuming you are logged in). Just click on the hyperlink, and you'll find yourself on a page filled with tempting things you might like. This eBay feature is very much like the buying suggestions some other online shopping destinations offer. You may enjoy getting this free advice, and you may actually like the things eBay's computers offer you. On the other hand, this may make it so easy to shop that you forget those three magic words: budget, budget, budget!

eBay Express

eBay auctions are great fun when you're in the market for funky collectibles and great deals on all sorts of used items, from clothing to books to cars. But what if you just want to order that cell phone your husband has been asking for, and you don't want to go through the auction process? There are *some* Fixed Price items for sale on eBay (you now know about Buy It Now items), but eBay's strength is in its auctions. So you're more likely to turn to "traditional" e-commerce sites when "you want it new and you want it now."

Thanks to a new service called eBay Express, you can buy new items at fixed prices through eBay, just as you can through any other Web site. No more waiting for auctions to end. You hop on eBay, click on eBay Express, search for what you want to buy, and order it. Simple as that.

Okay, buying things this way isn't as much fun as going through auctions. You may get a better price than you could through Target, let's say, but you're not likely to find the true bargains that you can sometimes scoop up through eBay auctions. But, as we said, you can buy things more quickly this way. Fraud may be less of a concern, too. eBay Express sellers have to meet stringent guidelines: They must have a feedback score of at least 100, and a 98 percent positive rating. (We'll explain what these numbers mean in chapter 3.) You'll be able to pay for items with PayPal, just as you can through the main eBay site. With eBay Express, no matter what you're in the market for, you never have to leave eBay.

Now that you've learned how to find things on eBay through browsing, searching, and letting eBay do some of the work for you, you're ready to put your money where your mouse is and actually *buy* a few things. Or almost ready. First let's explore how to evaluate sellers, which is where the next chapter comes in.

WHEN DEB WAS A CHILD, her favorite book was *Mio, My Son* by Astrid Lindgren, the author of the Pippi Longstocking series. She bought a copy for our children when they were old enough to enjoy it, and she read aloud to them so that they could all share the experience. Unfortunately, our copy disappeared from our daughter's elementary school desk, lifted by some budding young thief who also thought it was a good read. When we went to replace it, we discovered that it had gone out of print and was no longer readily available. The kids were okay with no longer owning it, but Deb was pretty unhappy. It became something of a family quest to find a replacement copy.

We searched for it every time we went to antique shops, used bookstores, thrift shops, garage sales, flea markets, or junk stores. *Eventually, it will turn up,* we kept telling ourselves. We did find it available from time to time, but always at a far higher price than we were willing to spend on it. (Trust us, Deb would never be happy owning a book that had cost that much!) It was beginning to look as if this would forever remain on the list of things we'd like to find one day.

Brad set a Favorite Search on eBay for the title and then sat back to bide his time. Sure enough, eventually a copy appeared at a price he could afford. It was a little paperback and nothing fancy, but it was in great shape and well within the range he'd decided to pay for it. As you can imagine, it made for a very happy holiday the year he gave it to Deb. He's given Deb lots of gifts in the years they've been together, but few of them mean more than that little book she thought she'd never own again.

How Do I Know Whom to Trust?

SO YOU'VE TAKEN OUR ADVICE and learned how to browse and search on eBay, and you've found some things you'd like to buy. What now? First off, congratulations! You've already learned enough to navigate eBay and spot some goodies. Now comes your next challenge. Before you actually buy that fine Fiestaware plate from the 1930s or the terrific Thumbelina doll from the 1960s, you have a bit of work ahead of you. First, you want to be sure they really *are* fine and terrific. We don't want you to be disappointed when you get your eBay treasure. To ensure that you're not, you'll need to evaluate the sellers of the items you're interested in.

As any good consumer knows, stores have reputations. If you shop at Saks or Sears, Tiffany or Target, you generally know what kind of merchandise you'll find there and what to do if something goes wrong. eBay is a horse of a different color—in fact, lots of different colors. While no one knows for sure, ACNielsen recently estimated there are more than two million people selling things on eBay. Many of these sellers are not merchants with established businesses. Some are "here today, gone tomorrow"; others are new but very committed; still others may be well established on eBay and even PowerSellers. (We'll discuss eBay's PowerSeller designation in chapter 20.) While the great majority of eBay sellers are honest and will aim to please you, you must be aware that there are also a few bad apples.

In this chapter we'll arm you with the tools you need to judge a seller as best as you can, based on the information he provides through his listing and the insights that other trading partners provide through their feedback. We'll assume that you've checked out the item description page by clicking on the link in your search results. (After all, that's how you know you're interested in the item.) Later, we'll discuss in detail what to look for on that page, but first let's discuss how to understand and evaluate a seller's feedback.

eBay's System of Feedback

eBay's ingenious feedback system, while not perfect, is the place to start when you're deciding whether or not a seller is someone you can trust. We discuss feedback a lot in this book: how to leave it, what kind to leave, what to do if the feedback you receive is mean-spirited and untrue, and more. But here we're interested in how to evaluate feedback to determine whether or not a seller is worthy of your business.

On eBay, feedback consists of the comments left by the partners—buyer and seller—in an eBay transaction. There are two components to it: the number of distinct feedback comments (which appears in parentheses after a seller's member ID), and the percentage of that feedback that's positive. When we were in school, of course, a person with an average of 90 percent or above was an "A" student. eBay is nothing like school! On eBay, a positive feedback rating below 98 percent should make you stop and wonder. That's how high your expectations should be for the person you're willing to trade with. If her rating is less than 98 percent, you may very well have found someone who isn't worthy of your trust.

How Feedback Works

Here's how it works. Ms. Jennifer Collector buys a Fiestaware plate from a seller we'll call oldtimeplates. After she receives her dinner plate, she can leave a comment rating the transaction (that comment is her feedback). First, she may rate the overall transaction as positive, negative, or neutral. You can imagine what these terms mean. Most transactions are rated positive, indicating that the seller delivered as promised (or the buyer paid on time and was pleasant enough to deal with). If things didn't go well, one of the partners may rate the transaction as negative. Negative feedback is a strike against your eBay record and is taken very seriously by the eBay community. Off eBay, neutral may seem to signify no strong opinion either way, but on eBay it does actually have a negative connotation, so neutral feedback must also be taken very seriously.

Aside from that one-word label, the participants in a transaction may leave a comment in the comment box of up to eighty characters in length. There they may elaborate on what they meant by that positive, negative, or neutral rating. Here are some examples of actual comments.

Positive: Very Fast shipment. Outstanding for eBay. Will buy from again!!!!!
Neutral: Never got Item. Money refunded.
Negative: Took over a month to receive. Unfriendly e-mails. Will never order from again.

Each trading partner can only affect someone's feedback by one point: plus one, zero, or minus one. That's to keep the tally balanced, so someone who does a lot of business with a particular buyer or seller can't skew the rating one way or another. For example, if you buy from a particular seller and leave feedback on three separate occasions, eBay will only count your feedback ratings once in determining his score. Suppose you buy three items from todaysdvds. One transaction is perfect, but two were disastrous. You would probably leave a positive on the one occasion but two negatives for the others. The positive will count once (+1), but so will the two negatives you leave (–1). So, if her score was initially 45, her score after your three feedback ratings will remain 45.

Now, looking at a typical eBay item page (Figure 3-1), notice the Meet the Seller section on the top right-hand side of the page. Next to the username (in this case brads87901) you'll see a number in parentheses (260). That represents the number of individual trading partners who had a positive experience with that eBay member. To arrive at this number, eBay subtracts any negative comments from the total number of positive comments from all trading partners. The next line is where the overall percentage of positive feedback the member has received is displayed. Here it's 100 percent.

Figure 3-1: *Notice the Meet the Seller box on the right. From there you can get a quick handle on the seller's reputation.*

The Member Profile Page

If you click on the feedback number in parentheses you'll find yourself on the seller's Member Profile page (Figure 3-2), where you can see a summary of the seller's feedback record and the comments trading partners have left. It's very important that you read some of these comments to get a snapshot of the person you're thinking of doing business with. For the most part, you see only the comments other people have left for the member, but you may also find more. The member who has received the feedback may also leave a comment in response to that feedback. This most often happens in the case of negative feedback. Many sellers will respond to those comments to explain what happened.

When you look at Figure 3-2, you'll notice that there are four tabs above the comments: Feedback Received, From Buyers, From Sellers, and Left for Others. By default, when you first go to a Member Profile page, all the member's feedback comments are displayed—both from buyers and from sellers. As a potential buyer, you're especially interested in the comments other buyers have left, so to start you'd want to click on the From Buyers tab.

Also of importance is the Recent Ratings box on the top of the page shown in Figure 3-2. That's where feedback from the past year is tallied and broken down by

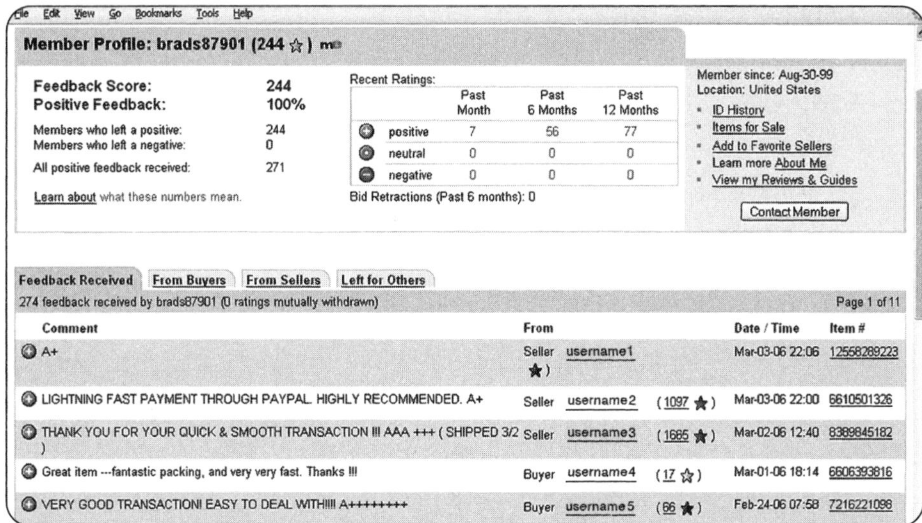

Figure 3-2: *The Recent Ratings box, which appears to the right of the feedback score in this figure, gives you a quick fix on someone's feedback record for the past twelve months.*

positives, neutrals, and negatives. Let's consider a couple of scenarios now, so you'll know how to evaluate a seller's feedback and how to proceed from there.

Evaluating a Seller's Feedback

If the seller has 100 percent positive feedback (and that's not that unusual), your job is easier. This rating means that it's likely this seller will be a good partner for you. However, you should still look into a couple of things before you click on that Place Bid button. First off, how many transactions has he had? Obviously, someone who has had five thousand transactions and still has a 100 percent positive rating should be viewed differently than someone who has completed only five transactions and has that same rating. The newer seller's feedback must be evaluated carefully, because doing business with a novice seller carries more risk than doing business with that experienced seller with a feedback score of 5,000.

Sticking with our example of a seller with a 100 percent positive feedback record, take a look at some of the comments partners have left. Those comments are shown in reverse chronological order, meaning they go from the most recent to the oldest transactions. (Bear with us through this; we know that great MP3 player you found is calling to you.) First, click on the From Buyers tab, since that will limit the comments displayed to just those from other buyers. Scrutinize the comments themselves. Buyers judged their transactions as positive, but how enthusiastic were they? Did the seller get a lot of "OKs" and "item as described," or did more than a few buyers sound positively effusive: "wonderful, would do business with this seller again." or "highly recommended!"? It's worth considering the level of buyer enthusiasm in the feedback, especially if you're thinking of buying something for $50 or more.

Now check out some of the items for which comments were left. Here's why: Suppose you're buying a $200 collectible doll, but everyone else has left feedback comments for much less expensive postcards, used toys, or CDs. In that case, you may be less secure about going through with the purchase than you would if many of the comments were for items comparable to the one you're considering. How do you tell what the comments were for? Look for the item number column on the far right of Figure 3-2. If you were online, you could click on the item numbers that were hyperlinks (as opposed to any that were "grayed out"). Doing so would take you to the sold item's original description page, where you could see for yourself what the buyer bought.

Okay, so you've found out that your seller has done a lot of business and a very high percentage of her partners left positive feedback (we recommend at least 99 percent). You've also learned that she has sold items like the one you're now interested in buying. You're still not quite finished with the feedback page. Click on the last tab, Left for Others. That pulls up the comments the seller herself has left for her trading partners, whether they were buyers like you or other sellers. Pay attention to the tone of the comments. How do they strike you? Are they friendly, efficient, and courteous, or, in the case where a transaction was negative or neutral, did the seller get belligerent and nasty? Was she drawn into public spats, or did she maintain her professionalism and composure, keeping her comments businesslike? This is also important information for you to note.

What if our seller had a feedback rating below 100 percent (also quite common), meaning some negative comments had been left for him? This doesn't necessarily mean you shouldn't do business with him. But you should take a look at some or all of these comments. Proceeding from the Feedback Received tab again, you should scroll down until you get to some of those negative comments (neutrals also), to see what the buyers' complaints were. Was a particular grievance frivolous, or did the buyer point out something that should give you pause? Is there a pattern among the negatives (Item never arrived, Item not as described, Avoid this seller)? You get the idea. If you see a troubling pattern, you may want to move on to another seller. Remember: Unless you're shopping for something quite rare, if this seller isn't right for you, there are probably many others who are.

The Item Description

Let's assume that your seller has passed the feedback hurdle. Now let's take a closer look at that item description. Let's move past the price and seller information, down to the item description itself. Carefully reading this information tells you a lot about the seller. (We'll get into the specifics of what to look for in a moment.) Be sure to read the entire listing description, including all the policy information. It may surprise you, since you're new to eBay and working hard to do everything right, but many, many buyers neglect to read the entire listing. Then, when they receive their item and are disappointed, they become angry with the seller. It's easy to get so caught up in the excitement of finding that rare collectible you've been searching for that you just skim through the listing. While we certainly understand that tendency, you must avoid falling into that pattern. We urge you to find out everything you can about the item and the seller, and the item description offers valuable information about both. (Okay, now we feel better. Let's move on!)

Language and Tone

We're not all great spellers or grammar geeks. Brad sure isn't, and he writes for a living! But a description that's riddled with typos and other mistakes shows a certain sloppiness on the seller's part. After all, it's easy enough to run a spell check these days on anything you write. But does a carelessly written item description translate into careless packaging, for example? It certainly may.

Now consider how the item is described. Does the level of detail the seller provides show that she has a lot of experience handling similar items, or did she just happen to come across this item, having never sold one before? It just feels safer buying from someone with experience selling authentic Roseville pottery, for example, rather than someone who happened to come across a Roseville vase at a yard sale. Simply put, her comments regarding an item's condition and background will have more authority. Not only that, since she's sold similar items, she probably has the proper packing materials on hand to ensure that your item arrives intact.

EXAMPLE OF A POOR ITEM DESCRIPTION

Suppose you collect old comic books, and came across two separate listings for Action Comics #252, a highly prized issue because it introduces Supergirl. (Action #252, published in 1959, is worth $3,000 in Near Mint condition!) The first listing reads as follows:

> Here's an old "Superman comic," Action #252. I found this when I came across some old comics at an estate sale, but I'm not very knowledgeable about these things. This comic appears to have all of its pages and seems to be in good condition. There are no tears, and from what I can tell there are no markings on any of the pages. I think it looks really pretty good for its age.

EXAMPLE OF A GOOD ITEM DESCRIPTION

Now consider the second listing for comparison:

> Action #252, Silver-Age "key." In solid FINE condition, per Overstreet Guidelines. The staples remain intact, and the covers still retain some gloss. It lays flat, and there are no tears or markings on the pages or covers. I will ship the comic bagged and boarded, and ready to be slabbed by CGC.

Price aside, it's clear that the second guy knows what he's talking about, while the first seller really doesn't know what he has. Seller #2 refers to "Overstreet," the standard price guide for the field. By saying the comic is in FINE condition, astute collectors would recognize he's using the commonly accepted grading system for the field. Furthermore, he notes that the comic is a "key" issue from the "Silver Age." If you were in the market for this comic, wouldn't you feel more comfortable shopping with Seller #2? Even if Seller #1 were offering the comic at a lower price, you just couldn't feel certain that there wouldn't be unpleasant surprises when your comic arrived.

Item Condition

If the description indicates that the item is sold "as is," you may be out of luck if the clock doesn't work when you get it, or that comic book isn't really in "fine" condition. Someone selling an item "as is" is putting the responsibility clearly on your shoulders for judging the item based on the information (and presumably pictures) that are there. If you regret your decision after getting the item, such a seller probably isn't willing to give you a refund. Just know that going in.

Seller's Policies

In evaluating your seller, it's not just the item description you have to consider. Scroll on down to the Shipping, Payment Details, and Return Policy area. Is the shipping cost reasonable? Sellers are entitled to add a reasonable handling charge to cover packing materials and time spent preparing the item for shipping. But if this shipping and handling charge strikes you as out of line, it probably is. In fact, some sellers will charge a very low price for an item, but an absurdly high shipping charge. For example, we did a search for new Pink Razr cell phones, available as Buy It Now items. The phones were in the $200–$300 range, but the shipping charges varied from free to $80! If someone is charging $80 to ship a cell phone to you, they're not only overcharging you, they're breaking eBay's rules. Since listing fees are based on an item's starting price, a low starting price means lower fees for the seller. Such sellers, in an attempt to keep their listing fees as low as possible, will simply charge more for shipping in order to bring the final price up to where they want it to be. eBay calls this practice *fee avoidance.* If they're willing to cheat eBay, who else do you think they'll be willing to cheat? In June 2006 at eBay Live (the company's annual confab for buyers, sellers, and other members of the community) eBay pledged to crack down on this practice, but how effectively the company will be able to do that remains to be seen.

What about the return policy? Is one specified? Under what conditions may an item be returned? Here are some actual policies from auctions.

- All eBay items are a FINAL SALE.
- Absolutely no returns!

- If you did not purchase insurance—then you are out of luck.
- If yours arrives damaged, it's not our problem.
- Don't waste our time and yours with Buyer's Remorse.

If you come across statements like these, you can bet that customer satisfaction isn't at the top of these sellers' agendas. It's more likely they're primarily interested in getting paid and moving on quickly to the next transaction, rather than developing repeat business. Now we've spoken to a lot of sellers for our other eBay books. And we've bought and sold hundreds of things on eBay ourselves. We know that you're not stuck with sellers like these. You have options. Here are some of the policies that *other* sellers told us they live by.

- I have a simple saying, "The customer is not always right, but they are always the customer."
- Give as much to your customer as you can, because that's the person who will buy from you again. We practically gift-wrap everything.
- I want my customers to be satisfied. Any issue, problem, or concern, I will address it personally, even if I lose money.

You can decide for yourself which of these groups of sellers you'd be more willing to trust, but as for us, we've already made that decision.

Ask a Question

After evaluating a seller's feedback, and scouring the item description and the seller's policies like Joe Friday, you may still have questions. There may be some detail about the item (condition, size, vintage) that's unclear from the description. If you were in a real-world store, you could ask the storeowner or clerk a question. On eBay you can do the same thing.

Let's return to the Meet the Seller box we looked at before in Figure 3-1. Notice the second bulleted item—Ask Seller a Question. If you click on this link, you'll get a screen that looks like the one shown in Figure 3-3. Just use the drop-down menu to select the appropriate subject, and type your question in the box. Decide whether you want a copy of the question sent to you, and if you'd like the seller to know your complete e-mail address, rather than just your eBay member ID, and click in the corresponding boxes if you choose either or both options.

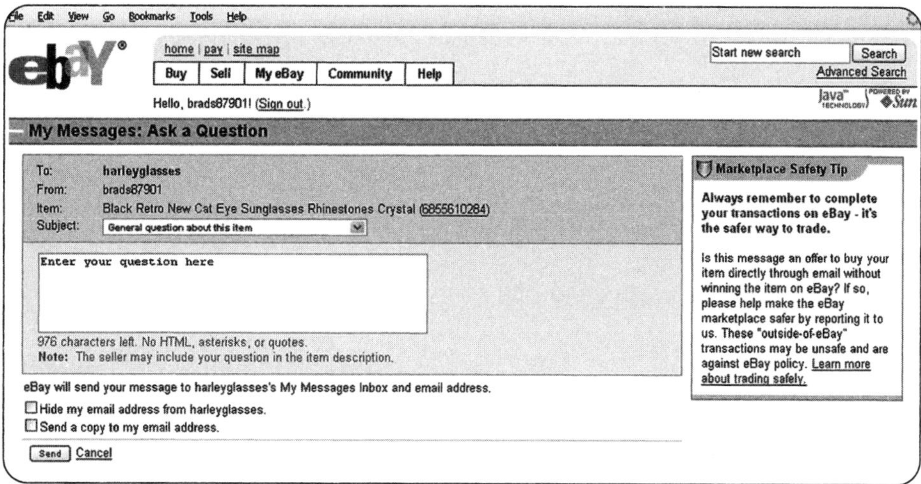

Figure 3-3: *The Ask Seller a Question page. Never hesitate to ask before you bid!*

Before we go too much further, we should explain why eBay gives you the option of either sharing or not sharing your complete e-mail address with a seller. Any communication you initiate through this form goes through eBay. When you get your e-mail response, it will come from eBay—not directly from the seller. This is to protect both you and eBay. You're protected because your full e-mail address isn't available to every trading partner you consider shopping with. Some of them may take advantage of you by putting you on unwanted e-mail lists or using your e-mail address for scamming purposes. eBay would rather not give out this information freely, because it doesn't want people to circumvent the site and complete a transaction outside its service by communicating with each other directly. If that happens, eBay doesn't earn its fees, and you don't have any protection under eBay's Standard Purchase Protection program if something were to go wrong. On the other hand, if you don't let the seller communicate with you directly, you may not hear back as quickly. If you're working with a high-volume seller, he may use an automated e-mail system that doesn't work without your e-mail address. In that case, the e-mail sent by eBay on your behalf may end up in a "junk" pile and go unanswered. So think carefully before you click the link to hide your e-mail address.

As a new buyer, you may also want to use the Ask the Seller a Question form even if you don't have a pressing question you need to ask. Just ask something related to the item or something that's not 100 percent clear to you regarding the seller's policies. This way you can get a feel for how responsive the seller is, and how interested she is in your satisfaction. A quick, friendly response can really help sway you here. But remember, many sellers—especially the larger ones—are busy, and may not be pleased if you ask something that's stated right in their auction listing. A slow or grumpy response may only indicate that she's preoccupied, not that she's unworthy of your business. Don't let that intimidate you. You're a new eBay member and most sellers understand that you may need a little more attention until you're comfortable shopping on the site. They were new once, too, so most are considerate of your lack of experience, as long as you're friendly and polite.

As a new buyer with little feedback, you may need to contact a seller anyway, especially if a higher-priced item is on the block. Some sellers are reluctant to do business with someone who doesn't have much of a history on eBay yet (say ten or fewer transactions). In fact, sellers are free to block certain bidders from placing bids on their auctions, and can even cancel bids from "unwelcome" bidders.

So a note introducing yourself may allay *their* concerns. And if you bid on an expensive item without contacting the seller first, you may get an e-mail from him to make sure you're clear about the transaction.

Signs You Can Trust

You'll come across some icons or logos in the item descriptions you read that help you feel more secure about shopping with individual sellers. These symbols indicate that a third party has verified that these sellers meet certain standards of professionalism and customer service. When you see them, you know that this person has made more than a casual commitment to the life of eBay selling, because none of these symbols comes free of charge.

SquareTrade

SquareTrade is a privately held company that specializes in verifying the safety of online shopping. The company offers services that include seller verification, post-

TRUST YOUR NEW NEIGHBORS

One of the best ways for you to get comfortable in any new neighborhood is to get to know your neighbors. You'll find a dynamic, friendly, and welcoming community on eBay. There are discussion boards, groups, and chat rooms for you to visit in search of answers to your questions, and new friends just waiting to be met. Spend some time exploring, and you're bound to find a corner of eBay that feels familiar and secure. Plus, you can easily reach these resources from any eBay page. Not surprisingly, you'll find all of them all under the same eBay hyperlink: Community.

Discussion Boards

Here's where you'll come to share ideas, information, and observations with other eBay users on just about any eBay topic you can name. You can find a discussion board for every category of item for sale on eBay. You can also find topic-specific boards for everything from About Me pages to Trust and Safety. There are even specific boards for just stopping in to chat, like the Front Porch or Night Owls Nests.

Groups

Groups are a little more specific than the discussion boards are. You'll find groups for special interests, such as gardening or stay-at-home parents; and groups for news announcements, mentoring, and collectors. Groups also include dynamic discussion boards; newsletters, photos, and group polls. Some of the groups are private. That doesn't mean you're not welcome; it just means the group gathers for very specific discussions. An example of a private group is the Beatles collectibles group, which is only open to "true" Beatles fans interested in comparing item prices. If you come across a private group that interests you, don't be put off; just send the group leader an e-mail to request membership.

The Answer Center

The Answer Center is a great resource when you come across an issue on eBay that you don't quite understand. You can freely come here and post your question. Other, more experienced users will be happy to help you. It's remarkable how giving this community is when it comes to advice and support. This is a perfect destination for newcomers, because it's designed specifically to answer those detailed questions that only occur to you once you start using the site for yourself. The FAQ in the Answer Center is a great place to start.

Chat Rooms

Pop into the live chat rooms. You'll discover individual rooms for general topics and for specific categories.

purchase protection, and dispute resolution. When a seller submits to the verification process, she agrees to meet certain business standards. Her identity is verified and so is her selling history. She also agrees to abide by the SquareTrade dispute resolution system. SquareTrade reviews her listings to ensure that they are complete, both in the description of the goods or services for sale and the policies by which she operates. She must also be willing to disclose all her contact information to her buyers.

Before granting verification, SquareTrade looks at the seller's current and previous listings. The company makes sure that the seller is peddling legitimate items and that the items he currently sells are in keeping with the items he sold previously. This eliminates the sellers who might pad their feedback by selling items for a dollar, only to switch to selling flat-screen TVs they don't actually own! (Note that SquareTrade monitors its sellers for "ongoing compliance" even *after* they've qualified for the SquareTrade seal, in part to prevent this type of abuse.) SquareTrade checks to see how long the seller has been on eBay, if he has a business offline, and if he's made good faith efforts to resolve disputes with his customers.

Once a seller passes the verification process, she can include the SquareTrade seal in all her listings. That seller pays SquareTrade $9.50 per month to maintain the seal and access SquareTrade's seller services. For buyers, there's comfort in the seal, and in knowing that this seller has met the requirements to earn the seal and is willing to pay the monthly fee required to maintain it.

BuySAFE

BuySAFE is a third-party bonding service for online sellers. Just as you would expect your roofer or plumber to be bonded, you can also shop with eBay sellers who have had their identities verified and their backgrounds checked. In return for submitting themselves to BuySAFE's scrutiny, sellers are entitled to use the BuySAFE icon that verifies them as bonded sellers. In order to qualify for the BuySAFE seal, sellers must pass the bonding inspection and agree to meet certain business standards, including the assurance that they will abide by everything they state in their listing descriptions and policies. In return, BuySAFE offers those sellers' customers a ten-point guarantee that includes assurances that the BuySAFE-vetted sellers will ship their items when they say they will and will be willing to resolve any dispute that might arise from a transaction. Finally, BuySAFE bonding includes $25,000 in financial protection for each transaction.

These guarantees are free for you, but your seller pays for them. That payment rate is 1 percent of the final value fee for the item sold, excluding taxes, shipping, and handling charges. So you can be sure that the seller who uses the BuySAFE program is going to some expense and trouble to make certain you feel comfortable shopping with him.

About Me Pages

There is one more place you can explore to learn even more about the seller you're thinking of shopping with, and that's the seller's About Me page. Not every eBay member has an About Me page, but it's a good idea for both buyers and sellers to create one. It's especially important for sellers, because it helps personalize the transaction, making the seller seem more like a real person to prospective buyers. In chapter 5 we'll tell you about creating one for yourself, but let's take a look at one now to see what you can learn about a prospective seller there. Figure 3-4 shows the About Me page of seller Stephintexas, known in the real world as Stephanie Inge. As soon as you arrive at her page, you'll see that Stephanie is a serious seller. As a matter of fact she's a PowerSeller.

In addition to her picture and logo, she offers you tabs that run across the screen to link you to her feedback history, her listings, her store, and some eBay pages you may find interesting. At the very top of the screen, notice that she also supplies you with her telephone and fax numbers in case you need to get in touch with her directly. As you scroll down her page, you'll find lots of information about her business, her services, and even her family. By the time you've reached the bottom, you will have even seen a picture of her as a schoolgirl! You can't help but read through her page and feel as if you've gotten to know the person who is behind the listing you were looking at just a few minutes before.

You can feel secure that anyone who has spent this much time and energy establishing her presence on eBay will also devote herself to providing great service to her customers. That's not to say that a great seller can't exist without an

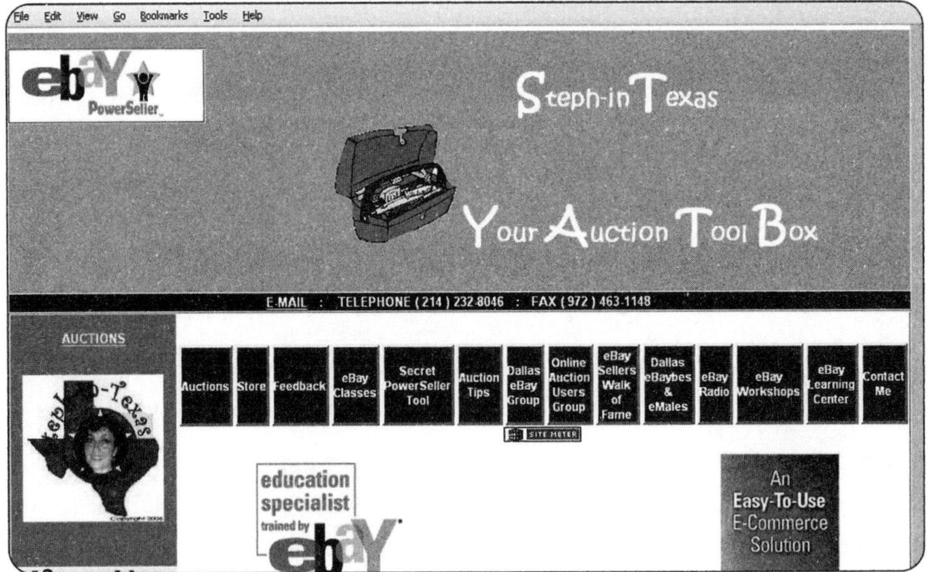

Figure 3-4: *Review a seller's About Me page to help decide if you've found a good trading partner.*

About Me page, but expending the time and effort to create a dynamic page introducing yourself to your customers is one way to distinguish your business from the millions of others on eBay. A seller like that is more likely to be on eBay for the long term and more likely to be someone you can feel good about dealing with.

eBay does not allow sellers to insert links to off-eBay Web sites directly into their auction listings. However, an About Me page may include links to anywhere on the Web. If you follow those links, you'll learn even more about your prospective trading partner. That's especially true if the seller operates a Web store. Now you'll see that not only is your prospective trading partner working as a professional eBay seller, but he is working to support a Web-based business, too. That goes a long way toward assuring you that he is serious about selling. Even if the seller doesn't have a Web store linked to his About Me page, it's a good exercise to click on the links he includes to see where they lead. That way, you can learn something about what the seller is interested in and what he thinks is important. Remember: Anything you can do to make the seller seem more real in your mind will help you to trust him when it comes time to buy from him.

Buyer Beware

So now you're equipped with quite a few good ways to learn more about a prospective seller and to decide if you're willing to take a risk by making a purchase from her. In the end, risk is unavoidable when you shop on eBay. You can be as careful as possible, but the moment will come when you will simply have to trust someone enough to risk dealing with her. Everything we've talked about so far will help lessen that risk, but nothing you can do will completely eliminate it. Before we move on, let's take a look at some common scams and tricks criminals may use to try to tip the risk equation in their favor. We call them *criminals* instead of *sellers,* because that's exactly what they are. Just because someone uses eBay to steal from you doesn't make it any less of a crime than if he had reached into your pocket and taken your wallet. These thieves are no more sellers on eBay than a mugger is a friendly neighbor out for a stroll on a pleasant evening.

Bad Offers

There are definitely some offers you should refuse. Scammers have come up with a number of simple and ingenious ways of cheating unsuspecting buyers. Unfortunately, criminals tend to think of ways to steal with more diligence than honest people think of ways to conduct fair and equitable trades. That means you have to stay ever vigilant for potential fraud, including offers that seem legitimate but are designed to either rob you of your money or make you a conspirator in defrauding eBay. Here are a few potential red flags to watch out for.

"I'LL TAKE THE LISTING DOWN AND WE CAN COMPLETE IT JUST BETWEEN US"

If a seller contacts you after you make a bid and offers to take down the listing and complete it off eBay, decline the offer and report the seller to eBay (just click on the Security Center link appearing at the bottom of many eBay pages). The seller has already proven himself to be a crook, because he's offering to defraud eBay and rob the site of the fees he agreed to pay when he signed on. He's used eBay for his own profit and now wants to deny the company the fees it rightfully deserves. eBay has fulfilled its part of the agreement with this guy, by giving him a place to earn his money. Now that he has the customer he wants, he's willing to cheat the company that helped him get to this point. How do you think he'll deal with you if you have a dispute with him? He's already proven he's a sneak and a liar, so why should you trust him to treat you any better? Plus, if you do complete the transaction off eBay, you'll have no one to turn to if he does cheat you. eBay is under no obligation to come to your defense when you complete a transaction off the site, and the company won't. You'll be strictly on your own.

SECOND CHANCE OFFERS

A seller can legitimately choose to make a second chance offer to a bidder under a number of different circumstances. If the winning bidder fails to complete the sale, the seller may approach the next highest bidder to see if that person still wants the item, at that bidder's highest bid. This is a good deal for the seller, even if that second bid was lower, because it saves her the trouble of having to run the auction listing again, and it lets her complete the transaction without incurring any additional fees or spending any more time on the sale. It's also good if you were the second highest bidder, and you really wanted the item. The seller can also extend a second chance offer to the highest bidder in a reserve listing if the auction ended without the reserve price being met. (A reserve listing is a listing in which the seller has set a minimum price for which he will sell his item. If no one meets that minimum, the auction ends without a sale. We'll discuss reserve listings in depth in chapter 4.) The seller might have a change of heart and decide that the highest offer was close enough to the reserve price to just go ahead and complete the transaction. Finally, if a seller owns two identical items, but only lists one of them, he can contact the next highest bidder to see if that person still wants to make the purchase. So, as you can see, second chance offers aren't bad in and of themselves.

The problem occurs when a second chance offer comes from someone other than the original seller. This is especially true with high-priced items. Some scammers and criminals watch auctions for expensive items so they can spot a victim just ripe for a fake second chance offer. It works like this: Suppose you were bidding on an expensive watch, and you lost the auction to another bidder. Suddenly you get an e-mail from the "seller" saying that he has another watch just like it and asking you if you still want to buy it. When you express interest, he'll direct you to send the money and promise to send the watch. The problem is, he doesn't own the watch, and you'll never hear from him again once he has your money. So how do you protect yourself from this scam? How do you tell a good second chance offer from a bad one? It's easier than you think. Any legitimate second chance offer will come directly through your own My eBay page. (Click the My Messages tab that appears on the left-hand side of the page. That's where you'll find all authentic e-mails from eBay and eBay members.) Then it's all happening on eBay, and you'll have all of eBay's Buyer Protection behind you. If it comes to you via regular e-mail, you know it's a fake, because any honest seller will know enough not to contact you that way with a second chance offer. So problem solved. Until, of course, the next scam.

"YOU'RE BIDDING ON A FAKE"

Another way for you to be victimized by a bad offer is to have someone contact you and tell you that you are bidding on a fake item from a fraudulent seller. Again, this is most likely to happen when you bid on expensive things; there are criminals who watch those listings just looking for someone to approach for a scam. The e-mail will seem like a friendly warning. It will say that you are lucky this person saw your bid, because he's been scammed by this seller before, and he's trying to protect others. He'll tell you that the expensive collectible you're hoping to purchase is fake, and you should withdraw your bid. Of course, as luck would have it, he has one just like it that he'll be happy to sell to you!

You might wonder why people would fall for this scam, but you'd be surprised how vulnerable people are to fraudulent deals. After all, you're already taking a risk by shopping on eBay. It's not that difficult to believe that someone, especially someone who is new to the site, might feel spooked by the thought of getting cheated. To have someone friendly approach you and offer to help you avoid a costly mistake that he himself just made could easily tip the balance in the crook's favor. If you get an e-mail like this, contact the original seller and eBay, too. Tell them both about what's happened. eBay will want that e-mail, and the seller, if he's legitimate, will do everything possible to reassure you that all is well.

Other Warning Signs

You may not always get an offer that smells bad to warn you of potential danger. There are other aspects of a potential eBay trade that should set your alarm bells ringing. Criminals have found ways to use eBay's own offerings to defraud unsuspecting buyers, and their ingenuity and creativity are only outpaced by their dedication to the task. Here are a few other cautionary notes you can add to your armor as you venture out into the fray.

ONE-DAY LISTINGS

Just like a second chance offer, a listing that lasts only a single day may be completely legitimate, but you should be careful when you're thinking of bidding on an item that will only be available for one day. An auction that begins and ends that quickly isn't around long enough for it to be discovered to be crooked. It's gone before most people notice it's even there. That's exactly why criminals sometimes use them. If you're shopping for something, and you see you only have today to decide on it, you may move more quickly than you should and buy impulsively. There's an added pressure not to miss the sale. That might just lead you to take careless shortcuts.

In addition, if the person is a crook, no one else selling in the category the item is listed in will have the time to detect the sale and notify eBay that it doesn't smell right. Sellers who work hard to earn their livings on eBay know the categories they occupy inside and out. They often act like neighborhood watch groups. They know who their competitors are, and they recognize buyers and sellers who operate within their neighborhoods. If a bad listing is up for three, five, seven, or ten days, the criminal who listed it is likely to get caught. But a one-day auction lets her hop on, find a victim, and vanish before anyone even knows she was there, except, of course, for the poor buyer who spent money on something that never arrives. So if you want to buy something that's only listed for a single day, be extra careful.

"WIRE THE MONEY TO ME, PLEASE"

One of the red flags of fraud that's easiest to spot is the old "wire me the money" scam. Never pay for anything through a direct wire transfer to someone's bank account. The money goes too quickly from being yours to being theirs, and you simply have no recourse if the seller turns out to be a crook. Even if you make a wire transfer through your credit card, you can't get your money back. That's because you willingly authorized the transfer, and that's all it takes for you to forfeit your protection through the credit card company. An easy way to be extra careful is to pay for your item through eBay's own service, PayPal. This can provide an extra measure of purchase protection, as we describe in chapter 8. There is really no legitimate reason for a seller to insist that you complete any transaction through a direct wire transfer outside of PayPal, so refuse to do it every single time.

Are You Buying a Fake?

One of the most difficult forms of fraud to protect yourself against is purchasing a fake item that is supposedly the real thing. Some categories are especially vulnerable to being plagued by copycat knockoffs. For example, "Oakley sunglasses" and "Louis Vuitton bags" are both frequently sold for bargain-basement prices on eBay. It's difficult for you to protect yourself, unless, of course, you know an awful lot about the luxury item you're shopping for. If you decide to come to eBay looking for bargains on these items, you must also be prepared to educate yourself to the point of knowing exactly what to look for and how to distinguish the real from the fake.

Of course, you'll take all the steps we've already outlined to try to determine that you've found a reliable trading partner, but then you'll also have to consider a few additional ones. If you're determined to buy a designer item on eBay, explore it outside of eBay before you buy. Go to a boutique that carries the item and note some specific details that will help you identify it when you see it on the site. Educate yourself about the item through the manufacturer's Web site so you'll be prepared to make a good evaluation of the item listed. You can even turn to eBay for some help with your education. eBay's Reviews and Guides area is a useful resource for learning how to evaluate products. You'll find it on the Site Map under Buyer's Resources. For its part, eBay states that it "does not permit" sellers to list counterfeits or fakes, and it will suspend a seller's account for violating this policy. Yet, many fakes are listed, and eBay explicitly states in its User Agreement that it has no control over and cannot guarantee "the quality, safety, or legality of items advertised" or "the truth or accuracy of listings." That pretty much absolves the company of any liability, a policy that some sellers, as well as large firms like Tiffany & Company, are starting to challenge in the courts.

Platinum-level PowerSeller Sarah Davis specializes in authentic, previously owned Louis Vuitton handbags, and she's written a guide for buyers who want to make sure they're getting the real thing. "Ninety percent of the Louis Vuitton bags for sale on eBay are fake," she told us. She's even had scammers steal her pictures of the genuine article to use in their listings for the fake counterpart! Reading her guide will help you recognize exactly what type of stitching a genuine bag should have, what the lining should look like, and even what the zipper head should be. You'll need to do that kind of research for any luxury item. Sarah asks a very good question we should all consider: When you know that Louis Vuitton doesn't sell seconds, returns, wholesale, or discounted bags, where do you think those cheap, brand-new, LV bags on eBay come from? Good point. So, basically, remember what your mother always told you: "If it sounds too good to be true, it probably is."

Now that you've learned how to find the things you want and how to effectively evaluate a potential trading partner, let's get to the real fun. Let's go see exactly how you can bid to increase your chances of winning the auction and finding the treasure!

HENDRIK SHARPLES IS A POWERSELLER who operates his business from the Pacific Northwest. His user ID is Hendrik. As a PowerSeller, he's had lots of experiences both selling and buying on eBay, and he's gotten to be very good at evaluating his fellow sellers. His favorite eBay purchase not only shows what fun eBay can be, but it effectively highlights the differences among sellers.

Hendrik bought a Mercedes-Benz on eBay. He was considering two different cars. One belonged to a dealer who was based in Texas, and the other belonged to a private individual in Florida. You'd think the seller in Texas would have been the safer bet, but Hendrik didn't agree. He asked each seller to do a mechanical check on the cars. The dealer said he was "too busy." The private individual agreed to take the car to his local Saturn dealer. For about $120, the mechanics completed the same type of check on the car that they would have conducted if it were being considered for a trade-in. The seller even paid for it. The car checked out just fine, and Hendrik completed the sale. He then located a transport company that was buying cars in Florida for delivery to his home in the Pacific Northwest. This made shipping the car across the country much more affordable. So Hendrik chose the smaller seller who seemed more cooperative and is now driving around in style!

How Do I Place a Bid?

BIDDING ON AN EBAY AUCTION is an art. If we just wanted to explain the mechanics of placing a bid on eBay that would be simple—this chapter would practically be over already. But there's more to bidding than clicking on the Place Bid button and typing in an amount. Before you offer to pay someone for an item being auctioned, you have to consider how much you should bid and when it's to your strategic advantage to place your bid. These may seem like straightforward issues, but they're not. There are many factors to take into account, including who may be bidding against you.

By the time you're finished with this chapter, you'll know not only the mechanics of how to bid, but also some strategies for determining how much you should bid and when you should make your bid known. We'll also introduce you to a type of software that will do your bidding for you. It works within the last few seconds of an auction, scooping up the item you want without your competition ever knowing you were after it, and giving you a distinct advantage over buyers who do not use this software. Our goal is to help you win as many auctions as possible and pay the lowest possible prices. Sound good? Read on!

How to Place a Bid

Before we start talking about bidding, let's first take a look at a simpler buying strategy: purchasing items outright on eBay as you would on any other e-commerce site. If you are shopping for items you can buy immediately, such as

Buy It Now items, or things listed through eBay Express, you have nothing more to consider. You're not bidding on these things; you're simply buying them. You agree to pay the price listed and move on to chapter 5 to communicate with the seller and get on with paying for your item. It's not much different from visiting any Web site to place an order. Of course, you've already done your homework to determine that this seller is trustworthy and is offering a good deal, but you really don't have anything to learn about this type of bid. eBay has purposely made this process very simple for you. And there's nothing wrong with these types of listings, especially when you're new to eBay and just trying to get your feet wet on the site.

If you're going to enter into an auction (and auctions are where most of the fun is), you must consider everything else we have to tell you about bidding. Now just because you may never have bid on an item on eBay doesn't mean you're a complete novice in the realm of auction bidding. It's really not much different from the live auctions you may have seen or attended. You know how bidding works there. The auctioneer calls out a starting price. Anyone who's willing to pay that price raises a hand, or a sign, or in some other way signals an agreement to pay that price. Bidding continues until no more bids are offered and the item sells. Well, the process is similar on eBay, except that eBay's computers do the work for you through proxy bidding.

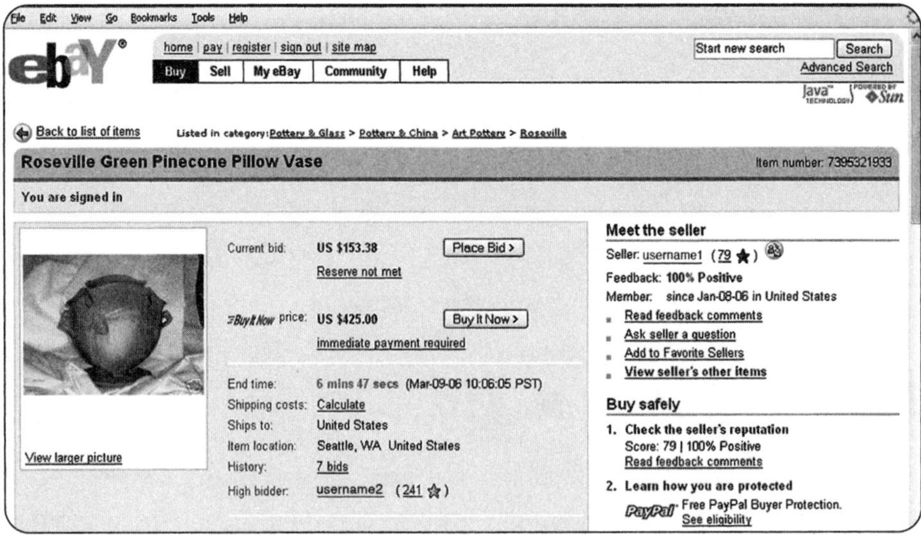

Figure 4-1: *This listing page is for an auction for a Roseville vase.*

So let's take a look at how you actually bid, and then we'll get to the inside advice. We'll assume you've found that beautiful Roseville vase you've always wanted (see Figure 4-1), and you want to try to win the auction for it.

You'll see right at the top of the listing the current price, how much more time remains in the auction, the number of bids received to date, and the member ID of the highest bidder. If you're ready to join the crowd, you can simply click on the Place Bid button next to the current price. Or you can also find the same link at the bottom of the page, after you've carefully read the item description, viewed the photos, and examined the seller's shipping, pricing, and return policies. Either way, once you indicate that you're ready to bid, the screen shown in Figure 4-2 will appear. Enter your maximum bid in the box, and you're now one of the group of people hoping to win the vase.

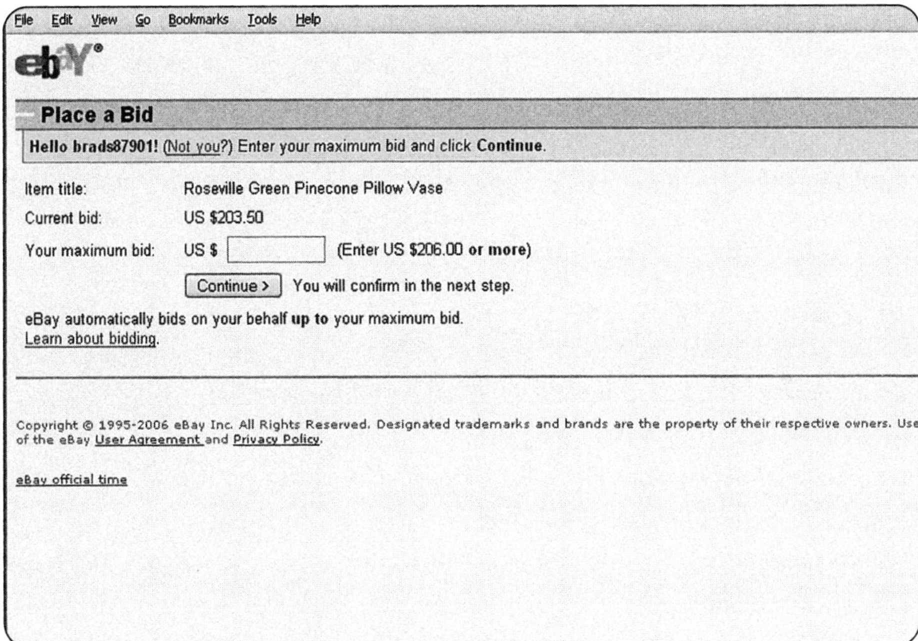

***Figure 4-2:** The Place a Bid page, which is where the rubber meets the road.*

Before you place your bid, be very sure you want the item. A bid is considered a contract. That was in the agreement you signed when you joined eBay as a buyer. Entering a bid means you've agreed to pay the price you've submitted, but it also means you've agreed to abide by all the policies the seller has listed in his item description. Bidding is a destination at the end of a considered journey you make toward acquiring something you want. You can't just say, "Oops, I changed my mind, didn't want it after all." At least you can't do that without suffering the consequences of becoming a nonpaying bidder, an outcast on eBay, and ultimately a former eBay member. eBay will revoke your membership for this.

You know all this, and you really want that vase, so you enter your highest bid and let eBay's computers do the rest. Through proxy bidding, eBay's computers keep up with the bidding on your behalf. The computers will track the highest amount you've agreed to pay and the amounts all your competitors have agreed to pay. With each new bid, the tally rises, and through this proxy bidding process eBay enters your next bid. Should someone enter a bid higher than your highest bid, you are out of the running unless you choose to bid again at a higher price. So, for example, if you were willing to pay up to $250 for that vase, you would enter that amount in the box where you place your bid. If the current bid were $203.50, your bid would increase by the applicable increment to $206.00, which would be listed as the new current bid. The proxy bidding would continue to go up in increments (as shown in the chart above) and you would remain a contender until your highest bid of $250 had been reached.

PROXY BIDDING INCREMENTS

CURRENT PRICE	BID INCREMENT
$.01 to $.99	$.05
$1.00 to $4.99	$.25
$5.00 to $24.99	$.50
$25.00 to $99.99	$1.00
$100.00 to $249.99	$2.50
$250.00 to $499.99	$5.00
$500.00 to $999.99	$10.00
$1,000.00 to $2,499.99	$25.00
$2,500.00 to $4,999.99	$50.00
$5,000.00 and up	$100.00

When Should I Bid?

There are two schools of thought about timing your bid. One holds that you set your maximum price early on, and then forget about the rest of the auction. Once you've determined that you are already offering to spend as much as you're absolutely willing to spend on the item, you really don't have anything more to consider until the auction ends and you get the notification that you've either won or lost. According to the other school of thought, you should watch the auction for a few days before bidding to see what the action is and then decide what you're willing to spend. In the latter scenario, you would place your bid closer to the end of the auction period.

Either method could be right for you. In the following pages, we'll look at the mechanics of an auction and both methods of bidding so that you can make your own choice. The first thing to remember is that the *auction* only happens in the last few moments of a listing's life. If you're interested in an item put up for a seven-day listing, all of the first six days and most of the seventh day are simply advertisement, designed to attract interested bidders. It doesn't matter if there is one bid during that period or hundreds of bids. Nothing has sold until the listing closes.

Both approaches to bidding begin when you determine the maximum amount you would pay for a particular item. Then you must stick to your decision. The same rule applies to auctions in the offline world, too. The auction attendee who loses all control and spends more than he ever planned is fodder for situation comedies, but it's not that funny in real life. eBay makes it very easy for you decide to bid just a little more, and then just a little more, until you've spent more for something than you know you should have—even more than the item might really be worth. So now we'll look at the psychology behind both methods of bidding on an auction item.

Bid Early, But Often?

Some bidders decide they want an item very early in the life of the auction. They do their homework, check out the seller, decide on a price, and enter the bidding. This is an effective strategy if you're the type of person who can establish a specific budget and then *stay within that budget.* Throughout the life of the auction listing, you'll be able to track your position in the bidding. If you are outbid, you'll also get an e-mail from eBay with a link that will let you bid more, just like that! These e-mails are designed to get your competitive juices flowing and strike back at the usurper who's bested you for the moment. If you set your maximum bid early and are then outbid, it's tempting to boost your bid just enough to keep on top, so you won't miss out on the item you've already decided you want. (Now you can't say we didn't warn you!)

Of course, if you have the willpower, this method can be great for you. You set your bid early, and then you can completely forget about it. At the end of the auction, eBay will notify you of the outcome, whether you win or whether you're outbid. But it won't matter—you've made your decision, and you're going to stick with it. It can be very calming on your nerves not to watch the action as the bidding continues.

Watch Early, Bid Later

Another option is to "watch" the item. In every auction listing there is a link, shown in Figure 4-3, that makes it easy for you to watch the action on the item. Click that link and the listing will appear on your My eBay page under "Items I'm Watching." Every time you log onto eBay and check My eBay, you'll see what's going on with all the items you've decided to watch. This is a great feature offered by eBay. It allows you to find some things you like, mark them so they don't get lost, and then keep track of how much demand there is for these items and what the final selling prices tend to be. It's a great tool, even if you're just thinking about buying something, but not quite ready to bid on anything. It helps you to monitor the life of an auction as it happens, without risking anything but your time.

If you watch the item for a while, you can monitor it while you do the rest of your

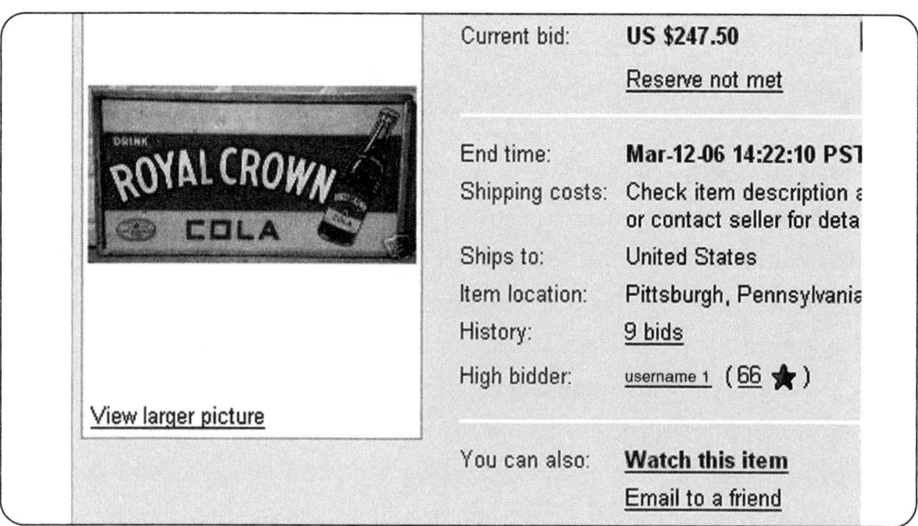

Figure 4-3: *Click on the Watch this Item link to track an auction through your My eBay page.*

research. You can investigate the seller, check completed auctions to learn how much similar items have sold for in the past, assess your budget, and take your time deciding if you want to bid and how much you're going to offer. If you decide to bid, don't worry about missing the end of the auction. eBay will send you an e-mail within a few hours of the auction's closing, reminding you that you're watching an item that's about to close and encouraging you to make your bid before it's too late.

One advantage to watching rather than bidding early is that while you're watching, only the seller knows that you're interested. He'll see that you're watching his listing through his own My eBay page, but none of the other bidders will know you're considering this item. If you bid early, everyone else who might be interested knows that you want that item. You've tipped your hand. If you consider it a while and come in late with a bid, you may just discourage an early bidder who was only bidding in hopes of getting a bargain and who isn't interested in competing for the item.

Early bidding definitely drives up the interest in an auction listing and can easily escalate the final price. It's human nature for people to want what others want, too.

Of course, waiting to bid doesn't eliminate the risk of getting caught up in the last-minute bidding frenzy and spending too much. But if you haven't yet bid on an item, you don't have quite the same connection to it. You may certainly watch the bidding move beyond the upper limit you've determined, and, because you haven't actually made your offer yet, you may be better prepared to let the auction end and the prize go to someone who is simply willing to pay more.

Either Way, Don't Get Too Attached

There is definitely psychology involved in eBay bidding. We've outlined two very different approaches for you to consider, but in the end neither one of these strategies will guarantee that you get what you're hoping for. When the auction ends and you're not the highest bidder, the disappointment is real. It's very important for you to keep reminding yourself that whatever you find on eBay will be available again. The site is just too big and too dynamic for items to be put up for auction just one time and never seen again. Once you've bid on an item, it somehow feels as if it belongs to you, even if you keep telling yourself that you haven't bought it yet. Once you've decided you want something, it's easy to go after it. eBay itself contributes to the mentality of competition.

Competitive people thrive on eBay—the whole system is set up to encourage you to view an auction as a contest of sorts, with winners and losers. If you should win an auction, eBay will send you a congratulatory e-mail, calling you the winner. If someone bests your highest bid, eBay will let you know that as well, sending you an e-mail saying "You have been Outbid. Bid again now!" You can see how easy it is to get caught up in the competition and take this bidding stuff personally.

HOW MUCH SHOULD I BID?

Only you can determine the price that seems reasonable for any particular item that sells on eBay. Your price might be much higher than another bidder's, simply based on how much you want that particular item. If it has sentimental value to you or if it completes a long-held collection of yours, its actual value is greater to you than it would be to someone who is less emotionally invested in the object. Sometimes that reality works in your favor and sometimes it works against you, when it's your opponent who feels that way. Did you pay too much? Only you can decide.

Don't Bid in Round Numbers

When you make a bid, steer away from whole and round numbers. If you're willing to pay $60.00 for something, make your actual bid something like $61.07. That way, if someone else has bid $61.00 for the item, you'll still be the highest bidder. Every penny counts, so always add a few to your bid.

What If Someone Bids Exactly the Same Amount That I Bid?

In the case of two identical high bids, the one that was entered first will be the winner. That's one point in favor of an early bid. On the other hand, if you bid in odd increments, you're likely to avoid an identical bid from another seller.

Don't Forget to Consider the *Real* Cost of the Item

Don't get so caught up in the bidding that you forget what the item is actually going to cost you. It's easy to do this. In deciding on your final, absolute high bid, remember that you also have to pay shipping, handling, and maybe even sales tax if the seller operates in the state where you live. The combined total of those charges is your actual cost of the item. To prevent buyer's remorse, before you bid be sure you clearly know exactly what you'll have to spend to get the item.

Know Your Competition

When you decide to make a bid, you will be better able to figure the actual likelihood of winning the auction if you take some time to consider who else is bidding against you. In most auction listings, the bidding history is easy to see. Simply click on the hyperlink that shows the number of bids, and you'll see a list of who's trying to get what you want. Reading this list can be very educational.

You can see if there is a bidder who is really determined to get the item. That person may have been the first bidder and may continue to top whatever bid comes along. You'll see multiple entries for this member's ID, so you'll know she's trying hard to win. You can see the feedback numbers of the other bidders, too, so you can size up the competition in terms of who has the most experience bidding on eBay. Don't be discouraged if the competition has more experience. We watched an auction end for a Roseville vase and found the winner had one feedback comment and the other two bidders each had thousands to their names!

Beyond that, you can click on the feedback numbers and check out the other bidders' feedback pages. Once there, you can note their prior bidding patterns by clicking on items they've previously won. Do they place a bid and walk away? Or do they swoop in at the last minute? Now you'll know what your competition is most likely to do, and you can monitor the auction for the item you want with this in mind.

You can also see if you're going to be bidding against someone who you simply can't beat. Deb found a collection of eighty-five old photograph postcards. Since she's been collecting these for years, she thought she'd give it a try. Getting the whole collection would allow her to cherry-pick the ones she really loved for her collection and sell the others individually on eBay. She decided she'd spend about $30 for the whole lot. The bidding came down to just Deb and one other person. When she checked his feedback, she found that he was a dealer in old photographic postcards. So he would probably be willing to spend more than she would to win the auction. Paradoxically, however, this knowledge left her feeling encouraged. She saw that she'd really identified a great buy, and she was glad to know that she lost out to a professional. It also helped her control the impulse to overspend, since she could see clearly that she was playing and he was working!

Special Situations

We started this chapter by telling you about some sales on eBay that don't include bidding, such as Buy It Now, Fixed Price listings, and eBay Express items. There are also other types of auctions that require bidding but involve special bidding considerations. Two of them are Reserve Price auctions and Best Offer sales.

Reserve Price Auctions

A seller may designate any auction as a Reserve Price listing. That means when the seller creates the listing, he decides on a price below which he simply won't sell the item. If the auction runs its course and the bidding doesn't reach the reserve price, the item doesn't sell, even if the highest bid comes within pennies of the reserve price. Sellers use Reserve Price listings for a variety of reasons. Often, a new seller who doesn't want to risk selling something for less than he feels it's worth will include a reserve. A Trading Assistant who is selling something precious to a client may also use a reserve price to ensure that his client won't be disappointed with the final sale price. If the seller has set a reserve, the listing will indicate that a reserve price exists but, generally speaking, the reserve amount is not specified.

If you want to bid on a Reserve Price listing, and the amount of the reserve doesn't appear in the item description, send the seller an e-mail and ask what the reserve is. There really is no reason for him not to tell you. If he does, then you'll know whether or not it's feasible for you to win the item. We say *if* because some sellers are a little overprotective of this kind of information and will refuse to reveal it. Then you'll have to decide if you want to take your chances by coming up with your best bid and going after the item in hopes that your best will be above the reserve. Note that once a reserve price is met, the listing continues on as a regular auction would, with the highest bidder ultimately winning.

Best Offer

Another interesting choice for sellers is to designate an item as a Best Offer listing. Let's suppose a seller has a jewelry box that she'd like to get at least $75.00 for, although she believes it to be worth more. She can list it at $89.99 with a Best Offer feature. Then she can attract interested bidders hoping to scoop up the jewelry box by making a low offer. She doesn't have to reveal the price at which she'll sell the jewelry box. She also doesn't have to accept any bid below $89.99, but she may accept one that gets close to her hoped-for price of $75.00. If you see a Best Offer auction, you know you'll have a little wiggle room with the starting price. So come up with what you think you'd be happy paying for the item, and send it along to the seller as your Best Offer. You may just wind up with a bargain, making you and the seller both happy.

Sniping Software

When we first started selling on eBay, one of the things we sold was an old TV repair manual to a buyer in England. We remember the sale because the bidding was very healthy, and the guy who won said he had "sniped" the auction. Sniped? We had never heard the term before, and it sounded vaguely unethical. After all, *sniped* sounds a lot like *swiped*. When we looked into it, we learned that the practice is perfectly legal and a lot of eBay buyers do it.

How It Works

Sniping software automatically places your bid for you within the last few seconds of an auction's closing. This means you don't have to be at your computer, waiting for an auction to end. You use sniping software to avoid tipping your hand by placing a bid before you have to, and therefore letting others know you're interested in the item. Less competition means lower prices, so using sniping software can give you a competitive edge, and help you win your items for less. It also means you don't have to worry about getting beaten in the last few seconds of an auction by someone with a faster Internet connection. Of course, if you don't bid high enough, you still don't win—simple as that. Let's see how this strategy works by walking through an actual snipe.

We're going to use BidNip as our sniping program, although there are many other programs available and they all work pretty much the same way. Some are easier to use, though, and we think BidNip's in that category. BidNip is Internet-based software, meaning you don't download a program to your computer—it resides on the BidNip Web site (http://bidnip.com/). Other sniping software is "desktop-based," meaning you need to download a program and your computer must be on when the auction is scheduled to end.

To begin, go to the BidNip site and register. You will need to enter your eBay user ID and password as part of this process. Don't be concerned about parting with this information; BidNip needs these details in order to bid on your behalf. As a new user, you will receive five free "snipes." Now let's assume that you have located something on eBay that you'd like to bid on. Highlight and copy the item number, which appears on the right of the description page, on the same line as the title. You'll need to enter that number in the item number box on the main BidNip page. Paste it in that box, and click on the Snipe It button. That will bring up a page where you'll need to enter your e-mail address and the password you created when you first registered with BidNip. The next page will look like the one shown in Figure 4-4. Enter your maximum bid in the box, and you're done! Your bid will automatically be placed from one to thirty seconds—whatever increment you've specified—before the auction ends.

During the course of an auction, you can edit or delete a snipe, so don't worry that you're locked in. BidNip will send you an e-mail at the end of the auction letting you know whether or not you won the item (just as eBay does). If you win the

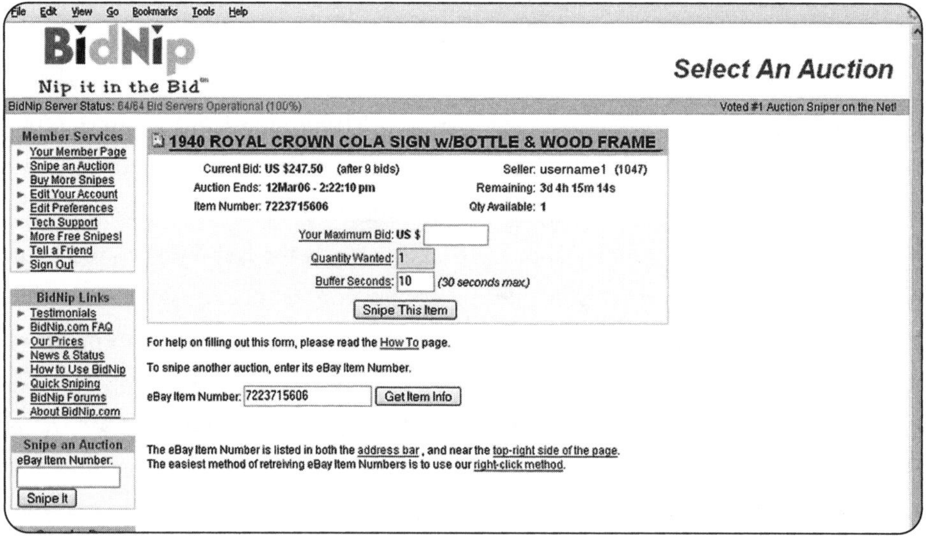

Figure 4-4: *With sniping software like BidNip, you can place your bid in the final few seconds of an auction, even if you're nowhere near a computer.*

item, it will cost you one of your free snipes. If you lose, all your free snipes remain. *Note:* You should monitor your ongoing auctions through BidNip, because if you're outbid before the auction ends, BidNip doesn't notify you of this.

Can I Cancel My Bid?

The short answer to this question is yes, but it's a little more complicated than that. If you're buying real estate or a business on eBay, your bid isn't binding. The same is true if you've bid on something that is prohibited from being sold on the site by law or by eBay's User Agreement. For all other circumstances, retracting a bid is not something to be done lightly, and there are only certain situations whereby eBay will allow you to legitimately back out of an offer to buy.

Typos

If you accidentally key in the wrong amount, you can reenter the correct amount if you do it immediately after you retract the mistaken bid. (You can retract a bid by going to the Site Map and clicking on Bid Retractions under Buying Resources.) If you just retract the bid and don't make a corrected one immediately, you will be in violation of eBay policy. So be very careful when keying in the bid you wish to make!

Description Changes

If you've bid on an item and then the seller significantly changes the item description during the auction, you have the right to retract the bid.

Seller's Gone Missing

If you try to contact the seller and you can't reach her, you are allowed to retract the bid. That means you've sent the seller an e-mail that bounces back to you as undeliverable or you've tried to reach the seller by phone, but found the phone number wasn't valid.

Criminal Bids

If someone has bid on an item using your user ID and password without your permission, you can cancel the bid.

You also have to consider *when* you make the retraction. If you place a bid before the last twelve hours of an auction, you may retract it up until the last twelve hours for any one of these legitimate reasons. Beyond that twelve-hour window, you cannot retract. When you retract a bid before the last twelve hours of a listing, you also cancel all the other bids you've placed on that item. If you've retracted to correct a bidding error, you'll have to start all over and bid again.

If you bid within that twelve-hour time frame, you may only retract a bid within a single hour of placing it. After that, it's too late to take it back. In this scenario you only eliminate that last bid. All the bids you placed before this deadline still count.

When you cancel a bid, no matter what the reason, that bid retraction becomes part of your member profile. eBay keeps track of how often you do this and will definitely take action if the company finds you habitually retract your bids.

Well, you must be feeling pretty good by now. You've learned to find items on eBay, research whether or not they're a good deal, and place a bid. You'll be winning auctions in no time and that means interacting with sellers, the subject of the next chapter.

RACHEL GELHAUS LOVES EBAY. Not only does she buy frequently on the site, but she's also adept at selling. Her favorite buy was an item that had great personal meaning to her. It was worth even more to her than it was to the other buyers trying to compete against her. It all started in college.

Rachel was studying design in college. She was selected for an internship to work with a design house in New York City. It was a wonderful opportunity for a young woman interested in the field, and she settled in quickly, learning the details of designing handbags and clothing. Her prized project was a yellow shirt with hearts that she designed herself. It was selected from the group of student projects to be manufactured by Odille Manufacturing, and Rachel wore hers with great pride. It was a thrill to see her creation for sale in stores.

But the life of a college student has its share of disappointments, and Rachel was heartbroken when someone stole her special shirt from the community laundry room. How could the thief fully appreciate the real value of that shirt to its rightful owner? So Rachel started looking on eBay in hopes of finding a replacement. She actually did find one, but she lost the auction and it went to a higher bidder. Not to be deterred, Rachel contacted the winner and appealed to her to sell the shirt. Unfortunately, the winner wasn't moved by Rachel's story. She liked the shirt too much herself! She promised Rachel she'd get in touch if she ever decided to sell it, but Rachel never heard from her again.

She kept scouring eBay. She listed it as a Want It Now item. Finally, after two years of dedicated searching, another shirt came up for auction. Rachel wasn't going to miss it this time. She entered into competition with twelve other buyers who also wanted the shirt, but this time she prevailed! She received a slightly used, but perfectly acceptable version of the shirt she had designed, and she still wears it proudly to this day. In good time, practically everything turns up on eBay. None of those other bidders ever stood a chance of winning that auction, but they had no way of knowing that the rightful owner would prevail this time.

Chapter 5

Effectively Communicating with Sellers

COMMUNICATION CAN MEAN EVERYTHING on eBay, where the person you're doing business with exists only behind a computer screen. This chapter will show you how to communicate effectively with a seller, not only through your own correspondence, but also through the image you project with your About Me page. Through this Web page you create right on eBay, you let the community know a little bit about the person behind your computer screen. We're all for anything that aids communication between buyers and sellers. It can mean the difference between a perfect transaction, in which you receive just the item you expected to receive—in a timely fashion, with no surprises along the way—and one you'll regret.

The Internet and eBay being what they are, you're unlikely to hear from a seller until you've bid on and won his item. Of course, you saw in chapter 3 how important it is for you to understand clearly the terms of a sale and how easy it is for you to ask a seller a question (we'll repeat) *before* you bid. After you've won an auction, you may exchange lots of e-mails—to confirm that you've paid for the item, note when the item is shipped, and finally to leave feedback for one another.

Effective E-mail Communication

The great majority of messaging among eBay partners—more than 90 percent—occurs via e-mail, and we don't have to tell you that e-mail has its limitations. In the real world, your body language and tone of voice can actually convey more than your words. That's why you have to be especially careful about the content and tone of your e-mail, since it is missing a lot of the nuances that you would convey over the phone or in person.

Your e-mails should usually be short and to the point, professional, and unemotional, especially in the case of a disagreement. They should be short because many sellers are busy and don't have time to wade through extraneous stuff like how much you like the item, who it's actually for, and how much fun it is shopping on eBay. They should be to the point, professional, and unemotional because it's easy for misunderstandings to occur. This is one reason why eBay encourages trading partners to call one another to try to resolve any misunderstandings. In fact, to make calling cheaper and as convenient as possible, eBay bought one of the leading Internet voice communications companies in the world, Skype (more on this shortly).

Notice that we said your communications usually should be as we described; we didn't say always. We don't want to imply that every e-mail you send a seller must be devoid of emotion and personality. After all, one of the benefits of doing business on eBay is the chance to interact with so many different types of people from all over the world. Many people enjoy this part of the eBay experience very much, and we don't want to deny you this. You can tell a lot from a seller's description and About Me page, including whether or not she's receptive to chattier communications, or whether she is all business. We just ask that you consider that when dealing with each seller.

Communicate *Before* You Bid

This point is crucial. We advised you to do this in chapter 3, when we talked about evaluating a seller. We discussed it in the last chapter, when we told you how to bid. But just to be sure that you avoid one of the most common mistakes new eBay users make, we'll repeat it just once more: Once you've committed to buying something, it's too late to ask about things that you should have asked about before making the purchase. You've already bought the item! Your bid is a legally binding agreement between you and the seller. To be a well-respected and honored member of the eBay community, you must follow through with every transaction you win. So ask *before* you bid.

Let's take a look at some of the most common reasons why you might have to "talk" to the seller before you bid.

Questions About the Item Itself

What condition is the object you desire in? In the case of valuable collectibles, such as coins, for example, the difference between something that's in fine or very fine condition can mean a good deal of money. You need to know these things for certain. You may also have questions about size, age, or other factors that would enter into your decision to buy a particular item. You may want to verify that you completely understand the nature of any flaws in the object.

Shipping and Handling Questions

Sometimes these fees are not specified. You don't want any surprises here because these charges vary widely—from the reasonable to the almost obscenely ridiculous. You also want some idea of when the seller will ship the item. Some sellers will ship as soon as they receive payment; others may only ship on designated days of the week. Again, this is information you may want to have before committing to a purchase, especially if the item will be a gift. Shipping costs appear right under the price and "end time" of the auction near the top of the page. If the seller has not specified shipping charges, the listing will instruct you to "check item description and payment instructions or contact seller for details." So be sure you do that.

What's the Return Policy?

Knowing these policies is absolutely crucial. They vary widely, from "satisfaction guaranteed, all returns accepted without question, we will gladly pay postage both ways" to "absolutely no returns under any conditions!" The return policy may be specified in the Buy Safely area of the item description page. This section tells you at a glance about the seller's feedback, and what protection is available to you should something go wrong. If the return policy is not there, or if you still have questions after reading it, again, *this* is the time to get clarification—not after you have committed to buy.

Before clicking on that Ask Seller a Question link, please be certain that the information you're asking for doesn't already appear somewhere on the item page. Also, sometimes a seller will refer you to a linked page, such as his About Me page, for policies. Sellers complain a lot about buyers who don't read these before firing off questions, and we don't blame them. eBay sellers often operate on thin margins, and they just don't have the time to answer questions for which the answers are clearly stated.

Evaluate the Seller's Response Before You Bid

You're after more than just the black-and-white answer to your question when you communicate early on with a seller. How and when that seller answers can tell you a lot about the person you're thinking of doing business with. As far as speed, it's not at all uncommon to get a response to an e-mail within hours of contacting a seller, or certainly within a day or so. Sellers strive to answer your questions before you grow bored and move on to another item.

But things don't always go this smoothly. Sometimes the seller will not directly respond to the question you've asked. Or she may seem annoyed that you have even posed a question. The seller may take days to get back to you, or not respond at all. These scenarios are red flags, and you should reconsider whether you want to do business with such a seller.

When you do get a response, you can feel better if the seller is friendly and helpful. The most successful sellers consider a query like yours as an opportunity to "smile" at a customer. They'll thank you for getting in touch with them, answer your question completely, wish you luck on the bidding, and provide contact information for reaching them again if you need to. That's a seller who is interested in pleasing his customers. If you've carefully checked the seller's feedback numbers and comments, you shouldn't have any surprises down the road. We've bought many items on eBay, and most of the e-mails we've gotten, as well as packing slips and other written correspondence, have been helpful and friendly.

After-the-Sale Correspondence

As you gain experience and confidence in your eBay shopping, you'll find that often the first time you hear from a seller is when she sends you an invoice after the purchase. Even at this point you may not hear from a seller, because eBay automatically sends you a message if you've won an auction. Within that message you can click on the Pay Now button to settle your bill. But sometimes the seller will send you an invoice, and will even specify in the auction that you should wait for this invoice before paying. That just reflects how her accounting system is set up.

Many of the types of e-mails we're about to discuss are automatically generated, either by the seller's auction management software (a subject we cover in chapter 12) or by eBay itself, so don't be put off if they seem impersonal. Their purpose is simply to transfer information to you. Of course, a savvy seller will still include a "Thank you!"

After You've Paid

Once you've paid for your item, you're likely to get another e-mail, thanking you for your payment, confirming that payment has been received, and telling you when the seller is expecting to ship the item. If you pay through PayPal, you'll get a receipt for your payment e-mailed to you right away. By contrast, if you mail a check or money order, your seller may skip this e-mail notification and get in touch with you only when he's ready to ship your item.

When Your Item Is Shipped

Many sellers will notify you when they ship your item. That way you can be prepared to watch for the package delivery. If you or the seller paid for tracking, the seller will also include the tracking information in this e-mail, so you can watch your package make its way from your seller to your door.

This e-mail may also include an offer from the seller to leave feedback for you and a reminder for you to please do the same. We will talk a lot more about feedback in chapter 7, but you already understand how important feedback is to all eBay users, especially sellers. The savvy seller will politely suggest that you "let me know you've received your package and are pleased with your purchase by leaving feedback." Then, of course, he'll offer to do the same for you in return.

Don't Be Afraid to Call

In some cases you may want to telephone the seller. It seems old school even to suggest this in a world where telegrams are a thing of the past, and almost no one writes letters delivered by mail carriers instead of computers. But if you would feel better hearing someone's voice, just to make sure that there really is a trustworthy seller at the other end of the transaction, then go ahead and call. This is not at all uncommon or out of the ordinary for eBay sellers. Many big sellers include their phone numbers, if not in their auction listings then on their About Me pages or in their eBay store policies.

If you want to talk to the seller after you've placed a bid, the process is very simple. Once you're engaged in a transaction with another member, you can request that member's contact number directly through eBay by clicking on the Advanced Search link and then clicking on Find Contact Information. When you do, you and the seller will receive e-mails notifying you both that contact information has been requested. That's to protect the privacy of both parties.

If you really feel that it's important to talk to a seller before you bid, use the Ask a Question form to request the seller's phone number. You may want to specify that you have a few questions about the item and would like to talk about those questions. If you're willing to pay the long-distance charges, most sellers will also be willing to take the time to talk to you on the phone. If they don't, or if their tone is nasty, you can decide then not to make an offer. We know of one prospective buyer who heard the following message when calling a seller: "You've reached so-and-so. Leave your number and, if I feel like it, I'll call you back." Of course this buyer never bothered leaving a message—and he decided to pass on the seller's item!

What About Skype?

The media and even many eBay PowerSellers raised a collective eyebrow when eBay announced it was acquiring Skype, a company providing the means to make voice calls over the Internet. It was an expensive and high-profile acquisition, even for a high-flying Internet company like eBay. So why did eBay do it?

Skype removes some of the barriers to telephone communications. When you use Skype (which is software that you can download at no charge from http://www.skype.com/), you can communicate by voice over the Internet with another Skype user for free. Also, since you initiate the call right through your computer, it's easy to get in touch without disrupting your workflow. Aside from the free Skype software, the only other thing you need to use Skype is a microphone or (even better) a headset. At the time of this writing, only a few eBay sellers are set up to use Skype, but we think it will be a commonplace part of eBay one day.

Your About Me Page

eBay gives you the chance to create your own Web page where you can tell the rest of the eBay world something about yourself and what makes you tick. As a buyer, this is your chance to convey an image of yourself as a real person and a trustworthy and responsible trading partner. It's especially important for you to find a way to personalize yourself on the site before you've built that feedback record we've been taking about. Sellers will sometimes look at your About Me page to get a feel

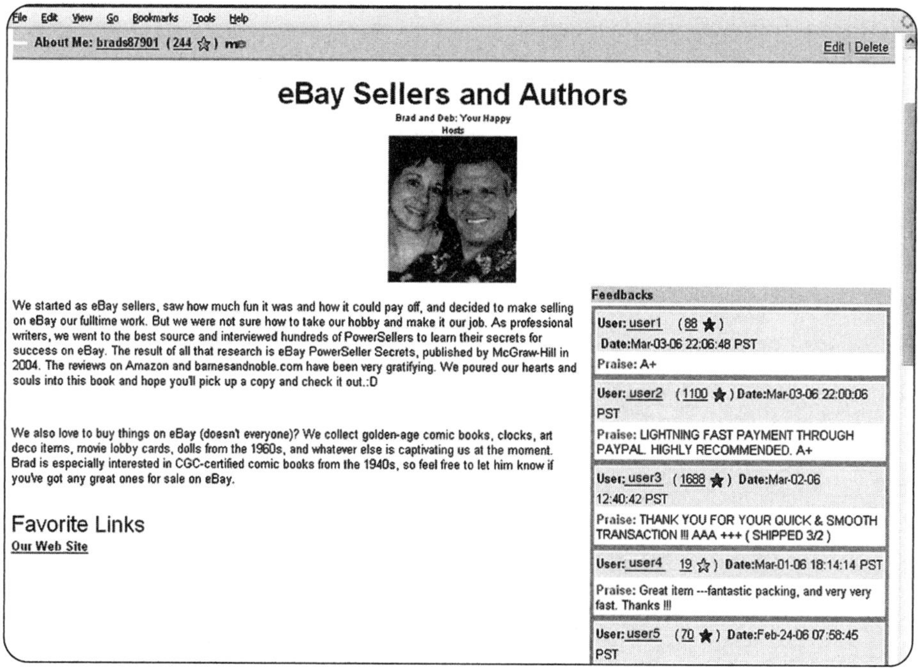

Figure 5-1: *A sample About Me page (ours!).*

for the type of person you are, especially when you've bid on a very expensive item. It reassures the seller, just as checking her About Me page reassured you. When you start *selling* on eBay, your About Me page is even more critical. Once you've created your About Me page, eBay will place a blue-and-red ME icon next to your user ID. It's a hyperlink that will take fellow eBayers right to your page. See Figure 5-1 for a sample About Me page.

Creating an About Me Page

Creating an About Me page involves two separate elements: the mechanics of creating the page and the content you wish to include. The mechanics are quite simple, so first we'll take a look at the content. Your About Me page is your own little space on eBay. It's your opportunity to let the eBay world know a little about yourself. Although you don't want to list information here that's so personal and specific that you leave yourself vulnerable to being identified and stalked in the real world, feel free to include some of your personal interests, hobbies, and passions. If you collect items that you'll be looking for on eBay, go ahead and talk about your collections. If you have a favorite charity that you support, you can spread the word on your About Me page, and even include a link to the Web site for that charity.

Adding pictures to your About Me page is simple, so don't hesitate to include your favorite shots of your pets or a photo from your most recent family vacation. Make your About Me page a pleasant reward for the person who stopped by to take a look. Anything that makes you seem more genuine and familiar will make your trading partners more comfortable doing business with you. So ask yourself, "What do I want people to know about me?" Then go ahead and tell them!

Luckily, eBay has made creating this page very easy. You simply type your content into eBay's own template (see Figure 5-2). You'll find plenty of information about creating your page at http://pages.ebay.com/community/aboutme.html. From there, getting started is as simple as clicking a button. You can create a great page by using eBay's easy-to-use forms. If you'd prefer, you can also do it yourself by entering your own HTML code. (HTML stands for Hypertext Markup Language. That's the programming language Web pages are written in.) While we'll discuss HTML briefly in chapter 12, for now we're going to assume that you'll use eBay's method to build your first About Me page.

File Edit View Go Bookmarks Tools Help

About Me: Enter Page Content

1. Choose Page Creation Option 2 Enter Page Content 3.Preview and Submit

Fill out this form with the information that you want on your About Me page. When you're ready, you can preview your page by clicking the Continue button below. Read tips on creating a good About Me page.

Add Text

Personalize your About Me page! Be creative with the title and your story.

Page Title:

Example: Adventures with Antiques, Bob's Books and Comics, etc.

Paragraph 1:

Enter either plain text or HTML.

Paragraph 2:

Enter either plain text or HTML.

Add pictures

Add your favorite pictures to your About Me page using these tips.

eBay Basic Picture Services | Your Web hosting

Label for Picture 1 | Picture 1 | Browse...

Example: The Real Me

Label for Picture 2 | Picture 2

Figure 5-2: *eBay's fill-in-the-blanks template makes creating your About Me page a snap.*

Because this is a "smart" guide to eBay, we're not going to step you through the process. Building an About Me page is simple to do, and we have so much confidence in our readers that we'll leave the details in the capable hands of eBay. We're here to encourage you to have some fun and enjoy the pursuit of creating the page. We're willing to bet there was a day when you never dreamed of having your own page on the Web. So make the most of it!

STEPHANIE SORKOWITZ IS A COLLEGE STUDENT. Like so many kids getting through college, her budget is tight. That's especially problematic around the big gift-giving holidays. Now consider that Steph has a boyfriend, a really special guy who means a lot to her. She hoped to be able to get him a corduroy blazer as a gift. She and her mom started shopping for such a treasure during the Thanksgiving weekend. It didn't take too long to discover that, in order to get one worthy of a gift, she'd have to spend about $140. That's far more than she could possibly afford, even for a special present. Oh, yes, one more detail we should mention. This fellow is six-foot-three-inches tall and weighs all of about 130 pounds. Fit is a challenge.

Discouraged and frustrated, Steph started thinking of other alternative presents, but she really had set her heart on this particular blazer. That's when her mom suggested eBay. Steph had poked around on the site, but she'd never done any shopping before. Mom and Steph started checking out listings to see what she might be able to find. She looked at quite a few jackets, but then happily found a brown corduroy blazer made by Abercrombie and Fitch. It was listed as new with the tags. Here's the perfect gift for a college guy! She had the choice of two sellers, one offering a medium and one offering a large. She e-mailed both of them to get specifics about which jacket would be the better fit.

The seller with the medium jacket sent back a quick note saying the medium would be perfect. Steph was a little skeptical about the sleeve length. The other seller sent back an e-mail with complete measurements, including those from the neck to the tip of the sleeve. Using her dad as a model, she quickly saw that the large would be the better choice. She also felt reassured that the seller had been so accommodating in his reply. For a Buy It Now price of $65, plus shipping, she was able to afford her first-choice gift after all! When it arrived, she found that it was just what the seller had claimed it was, and everyone had a happy holiday.

Paying for Your Items

AFTER MUCH BROWSING AND SEARCHING, checking and comparing, researching and pondering, you've found just what you want to buy on eBay. Congratulations! You've either won an auction or you've chosen a Buy It Now item from a seller you can trust. It's time to pay for that special something. Until now, weve focused our discussions on the risks that you take when you pick a seller to do business with. Ironically, at this point *you* are the one more likely to be suspect in the transaction. Now the seller has to trust you to be an honorable trading partner. This is the moment when you both have to take that leap of faith and trust each other.

Paying for what you've bought seems simple, and yet it's not as easy as just following whatever payment options the seller has specified. That's the beginning, but you'll have to decide which of those options best suits your needs, and follow whatever instructions he's listed. Now is not the time to get careless. Things can still go wrong this late in the game, and although the vast majority of transactions come off without a hitch, our job is to make sure that's the way things go for your transactions.

Seven Days to a Successful Sale

Unless the seller specifies immediate payment in the auction listing, you generally have seven days after the auction ends to get in touch with the seller and send your payment. Of course, you may well hear from the seller much earlier, but until seven days have passed, you're still within a grace period. After that week is over, the seller can file an Unpaid Item dispute against you and relist the item you won. Why would a seller skip the seven days and specify immediate payment only? If you're purchasing a time-sensitive item, such as concert tickets, that seller has a lot to lose if you don't pay for the item within those seven days. By then, there's very little time left for her to relist those tickets and make her sale, so she's likely to require immediate payment to protect her investment. That's not to say that the seven-day period is cast in stone. That is the reasonable expected time for the seller to receive payment, but if you get in touch with the seller during that time and request some extra time to pay for a specific reason, the seller may be willing to accommodate you. Once again, as in all things between trading partners on eBay, it's a matter of good communication.

Of course, that good communication started before you ever bid on the item you've won. The seller communicated his payment policies clearly in the item description. You read them and were certain that you clearly understood them before you bid. If you had any questions about those policies, you asked them *before* you bid. Most experienced sellers make their policies as clear as possible in their listings to avoid unnecessary e-mail transactions. Their businesses run more smoothly if you can get all the information you need upfront.

Once the sale is complete and you're ready to pay, you are only obligated to pay the seller by the methods specified in his listing. If, after you contact him, he asks you to pay in some other manner, you are free to refuse. Insist that the transaction be completed by the methods he specified, and don't be intimidated into making a change. Just as you entered a legally binding agreement when you bid on his item, he made legal commitments to you when he spelled out his payment policies in the listing.

The mechanics of paying for your item couldn't be simpler. Just click on the Pay Now button that appears in a number of different places. You'll find it on the item page itself. It appears when you check the item and see that the listing has closed. It is also on your My eBay page under the "Items I've Won" section. The confirmation e-mail eBay sends you, telling you that you've won the auction, includes a payment button, and this button also appears in the invoice e-mail eBay sends on behalf of the seller. So, as you can see, it's perfectly clear what you have to do next. Click that button and proceed, step by step, through the checkout process to pay for your item. But, assuming that the seller offers you an array of options, which method of payment should you choose? That question is a little more complicated to answer. Of course, we're here to help.

Before we discuss different payment options, we should mention that some sellers have their own "checkout" procedures that may differ from those we describe. That may be because of the software they use to post and track their eBay items. In this case, they may ask you to wait until you hear from them before proceeding with payment. So again, be sure you've read the payment instructions carefully before you click on that Pay Now button.

PayPal: Your Best Option

From your point of view, nothing else comes close to PayPal for convenience and safety. As the buyer, you get access to all of PayPal's many benefits, and you don't ever have to pay anything for them. When you use PayPal, you make yourself more desirable to the sellers who prefer PayPal payments. Sellers can actually choose to block buyers who don't have a PayPal account. Plus, you get PayPal's buyer's protection with every transaction you make. We'll explain.

PayPal is an eBay company. Once you register with PayPal and set up your account, everything you buy through PayPal falls within eBay's protective borders. You'll have fraud protection of up to $1,000 should the seller turn out to be dishonest, and you'll have access to PayPal's dispute resolution service should you have a bad experience with a transaction. After you sign up with PayPal, you'll be able to pay for everything you buy with your credit card, without ever giving out your credit card information to a seller. Your information resides on PayPal's own computers, and only authorized PayPal employees have access to it as they complete transactions on your behalf. These records aren't even stored on the Internet. They're that secure. Plus, PayPal will never sell your name or any of the information the company holds about you to a third party.

Signing up for PayPal couldn't be easier. Simply go to the homepage at www.paypal.com, shown in Figure 6-1, and click on the Sign Up Now button. The step-by-step instructions are easy to follow, and signing up for an account is

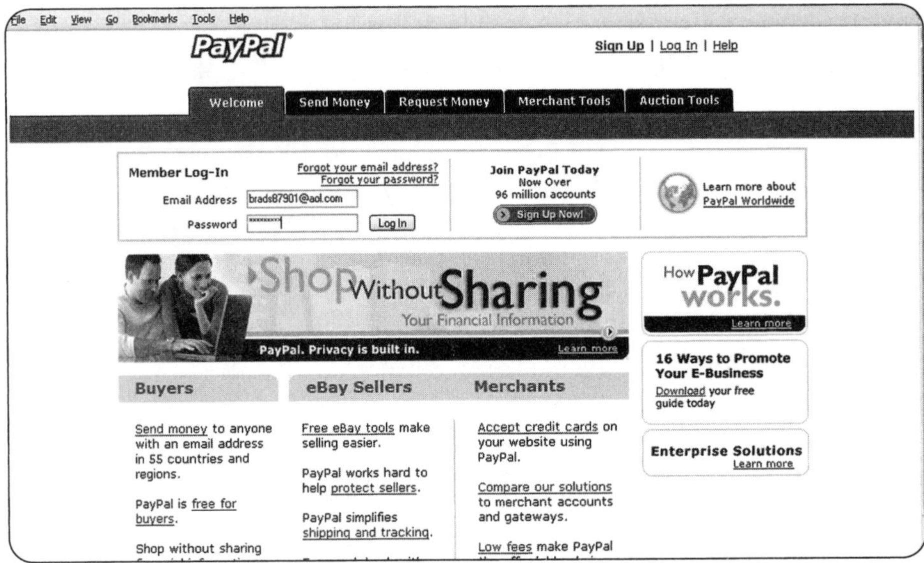

Figure 6.1: *PayPal's homepage. Sign up and live happily ever after on eBay.*

free. You can choose to sign up for a Personal account, a Premier account, or a Business account. For your purposes, as a buyer, either the Personal account or the Premier account will be sufficient. The Personal account will allow you to safely make payments directly from your bank account, or from the credit card or debit card you have on file with PayPal. You won't be able to *accept* credit card payments with this account, but if you only want to buy on eBay, that may not matter to you. With the Premier account, should you decide to sell items as well as buy them, you'll also be able to accept credit card and other types of payments. Since both options are free when you buy, we recommend that you open the Premier account. That way, should you decide you'd like to try selling on eBay—and we think that's likely once you get the hang of it—you'll be all set to accept payments from your customers.

When you sign up for PayPal, the company will verify that your bank account information and address are correct. Soon after you complete the registration process, you'll find a deposit of a few cents in your bank account. That allows PayPal to complete a transaction and ensure that your banking information is correct. Now you can pay for your items through PayPal in three distinct ways:

1. You can keep a balance in your PayPal account and pay directly from that balance.
2. You can specify that the money you owe be taken from your bank account and transferred to the seller electronically.
3. You can have your purchase charged to your credit card.

By default, PayPal will take the amount of your purchase first from your PayPal balance. But if you don't have enough money in your PayPal account, the company will debit your bank account. If you want PayPal to charge your credit card instead, you'll have to designate that when you complete a transaction. It's simply a matter of clicking a button to route the charge to your credit card, but if you fail to specify that, you can easily debit your bank account, thinking instead that you're paying with a credit card.

Confirm Your Address

PayPal offers address confirmation for buyers, a service that is important to both buyers and sellers. If you don't have a confirmed address through PayPal, your trading partner is taking a risk when she ships your item to you. If she ships to an "unconfirmed address" and you claim never to have received the package, she has no protection against a chargeback of that fee to PayPal. Now you're not going to buy something, pay for it through PayPal, falsely claim that you never received it, and demand a refund. But some people do. It's a common scam against sellers. So to protect themselves, sellers often demand that, if you pay through PayPal, you have your address confirmed. How do you do that? It's quite simple. If you've signed up for a Premier account, your address will be confirmed automatically. As part of the process used in verifying your credit card information, PayPal representatives confirm that the credit card bill is sent to the address you submit to PayPal. If you open a Personal account without a credit card, you can still have your address confirmed, but the process requires an extra step. When you request address confirmation through a Personal account, PayPal will mail you a security code to the address you submit. When you receive it, log onto your PayPal account and enter the code. That will confirm that the address you specified is accurate. You can also apply for a PayPal credit card, which includes automatic address verification with an accepted application.

PayPal's Money Market Fund

If you'd like, you can stipulate that PayPal place your PayPal funds in its money market fund, keeping all your money for eBay shopping right in that account. PayPal consistently pays a competitively high-yield interest rate on cash placed in its money market fund. As we write this, it's 4.62 percent, which is good. To open the money market account, simply click on the hyperlink "Earn a Return on Your Balance!" that appears on your Account Overview page. Here you enter your social security number and date of birth on the form that pops up, and walk through the process to open your account. You will be prompted to read the prospectus before you join. As with any money market fund, be sure you read the details clearly so you understand exactly what you're getting for your investment. Also remember that money market funds are not FDIC-insured.

Here's one final word of warning. Although we love PayPal, especially for buyers, having a money market fund right on site can make it difficult to control your buying tendencies. If you have to add each purchase to a credit card statement at the end of the month or subtract each purchase from your household bank account, you may be more cautious in your spending. If the money resides on PayPal and is outside your family's ordinary budget, it may be easier to overspend than it should be. Only you can judge your individual situation (and your ability to put the brakes on spending), but we promised to warn you of potential dangers when you agreed to read this book, so we feel compelled to point out that you may not want to make it easy for yourself to buy more than you can afford.

Personal Checks

Many sellers still accept personal checks, because many buyers still like to use them. From your point of view, a check is easy. You win your item and notify the seller that you'll be paying with a personal check. eBay or the seller forwards his address to you, and you simply pay him the same way you pay your monthly bills. That's why buyers like personal checks. They're easy and familiar. Plus, once your check clears, you have proof that you've paid for your item, so you have a built-in receipt.

On the other hand, some sellers may refuse to ship your item until your check has cleared the bank. You can't very well blame a seller for insisting on holding on to her item until she's sure you've actually paid for it. If she sends it out when she receives your check and the check doesn't clear, she's lost both her item and her sale, and she has very little recourse for recovering either. When you've built a solid and reliable reputation on eBay, with many successful transactions and positive feedbacks behind you, you'll find sellers more willing to take a risk and send your item out to you without waiting for the check to clear. It's a courtesy a savvy seller will extend to a proven buyer. But, as a new user, you are very far from that status now. So pay by check if your seller agrees, but know in advance that it may hold up your delivery by as long as ten business days. Of course, you can always send a certified check, which will eliminate this delay, but then you'll have to go to the added expense and trouble of obtaining a certified check.

Money Orders

Money orders are less convenient for you, but they can be more secure for your seller. If your seller agrees to accept a money order, you may eliminate the required waiting period of a personal check, but only if you use a secure money order, such as one from the U.S. Postal Service. The incidence of fraudulent money orders has increased so dramatically in recent years, that now many sellers insist on holding your shipment until they're certain the money order has cleared! To eliminate that waiting period, you can simply buy your money order through the U.S. Postal Service. USPS money orders will provide your seller with all the necessary protection against a counterfeit payment, and give him the security he needs to ship your item to you as soon as he receives the money order. Of course, you'll have to go through the extra step and the added expense of going to the Post Office to buy one, but if that's not a problem for you, and your seller agrees, USPS money orders are a great alternative to personal checks.

Paying for High-Priced Items

In chapter 10 we cover shopping for high-priced items on eBay, such as cars and houses. We're not recommending that you do this for quite a while. The formal and informal rules for handling these transactions are different from those governing ordinary eBay sales. Plus, you're a lot more likely to come across fraud when the stakes are higher. As a new eBay user, we don't believe you're quite ready yet to take this step, but the day will come when you may feel ready, and we want to be able to help you take that next step when the time is right.

When you decide that you want to take on the big purchases, do it carefully and be smart. Insist that your transaction be completed through an escrow service, a third party that will hold your money until all the conditions of the sale have been met. You'll have to pay the escrow fees, but that is a small price compared to what you could lose if you send payment for your new car to a seller who hasn't provided any real proof that she owns the car you're trying to buy. Here's how an escrow sale works.

You enlist an escrow service to act as your agent in receiving the funds you've agreed to pay the seller. You transfer your money to the escrow service. The service notifies the seller that your payment has arrived, and the seller transfers the property you've purchased directly to you. You then have the right to inspect the item. If you're satisfied that everything is as you expected it would be, you authorize the escrow service to pay the seller for the item. If you're not satisfied, you return the item to the seller and get your money back from the escrow service. Your money doesn't reach the seller's hands until you're certain that everything has worked out to your liking. The protection this affords you is certainly worth the fee the escrow service will charge you for acting on your behalf.

We'll add just one more word of caution: If you do decide to use an escrow service and buy a high-priced item through eBay, make sure that you use one that is approved by eBay itself. (At the time of this writing, Escrow.com had eBay's endorsement for U.S.-based transactions.) You might be surprised to know that criminals have even found ways to establish fraudulent escrow services that take advantage of both buyers and sellers. So, again, if you're going this route, be sure to use an escrow service that's been approved by eBay. You can easily find this information at http://pages.ebay.com/help/tp/payment-escrow.html.

Wire Transfers

A direct wire transfer electronically moves funds from your bank account to another bank account. This can be a great convenience for you when you're paying your bills online, but paying a stranger this way presents real risks. The only safe way for you, as a new eBay buyer, to transfer money from your bank account to a seller's account is through PayPal. Don't make any mistake about that: There simply is no other way that you can do a direct bank transfer without risking a loss. There's also no reason why a seller should resist a PayPal bank transfer as a legitimate way to move money directly from your bank to his bank. If he doesn't accept a PayPal wire transfer, then refuse to pay for the item with any other form of wire transfer either. If he insists on a direct wire transfer, don't even bother to bid on his items. It's way too easy to find someone else selling the same thing and offering you a better protected means of payment.

Our PayPal Bias

Now that you've reached the end of this chapter, you've no doubt noted that we're biased in favor of PayPal. From the buyer's viewpoint, there simply is no other option that compares to PayPal in terms of making it simple for you to pay and ensuring that you're paying securely for your purchases. We admit it. We stand guilty as accused. We favor PayPal. But we're not alone.

In a recent survey of its readers, conducted by the online newsletter AuctionBytes, 94 percent of the respondents used PayPal. PayPal's own figures suggest that 90 percent of the items for sale on eBay can be paid for with the service. You will find grumbles and complaints against PayPal on eBay's discussion boards and in the groups, but that grumbling usually comes from sellers, not buyers. Sellers express frustration, at times, because they pay PayPal fees for every transaction. They also feel that PayPal's protection services are skewed toward the buyer. You'll even find sellers who no longer accept PayPal for these very reasons, although that's the extreme. These legitimate complaints are between large sellers and PayPal. The issues large sellers face are very different from the issues that concern you now, so none of those complaints has anything to do with you. Standing in your shoes, we unequivocally recommend PayPal.

Now that you've learned how to pay for your item, let's move on to the absolute last part of every eBay transaction: leaving feedback. It's important not to jump the gun on this last step. Chapter 7 explains why.

GARY RICHARDSON IS AN EBAY POWERSELLER who operates under the member ID harleyglasses. He is one of eBay's largest sellers of sunglasses. We asked him about his best eBay buy, and he told us the following wonderful story. We thought you'd enjoy reading it in Gary's own words:

> My best purchase led to the foundation of a strong eBay business.
>
> I had just started selling on eBay. I paid particular attention to how sellers operated. I watched what they did as well as what they didn't do. I would evaluate each seller to determine how much I wanted to be like them or not like them. I would learn from their mistakes and make sure that my business didn't do the same. When I bought something and the seller was above average, I would try to emulate him and exceed what he had shown me.
>
> I needed a digital scale for my business, and I went off on a search to find the ultimate scale, or at least what I thought was a great scale! I ended up purchasing an Ultraship thirty-pound scale that fits on my desktop. I found a seller with great feedback and nice listings who answered all my questions. The seller was a mega PowerSeller, and my previous buying experiences made me think that I would receive anonymous service, slow shipping, and all the other problems that came with buying from a large seller. Boy, was I wrong!

I decided to do a BIN after much research from a seller named Will Knott. I think my scale came to about $35, or a little over $1 per pound of capacity. Right off the bat, I got a funny e-mail thanking me for my purchase! Geez this was great—I hadn't even paid and the guy was thanking me! I paid for my scale, and I got another message thanking me for my payment. Boy, I was really feeling good about this purchase! Shortly afterwards, I got another e-mail telling me my item had shipped and how great of a time it had been dealing with me! All of the information he had sent was exactly what I wanted to know as a buyer. I knew this was an exceptional level of service. I also knew this was how I wanted to be treated as a customer and, more importantly, how my customers wanted to be treated! At that moment, I knew there was only one place I would ever buy a scale from!

A few short days later (three) I received my scale and had it working. He had sent some more information about how to contact him if anything went wrong, and he had sent a gift of a brass postal scale for weighing small packages. I really felt good about my purchase now!

Two years later we have weighed thousands of packages on that little scale; more importantly, I learned things from Will that just can't be gleaned from books. I've emulated his outstanding service and tried to exceed it. It's been a giant payoff for my business. You can go to just about any forum on eBay and tell people you're looking for a scale, and nine out of ten people will refer you to oldwillknott. I didn't know it, but not only did I buy a great scale, I bought some sound business practices!

Chapter 7

Feedback: Love It and Leave It

LOVE MAY MAKE THE WORLD GO ROUND, but feedback spins eBay. You've already seen how the feedback system works and how it allows buyers and sellers to evaluate each other. It is a vital part of creating the marketplace by which trading partners can risk trusting one another. If you're going to join the eBay community, you have a responsibility to participate in the feedback system. Even though feedback is technically voluntary, it's as much a responsibility to a citizen of eBay as voting is to a citizen of a democracy. So together we'll take a look at the details of the feedback you'll be leaving and receiving.

Feedback is a precious commodity to a seller, and we'll spend a good deal of time discussing it from that point of view in chapter 17, but as a buyer you'll find it's also important. As your feedback number increases and your positive rating stays high, you'll become a more competitive trading partner. Sellers feel more confident doing business with you as your track record grows. Some sellers may even take risks with you they are generally unwilling to take, such as sending your item before your check clears.

At the same time, we've noticed that new users often misunderstand the feedback system. They leave feedback for the wrong reasons. They leave it too soon. They leave it before they've given the seller a chance to respond to their concerns and correct mistakes. Interestingly, the vast majority of negative feedbacks are left by users with very low feedback numbers of their own. We're here to give you a boost and help you avoid this and other beginner's mistakes. By the time you're ready to move on to the next chapter, you'll be far more experienced in the whole feedback arena, even if you don't have a single feedback to your name as of now!

When Should I Leave Feedback?

As a buyer, timing your feedback is pretty simple, especially if you've decided to leave the seller positive feedback. When you receive your item and you're pleased, go to your computer and let him know. It's simple to do. You'll find a link reminding you to leave feedback for a particular transaction right on your My eBay page. You may also get a friendly e-mail reminder from the seller if you delay sending feedback. Many sellers use their feedback as a way to keep their records straight about which of their sold items have reached their destinations. With your positive comment, that seller can move that sold item from his "pending" file to his "completed" file. You may also find that leaving positive feedback for your seller results in very quick positive feedback on your own feedback page. Figure 7-1 shows a sample feedback page. Many sellers hold off leaving feedback until they've received feedback from you. It's then that they know their work is truly done, and the transaction is completed. Also, many large sellers who use automated e-mail

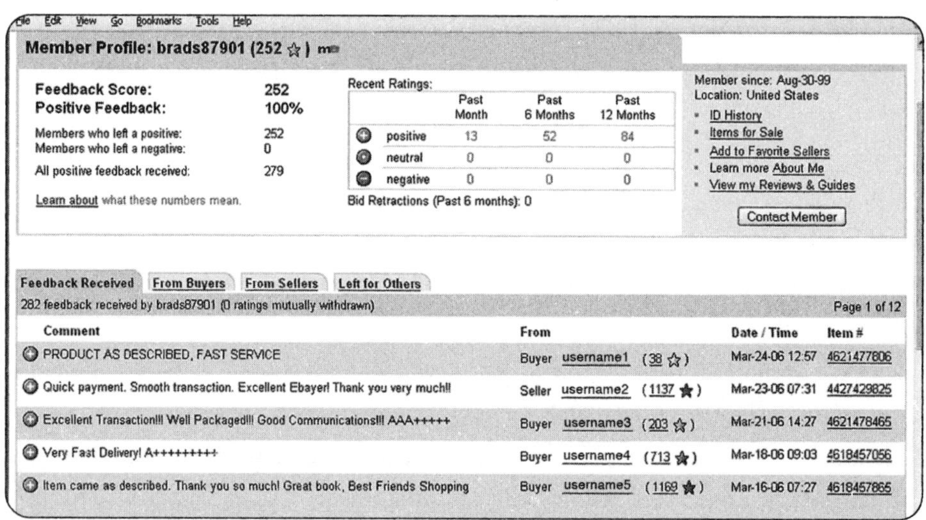

Figure 7-1: *A trading partner's Member Profile page displays the feedback comments he's received.*

and feedback systems have those systems set to send positive feedback to their buyers when they receive positive feedback from them. So don't wait for your seller to reward you. If you're happy, let him know it.

But what if you're not happy? What if you receive something that has been broken in transit? What if what you received is not what you thought it was going to be? What if you're completely disappointed? Then the answer is not quite as clear or straightforward. Your transaction isn't complete, and you're not ready to take any action at all in terms of feedback. There's more work to do, so take a deep breath and we'll look at what needs to happen next.

The first thing you have to do is figure out why you're not happy. Is the item different from what was described in the listing? Is it damaged? Be honest about the reasons for your disappointment. Feedback rates the transaction itself, not the item you bought. If you simply don't like the shoes, but you have to admit that they're just what the seller said they were, that seller doesn't deserve to have a negative mark on her record. Feedback is not a reflection of your disappointment. It's an assessment of how well the seller held up her part of the bargain.

You shouldn't have to ask yourself, "Can I return this?" You should already know that from having carefully read the listing and chosen your seller in the first place. But if you don't remember, go back to your My eBay page and check the listings, now under Items I Won. See what the seller's return policies are. If they're spelled out there, you will know, step by step, how to proceed. Sellers who offer 100-percent-satisfaction guarantees will accept your item for return within the time period they specify, even if you're returning it simply because you don't like it. You may be expected to pay for the return shipping, but you'll get the bulk of your money back when the seller receives your returned item.

Notice that we said the first thing to do is to recheck the seller's return policies. We didn't say the first thing to do is to go onto eBay and leave negative or neutral feedback for the seller! We'll repeat that: Feedback is the very last part of any eBay transaction. It happens only when the transaction is complete. If you've received something you're dissatisfied with, your transaction isn't complete. So recheck your facts to help guide you in your next step and then get in touch with the seller directly. By now, you've received e-mails from your trading partner, so you have all the information you need to contact him directly. Or, your seller may have included an invoice in your package that gives you specific directions for contacting him if you should have a problem. Give the seller a chance to make the sale right for you and see what he has to say. It's easy to be a good eBay seller when everything goes right, but you'll find the best eBay sellers are the ones who leave their customers feeling satisfied even when something goes wrong. So give your seller the chance to prove himself by showing you what he can do to fix a mistake. Get in touch right away, be polite, and explain your problem to the one person who can directly help you: your trading partner.

Ultimately, you can decide to leave negative feedback if you must, but once you do that, you can't undo it, so don't jump the gun. Leaving someone a negative mark is a serious act. If you do, you should be prepared to receive one in return. That's not a threat. We're just telling you the truth about what will probably happen next. We're not saying you should never leave negative feedback. Sometimes your trading partner absolutely deserves it, and you're not being fair to the eBay community at large if you don't have the courage to do it when you must, but it should be your last resort.

What Should My Feedback Say?

Leaving a feedback comment can be fun if you're happy, and challenging if you're not. When it comes to feedback, you have only eighty characters to make your point, so use those characters to get the most you can from them. Sure, you can just say something like "A++++++++++++ eBayer!" but the rest of the community will appreciate a little bit more detail than that. Think about when you were checking sellers' feedback ratings to decide which one you wanted to shop with. Wasn't it better to see specifically what the other buyers thought? So consider your feedback comment as an opportunity to help the next buyer who will check this page, looking for guidance about which seller to choose.

As you prepare to leave feedback, another thing to remember is that it's permanent. Once you make a comment, it can't be taken back (under most circumstances). In some instances, you can remove the score (a –1) if you've given a seller a negative, but you can't take back the comment. We'll tell you more about this shortly. So every time you leave feedback, remember that you're doing something that is difficult or impossible to undo. The feedback you leave for others becomes part of your eBay history, too; it is always available to be viewed on your feedback page. Make sure that you conduct yourself in a manner that will allow you to feel proud of your eBay presence.

Leaving Positive Feedback

When you're ready to leave a positive feedback comment, you can afford to have a little fun. It's a happy moment. Everything's gone right, and you can use your feedback comment to celebrate a little. Or not everything has gone right, but your seller did everything possible to fix the problem, and you're satisfied. Sellers will tell you that some of their best positive feedback came from buyers who were initially unhappy. They earned that positive score through good customer service. So praise your seller by citing whichever part of the transaction made you feel the best. Here are some examples of specific types of feedback comments that can really be useful to the next buyer who's evaluating your seller.

- Excellent packing. Lightning-fast shipping.
- Item just as described. Great job.
- Great communication. Love the item.
- Better than expected!! You can't go wrong!!!
- Great transaction. Professional seller!! Highly recommended!!

Or you can also decide to have a little fun. Make your seller smile with a comment she'll be proud to swap around the message boards. You won't be giving as much information about the transactions as you could with a more serious comment, but your happiness will definitely come through and speak volumes about the seller's ability to please a customer. Some of the ones we've found include:

- Oh My Gosh!! I'm in Heaven!!
- This was better than ice cream!
- I would marry this eBayer if I could!
- ***P***E***R***F***E***C***T***
- G☺R☺E☺A☺T!☺e☺B☺A☺Y☺E☺R!!!!

By now, you've gotten the idea. Express your good experience! Have a little fun, and reward a good seller with a warm pat on the back.

Leaving Neutral Feedback

As we said in earlier chapters, neutral feedback isn't so neutral after all. In the offline world, neutral means just that: It wasn't bad, but it wasn't great. It could even have a slightly positive connotation: It was what I expected it to be. It didn't disappoint, but it didn't thrill me either. On eBay, neutral is viewed as just one small step above negative. It doesn't alter the percentage of positives. It won't bump someone from 100 percent positive to 99.9 percent, but it doesn't do anything good for the seller either. It suggests that you weren't entirely pleased with the transaction, and perhaps the seller could have done better. So don't leave a neutral comment without thinking about it carefully.

Neutral feedback is an appropriate tool for certain situations. Not every transaction neatly fits into either the positive or negative category. We feel it's appropriate to leave neutral feedback if a major part of the transaction didn't go well, and the seller did not adequately explain what happened or correct the problem. For example, suppose you win an auction for a postcard, and it doesn't arrive for five weeks. In the meantime, you've contacted the seller to inquire about the item's status, but you haven't heard back from him. You give the seller another chance to respond, and still nothing. The item finally does arrive, and you're satisfied that it is as it was described. In this case, a negative isn't justified because you did get the item; however, the seller's slow shipping and poor customer service should be noted. This was not a positive transaction, yet it wasn't a completely negative one, either. Your fellow eBay traders should be forewarned that, in your experience, the transaction didn't go that well, and the seller didn't do all he could have to make your experience positive. Still, overall, he doesn't deserve a negative. A neutral rating would be just right.

Here are some good examples of neutral feedback comments that we found:

- Frames never rec'd, seller says damaged in transit. No comm. R'ecd full refund.
- Way too long to ship, NO Response to E-mails! However, satisfied with dvd!

- Disappointed not told earlier not in stock—needed it for a class.
- Item defective—sent bck W/ TRKG # but got lost in mail—had 2 argue 4 new one

Please remember that neutral comments do stand out, and potential trading partners will zero in on them when reviewing someone's feedback. Therefore, you should give the seller a chance to fix the problem before marring his feedback record with a neutral comment.

Leaving Negative Feedback

In our day-to-day lives, we are often reminded to "count to ten." Almost every time we react in anger without thinking, we're going to regret our actions. Humans aren't different when they begin to operate on eBay. Losing your temper and leaving negative feedback for a seller in anger is going to come back to haunt you. You will regret it, we assure you. That's not to say you should never leave negative feedback. We only advise you to be sure that your action is deliberate, and that you've thought carefully about what you're doing before you take this step. You have up to ninety days to leave your feedback, so there's really no need to be hasty. You'll know when you've reached the point where negative feedback is warranted, and we'll help you craft an appropriate comment for just that instance, but don't be too quick to act. As a new eBay user, when you do want to leave negative feedback, eBay will direct you to a tutorial for crafting and leaving your negative rating. The company insists that you read the tutorial before you proceed so that you can fully understand how serious the act of leaving a negative truly is.

In chapter 8 we'll take a good, hard look at what you should do if something goes wrong with a transaction, but for the sake of our feedback discussion, we'll consider the issue of leaving a negative comment here, too. The first thing you need to remember is that you should try to do everything possible to correct the problem before you leave negative feedback. A good seller will take a bad situation and find a way to make you so satisfied with her response that you have no need to leave negative feedback at all. So give your seller that chance to make it right.

If the seller is simply unwilling and/or unable to address your problems, and you've exhausted all your reasonable options to make everything right, then you'll be ready to leave a negative comment. Of course, by now, although you may be frustrated and disappointed, you're not raging mad anymore (so you're in a better frame of mind to post that negative). In leaving that comment, stick strictly to the facts of the transaction. Don't even consider name-calling, threatening, or character assassination. Remember: The feedback you leave is there for everyone else to see, so don't give anyone a reason to suspect that you brought your troubles on yourself by being a hothead and a jerk. If you get insulting and slanderous, eBay will remove the feedback, and you'll be the one held accountable for your actions. (We'll elaborate on eBay's feedback policies in a moment.)

So, once you've cooled off, leave a direct statement of fact, and move on. Here are some examples:

- Paid w/PayPal 11-15. Item not received by 12-15. Filed for refund.
- Item r'cvd. 12-05 broken. Seller never responded to emails.
- Item not as described. Seller never answered emails.
- Item delayed 6 weeks. Claimed new, but was used. Seller didn't respond.

As you can see from these examples, there was more than one problem with these transactions, and in each case, the seller was unwilling to rectify the situation. These occurrences would warrant negative feedback. You can leave your feedback knowing that you tried to work with the seller, but you simply couldn't get any satisfaction. When you leave your statement, you will most probably receive negative feedback in return, but you owe it to the eBay community at large to do so anyway. The feedback system only works when people are willing to take the risk of receiving negative comments to unmask a bad seller when they find one. Otherwise, feedback ratings are meaningless. If you leave a feedback comment that is simple, factual, and clear, anyone reading your feedback history will see that you conducted yourself well. That will go a long way toward placing your negative feedback into a proper context.

OUTRAGEOUS FEEDBACK MESSAGES

Most eBay transactions proceed without a hitch and feedback comments reflect that. "Great ebayer," "Fast Shipping," "A+++"—you'll see these comments many times, and that's a good thing. It's when a problem arises that eBay members show their displeasure, wit, and, yes, ignorance. Here are some examples:

- received item but broke after two days use
- "Sterling silver" turned my finger green the first day I wore it. Is now black.
- Haven't received item.Wont answer emails. Lives in GA. See ya soon.
- ordered diet pills but RECEIVED pen*s enlargement pills. But OK, friend wants it.
- Picture shows good stones, got very, very bad stones, not gem stones. Very bad
- 40 days without the item, i have a locked secure mailbox, maybe mailman stole it
- BIDDER'S COMPUTER IS INFECTED, THAT OR HIS MIND. OUR DISCS ARE 100% CLEAN!
- NIGHTMARE, THIEF, DO NOT BUY, WORST EBAY EXPERIANCE EVER
- Very Negitive and rude when my bid was declined. Called me a looser.
- Fast delivery, good communication; but item is broken and no help was offered
- beautiful ring. Not the right size. shipping kinda slow ... but sooo pretty!

Someone Left Me Negative Feedback! Now What?

Whether you receive your first negative feedback in retaliation to one you've left or under some other circumstance, it's almost impossible to live an active life on eBay and never receive a negative or neutral feedback comment. It happens to the best of us. When you do receive a negative, you can leave a brief response to that comment right below the comment. That will give you a chance to briefly explain your side of the story to interested parties. Again, be calm and reasonable, and stick to the facts. Potential trading partners will judge you by how you respond to a negative comment, along with the negative rating itself, so you'll have a quick opportunity to make a bad situation a little better. Then, move on and go about your eBay life carefully. Before you know it, that negative will become part of your history, and it will fade away from the first page of your feedback record. You *can* recover from negative feedback, even though it stings when it happens.

Can I Undo It?

Under a few specific circumstances, you can have negative feedback removed from your record, but it's not easy. eBay purposely makes this process very difficult. Feedback is a system that operates between eBay members, and the less involved the company is in the system, the more accurate and reliable the system is. There are just too many transactions every day for eBay to get involved in disputes between members, unless it's absolutely necessary.

It becomes necessary, however, when a member oversteps the bounds of safety or decency. Then eBay, after careful review, will remove the feedback and censure the offender with consequences that range from the loss of listing privileges to the loss of PowerSeller status. If someone leaves a feedback comment that contains profane, vulgar, obscene, or racist language, for example, it will be removed, once you notify eBay. The same is true if the feedback comment identifies you in the offline world by name, address, or contact information. That's just a matter of protecting your personal safety. eBay will also remove a comment under court order, or if the person who left it is not eligible to participate in eBay transactions at the time of the feedback. As you can see, these are rare and extenuating circumstances. For a complete list of reasons why eBay may remove feedback, go to http://pages.ebay.com/help/policies/feedback-ov.html. But you must assume that once you receive negative feedback, eBay will not intervene on your behalf to have it removed.

Try Mutual Feedback Withdrawal

You and your trading partner can agree to enter into a Mutual Feedback Withdrawal. That's not terribly likely if you've left a negative comment for someone the likes of which we've just described. That's because this process involves communicating with the seller, and our examples were clearly based on noncommunicative sellers. But, if you've lost your temper and you've left negative feedback in anger, receiving one in return, you may have some recourse. The first thing to do in this situation is to calmly contact the seller and apologize for your misstep. She doesn't want negative feedback any more than you do. If you're contrite and polite, you may find her willing to enter into a Mutual Feedback Withdrawal. Within thirty days of leaving the feedback, or within ninety days of the end of the transaction, you can complete the Mutual Feedback Withdrawal process. Once you and your trading partner have reached an agreement, you both submit a request for a Mutual Feedback Withdrawal. eBay will process the requests and simultaneously remove both feedback numbers from the total scores of both partners. If the negative feedback you received bumped your score from 100 percent positive to 99.9 percent, it will go back to 100 percent positive. Your partner's score will go back to its pre–negative feedback status as well.

Although your score will revert to what it was before you received the negative, the comment will still be part of your permanent feedback history. eBay will make a notation on that comment to indicate that it was removed through a Mutual Feedback Withdrawal, but the comment itself will remain. Again, that's why it is crucial for you to be careful about the words you choose when leaving feedback. They say a great deal about you, and you can't avoid them in the future. Still, most eBay users understand that negative feedback happens. If you've completed a Mutual Feedback Withdrawal, you've shown yourself to be a reasonable partner, willing to work on making a bad situation better. If you've left professional and businesslike feedback comments, you've also represented yourself well. The key to the overall feedback system is this: Always behave in a way that will make you feel proud of yourself later.

Now let's move on to chapter 8, where we'll learn some other techniques for dealing with problems, should they arise. As we've said before, most eBay transactions move along smoothly with no trouble at all, but if you should get yourself into a bad situation, chapter 8 will help you figure out how to get out of it.

LEW TENDLER, ONE OF THE FINEST boxers of the 1920s, is considered the best southpaw who ever entered the ring. As a boy, he sold newspapers from a Philadelphia street corner. Legend has it that he got into his first real fight when another boy tried to dislodge him from his corner and take away his business. That fight was the spark that led to a career in boxing, and forevermore he was known as the "Newsboy Boxer."

After he stopped working as a fighter in 1928, Lew opened four restaurants in the Philadelphia and Atlantic City areas (see Figure 7-2). Signed photographs of many of the great celebrities of Lew's era, such as the Three Stooges, the Marx Brothers, and Milton Berle, were displayed proudly on the walls of those restaurants. After the restaurants closed in the late 1960s and 1970s, Lew's family recovered just one of the pictures, leaving behind the other pictures and memorabilia that had graced the walls of all four restaurants. All this great memorabilia—the 1,001 things that made up Lew Tendler's restaurants and in many ways his life—were lost to the ages.

Until recently, that is. Thanks to eBay, Lew's granddaughter, Sharon Tendler, has amassed a priceless collection of matchbooks, dinner plates, postcards, photographs, menus, stirrers, and more from her grandfather's restaurants. More than collecting mere memorabilia, however, Sharon has recovered precious pieces of her heritage. Her grandfather was part of her life until she was twenty, and she has many fond memories of spending time with him at the Jersey shore.

Lew was quite a character. He had many trademark sayings, which he coined and quoted often, including the following:

The greatest sin..............................Fear
The best day................................Today
The best town...............................Where you succeed
The greatest troublemaker..............One who talks too much

The first thing Sharon looked for on eBay was a postcard or menu with some of these sayings on it, and, of course, she eventually found one. Sharon adds to her collection all the time, and sometimes makes new friends when sellers learn about her connection to Lew Tendler. When she's especially pleased with an item, she'll add to her feedback a comment like the following: "Thanks for the [matchbook] ... from Lew Tendler's granddaughter." Lots of people have contacted her as a result of those messages, which has led to more memories and pieces of her childhood returning to her.

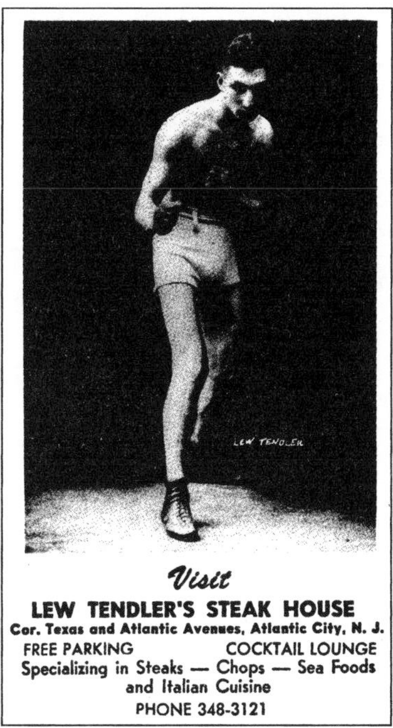

Figure 7-2: *Lew Tendler was one of the best boxers from the 1920s.*

Chapter 8

What If Something Goes Wrong?

IN 2001, NEW JERSEY POLICE OFFICER Stephen Klink bought a $75 speaker on eBay for his stereo system. When it arrived, he was surprised to see that it had been chewed up, he could only assume by a dog. He contacted the seller, who refused to do anything about it. "An animal must have gotten into the package during transit," the seller told the officer. Klink then contacted eBay, and company representatives told him to work it out with the seller.

That's when Klink got the idea to create a Web site to tell his story. Afterwards, he sent a link for the site to the seller, who must have paid a visit, because within days he refunded Klink's money! Klink reasoned that if the site could help him get his money back, he could help other eBay buyers who found themselves in the same unfortunate situation. That's how his new site, ebayersthatsuck.com was born.

Before you put this book down and head back to the mall, you should know that Officer Klink is still a huge eBay fan, although he's now read countless stories about eBay fraud. "I think eBay is fabulous, and 90 percent of the stuff I buy, I buy through eBay," he says. Klink's story points out two things. Number 1: Bad things can happen to you as a buyer (or seller) on eBay. And number 2: Number 1 doesn't have to keep you from using the site.

If something should go wrong with your eBay transaction, you're not all alone, provided you've been careful from the very beginning. We'll use this chapter to review the steps you can take to improve your chances of having everything go right, but we'll also show you what steps to take if it doesn't.

But first, here's a follow-up to Officer Klink's story. In 2005, Stephen and his brother Edward, a business writer, compiled some stories from their site into a book *Dawn of the eBay Deadbeats*. They started selling the book, on eBay, of course. And who do you suppose was one of the first people to buy the book? No, not the seller who started it all, but a member of eBay's own fraud department. They need help, too!

The Realities of Doing Business on eBay

eBay tries to create the illusion that the site is a safe place to buy and sell things, and you definitely get that impression everywhere you go on the site. eBay has a community feel about it, suggesting we're all in this together. However, should something go wrong, the reality is that you're the one who will have to work to make it right. eBay makes this perfectly clear in its User Agreement, which you agreed to before becoming a member. (Remember we told you how important it is to read that?) eBay states right there that it cannot guarantee that a given item is in the condition a seller claims, or even that it exists at all:

> We are not involved in the actual transactions between buyers and sellers. We have no control over and do not guarantee the quality, safety, or legality of items advertised, the truth or accuracy of listings, the ability of sellers to sell items, the ability of buyers to pay for items, or that a buyer or seller will actually complete a transaction.

That's not to say that eBay is some giant, unfeeling, corporate entity that doesn't care if you're happy or not, as long as you pay your fees. We don't think that for a minute. It's just that eBay has too many users and too many transactions to involve itself in every dispute between trading partners. If you take nothing else from this chapter, remember this policy before entering into a transaction with an unknown trading partner!

An Ounce of Prevention

And that brings us back to you and all the steps you have to take before you even bid on something you want to buy on eBay. In the offline world, you need to stay alert, awake, and vigilant as you go about your daily business. You have probably developed hundreds of big and small ways to protect yourself, from locking your car doors to putting your wallet in your front pants pocket, or having your keys out and ready as you walk through a parking lot at night. These things become second nature to us. On eBay, you have to be ever vigilant as well, just in slightly different ways. Let's review some of the things you should do to help ensure that you're entering into a safe transaction.

1. Research your seller carefully. Find out not only what her feedback score is, but also what her feedback history is in terms of what she's sold, and the comments she's sent and received as both a buyer and a seller.

2. Know what all her policies are for operating her business. Be sure that she accepts multiple methods of payment, but never demands wire transfers outside of PayPal. Be thoroughly familiar with her return policies and agree that they are satisfactory to you. Find out when to expect her to ship your item and what method she will use to send it.

3. Read through the entire listing carefully, word for word, so you don't miss something important. For example, as we write this there's a scam going on whereby some sellers of Xbox (gaming systems) are selling just the box to unwary buyers, not the actual games. This fact is mentioned in small print, buried deep within the listing, but some buyers miss it in their haste to scoop up a bargain.

4. Choose your eBay purchase with your head, not with your heart. Resist the temptation to buy that Mickey Mantle autographed baseball at any cost. Nothing is that precious. Anything that comes up for sale on eBay once will come up for sale again, so don't lose your head over something. That's when troubles can really begin.

5. Don't buy something expensive from someone with little or no feedback, even if it's just what you've always wanted. That person has no proven

track record, and you simply have no way of knowing if he is who he says he is.

6. Use an escrow service if you purchase something very expensive. Some of the stories we've read about people spending their life savings on vehicles that a seller never owned are heartbreaking. But these tragedies could have been avoided if the buyers had insisted on using an escrow service. Until you're savvy enough to navigate the high-end eBay market, don't even think of buying big-ticket items through eBay.

7. If it smells funny, it probably is. Sure there are some eBay sellers who don't quite know the value of what they have and who list items for ridiculously low prices. But the chances of that happening and you being the only one to spot that mistake are pretty slim. Just as in the offline world, you have instincts that alert you to potential trouble. Don't discount those instincts, because they're usually right. Even if they're wrong, you're still safer following them than dismissing them as groundless. The same thing is true on eBay. If you get that strange uh-oh feeling, don't ignore it.

In most cases of egregious fraud, buyers didn't follow one or more of these rules. That's not to say that their losses are any less frustrating or sad, just that perhaps they could have been avoided.

Types of eBay Fraud

Still, even the most careful among us can fall prey to the wrong seller, just as even the most careful among us can become the victim of a crime in the real world. So first, let's define *fraud* and *crime* on eBay. There's electronic fraud, which is a type of identity theft. Then there's the kind that follows a transaction and involves you and an unscrupulous trading partner. In the eBay world, electronic fraud includes e-mail ploys aimed at getting you to reveal personal financial data. Unfortunately, eBay and PayPal users are a prime target for this type of fraud. In a typical example, the fraudster will send you an e-mail, saying that your PayPal account information must be updated. You're then directed to a Web site to reenter credit card or other information that could be used to separate you from your money. The sites these charlatans direct you to look authentic enough, as do the e-mails. This is why you have to be extra vigilant in checking your e-mail carefully once you start trading on eBay.

Fake E-mails You Can Detect

If you are going to enjoy eBay, you must be aware of the dangers of fake e-mails. Fake e-mails are simply a fact of life on the Internet. The more time you spend in cyberspace, the more likely you are to become a victim of this type of fraud. Studies have shown that 70 percent of Internet users have received "phishing" e-mails, whereby a criminal "fishes" for their financial data. But the good news is that e-mail fraud isn't too difficult to guard against, as long as you know what to look for and what to do if you receive a fake e-mail.

SPOOF E-MAILS

We already told you about a few spoof e-mails in chapter 3. Those bogus second chance offers and that e-mail warning you that you're bidding on a fake are both examples of spoof e-mails, meant to gain your confidence and steal your money. These are only dangerous if you're not aware that they're fraudulent and you act on the suggestions they contain. If you receive a spoof e-mail like this, you can simply ignore it. Or, as we said, if you are now or were recently engaged in a transaction, you can go back to your trading partner and deal with that party directly. Of course, forward the spoof e-mail to eBay so the company can address it, too. You can easily do that by sending it to spoof@eBay.com.

PHISHING E-MAILS

Phishing is different from spoofing in that phishing e-mails ask you to disclose your personal information. Unfortunately, they are usually very polished and realistic looking e-mails, and it's easy to get caught by one. You may receive an e-mail ostensibly directly from a company claiming that your account information has been violated, and you'll need to respond to the e-mail to correct it. The e-mail may seem to come from PayPal or even your credit card company. It may contain the letterhead and the logo of the legitimate business, and look exactly like the e-mails you routinely receive. That's why phishing e-mails are so dangerous. eBay is among the top five companies most frequently targeted by phishing scams.

(The others are Citibank, U.S. Bancorp, PayPal, and AOL.) It's easy to see why eBay is a likely target, since almost all eBay communication occurs through e-mail. Here are some specific things you can do to protect yourself from phishing:

- Never respond to requests for personal information. If something were to happen to your account information on eBay, you wouldn't learn about it through a regular e-mail. Any legitimate message from eBay concerning your account will appear under My Messages on your My eBay page. So your My eBay page is the first place you should look before acting on such an e-mail. The company would also never ask you to provide personal information via e-mail outside of your My eBay page, so if that's the case, it's a fake.
- Don't click on any hyperlinks in an e-mail, unless you are 100 percent certain that you know who sent it. If you get an e-mail from PayPal, for example, and the directions tell you to click the link to process your information correctly, don't do it. That is a link to a fake Web site that has nothing to do with PayPal. Once you click on the link, you've made your computer and your personal information vulnerable to the criminals who set up the Web site expressly to "phish" for your personal financial information.
- If you want to visit the Web site questioned in any e-mail and verify that everything is okay, go to your browser and type the URL for the site, just as you would any other time—never click on the link provided in an e-mail. If it's true that your eBay account information has been violated, you won't be able to sign on to the site in the normal way.
- Forward all suspicious e-mails to those companies that the e-mails claim to represent. eBay, PayPal, and many other online retailers have departments working to protect their companies from online fraud, and they do investigate the fake e-mails they receive.

Frauds Involving Transactions

This is the real focus of this chapter. Unfortunately, buyers and sellers have come up with lots of ways to rip each other off on eBay. These criminals poison the well for everyone and, unfortunately, discourage people from shopping on eBay. Most of the troubles you'll have on eBay result from ineptitude rather than crime. You are more likely to receive something poorly packaged and therefore damaged or in some way significantly different from the item that was described in the listing. If it's a matter of ineptitude, you're not necessarily dealing with a bad person, just an incompetent seller. These sellers usually have feedback ratings that could warn you in advance, but not always.

The first thing for you to do is to politely attempt to resolve the problem directly with the seller. In most cases, it never has to go further than that. But some of the sellers on eBay are not simply incompetent. They are criminals. Don't confuse an eBay seller with an eBay criminal, because they aren't the same thing at all. Any seller can make a mistake that needs to be resolved, but the criminals aren't on eBay to conduct business. They're there to steal. If you fall prey to one of these criminals, your only true recourse is to have paid for your item with PayPal or your credit card so that you'll have the protection of these entities behind you. Other than that, you may find you've simply lost your money.

When Bad Things Happen

Bad sellers will send damaged goods, not send the item at all, send something much different from what the listing described, and ignore your e-mails. You'll know soon enough if you've come across a bad one, because you won't hear from that seller again. In the paragraphs that follow, we discuss what you should do, step by step, if you find yourself the victim of a shady or otherwise negligent seller.

Contact the Seller

By all means contact the seller first, in case there's some misunderstanding. Deb's mom used to say that you should never be too quick to judge someone on the basis of a single encounter. "Maybe he had a headache," she would reason. In that spirit, start off by assuming that the seller is not aware that there's a problem, and is an honorable fellow who would want to make things right. Once you've won an auction, eBay will send you the seller's contact information, so e-mail him at least three times before giving up. One of your e-mails may have gotten caught in his spam filter, for example, so maybe he didn't see it. If there's still no response, call him. (Once you're involved in a transaction with someone, eBay will send you his complete contact information, including his phone number if you ask for it. Just click on Advanced Search and then the Find Contact Information hyperlink in the left-hand column.) By taking these steps, you'll soon find out if your faith in the seller is warranted or not.

Document Everything

You have ninety days from the time the transaction ends to file a claim with eBay. If you haven't received your item or even heard from your seller within about ten days, it's time for you to get started. You don't have to be a lawyer to know that it's wise to keep track of all e-mail correspondence, and take careful notes if you speak with an eBay seller on the phone. Many e-mail programs will automatically save incoming and outgoing mail. Check that yours does this and that this feature is enabled. Otherwise, print out each e-mail you send and, more importantly, receive from your eBay partners. If you pay for your item with a check or money order, be sure to photocopy the check before you send it and keep all your receipts for your money orders. Do this with every transaction. You won't know whether or not you'll need the documentation until it's too late to go back and retrieve it, so make this your practice from the beginning.

Contact eBay and PayPal

Okay, so your seller has not responded to your e-mails, and you can't settle things through a phone call, either. Let eBay and PayPal know what's happening. This is important because, as *Dawn of the eBay Deadbeats* coauthor Edward Klink wisely suggests, you don't want your trading partner to be the first one to contact eBay or PayPal and say something that differs from your own account. So by all means follow procedures and contact eBay (and PayPal if that's how you paid for the item). Getting in touch with eBay couldn't be easier. Simply go to eBay's Security & Resolution Center (http://pages.ebay.com/securitycenter/), shown in Figure 8-1, and click on the appropriate problem you're experiencing. You can also reach the Security & Resolution Center from the hyperlink at the bottom of most eBay pages.

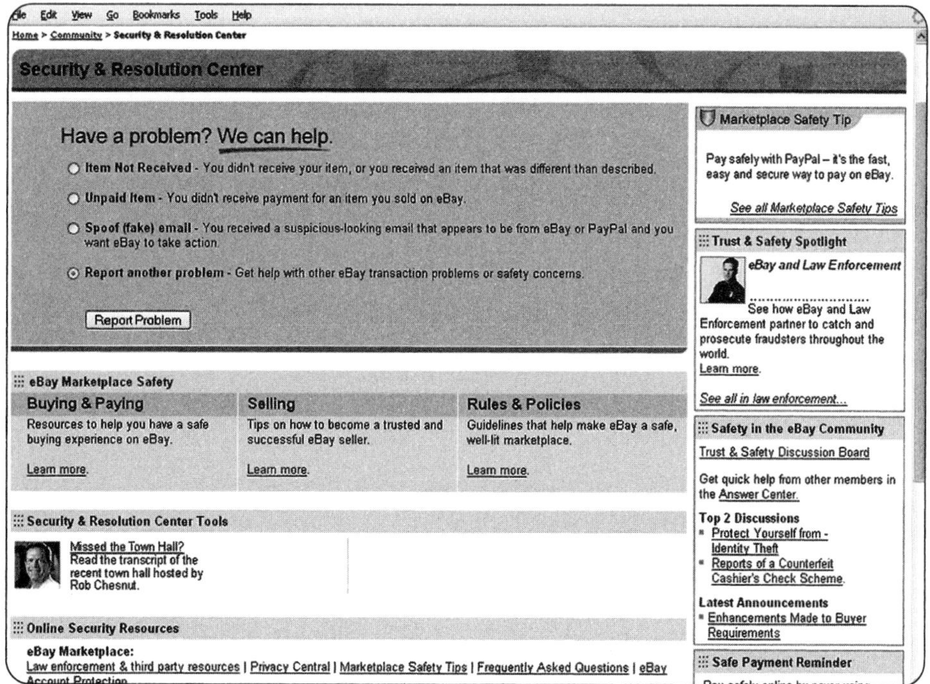

Figure 8-1: *eBay's Security & Resolution Center is the place to start if you run into trouble.*

eBAY'S BUYER PROTECTION POLICY

If you do not receive an item you paid for or you receive an item that's "significantly not as described," you are eligible for reimbursement through eBay's Standard Purchase Protection program. Once eBay verifies your claim, you will receive up to $200 in reimbursement, minus a $25 processing fee. If the item you purchased cost $500, you'll receive $175, the same sum you'd receive if the item cost $200. In order for the item to be eligible for purchase protection, it must have a final selling price of at least $25. Read what's covered and to what extent by going to http://pages.ebay.com/help/tp/esppp-coverage-eligibility.html. *Note:* eBay insists that, if you paid by credit card, you contact your credit card company first and seek reimbursement there before you file a claim with eBay. One more thing to consider: You can only file three claims per six-month period through this program. Don't let that trouble you, though: Most of your eBay transactions won't require reimbursement anyway.

PAYPAL'S DISPUTE RESOLUTION

If you paid by PayPal you were smart—PayPal can actually be a big help to buyers (not so much to sellers) when fraud occurs. Here you would work through PayPal's resolution process, and not the separate one for eBay customers who paid via another means. (While it's true PayPal is an eBay company, in cases such as this each has its own set of procedures.) Start by going to PayPal's Resolution Center. Get there by clicking on the link for it from your My Account page, which is the page that appears once you log in to PayPal. Figure 8-2 shows the Resolution Center. Once you're there, just click on the File a Claim link to get the ball rolling.

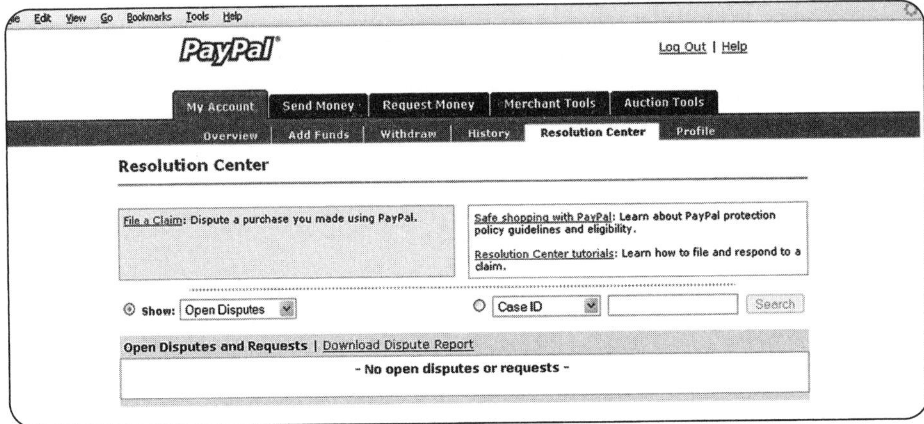

Figure 8-2: *PayPal's Resolution Center is where you'll go to file a claim.*

You have forty-five days from the end of the transaction to initiate a claim. Once you enter into a dispute resolution, PayPal will review your claim and reimburse you based on the eBay Buyer Protection policy described above. If you file a complaint with PayPal, you don't also have to file one with eBay. That will happen automatically. If you've paid for your item through funds from your PayPal account, you will only be reimbursed if your seller has the balance due to you still in his PayPal funds. If you've paid with a credit card, you may be eligible for further reimbursement through your credit card company. While eBay will tell you to contact your credit card company first, PayPal advises just the opposite. You should not initiate a claim with your credit card company until PayPal has completed your claim. If you do, you will void the complaint through PayPal. Most credit card companies give you ninety days to initiate a charge-back claim. That will be ample time for PayPal to decide the merits of your case.

PAYPAL'S BUYER PROTECTION POLICY

PayPal Buyer Protection is a program that your seller must qualify for by having at least fifty feedbacks, a 98 percent positive record, and by meeting other criteria. If your seller signs up for this program, as one of his buyers you'll have up to $1,000 of purchase protection on qualifying listings. To see whether or not your seller offers this protection, note whether the phrase "PayPal Buyer Protection" appears in the Meet the Seller box on the original listing. An item is eligible if you never received it or if it is significantly different from what was described in the listing. You can start the claims process by going through PayPal's Resolution Center. You may initiate three such claims in a calendar year. PayPal's Buyer Protection Policy is one more way to help you secure your purchases on eBay, but keep one warning in mind. The sellers who qualify for these services are not likely to be the most dangerous sellers on eBay. They have to have solid reputations and proven business practices before they are eligible for this program. So, by all means, consider them when you're shopping, but theirs may not be the transactions you need the most help with anyway.

Your Credit Card Company

If you've paid for your item with your credit card, but not through PayPal, you should notify your credit card company as soon as you suspect that you have a problem with the merchant. If the merchant is actually a criminal, intent on cheating eBay buyers, you've given your credit card information to the wrong person. Notify your credit card company to help protect yourself from credit card and identity theft, and to freeze further charges to your account. If your seller is just a bad seller, but not a criminal, you'll have to go through the process of trying to recover your funds through the credit card company. Most credit card companies will freeze the amount in dispute as soon as you notify them and not charge you any interest while the dispute is being reviewed.

You'll be asked to provide any documentation related to the transaction and your attempts to resolve the dispute directly with the seller, so, again, save everything. The types of documentation necessary will vary depending on the nature of your dispute and the item in question. For example, if you're claiming that the item you received is significantly different from what was described, you'll have to provide the original listing description and proof that what you received doesn't reflect the description. In the case of collectibles, you may have to provide an appraisal from a third party to verify that the condition of the item you received did not match the condition described in the listing. Contact your own credit card company for more specific information about what would be required in case of a dispute. Remember: It's always a risk to provide an unproven individual seller with your credit card information, especially when you can so easily pay for your purchases with a credit card through PayPal.

SquareTrade

Is your trading partner a SquareTrade member? SquareTrade has been working to make online commerce safer since 1999 through its verification and dispute resolution services. As you saw in chapter 3, SquareTrade helps to ensure that the seller you're dealing with is honorable and reputable. Now we'll tell you about SquareTrade's buyer protection services. Before you even bid, you can ensure that you're shopping for an item protected by SquareTrade because the listing will include the SquareTrade seal, shown in Figure 8-3. If that item is covered by SquareTrade's guarantee, you can sign up for the protection free of charge when you place your bid or until forty-eight hours after the end of the auction. Once you do, you'll have up to $10,000 worth of protection to ensure that the item is as it was described in the listing. You'll also have up to $100 worth of price protection if you find the item cheaper off eBay. (This is only for new items.) But these guarantees are only available to you if you're shopping with someone who has signed up for SquareTrade's program to begin with.

Sellers who qualify for SquareTrade's program are safe sellers anyway, since they have to maintain certain standards to qualify for SquareTrade's protection

Figure 8-3: *This SquareTrade Seal, appearing in a listing, means the item is "protected" by SquareTrade.*

services. They must submit to an identity and address verification through Equifax, a third-party identity verification service, to authenticate their identity and confirm that they have no prior history of fraud. The eBay history of anyone who applies is run through five separate background checks that include feedback quality and quantity and inventory inspection. Finally SquareTrade checks each applicant to see if she has a history of successful dispute resolution. So if you're dealing with a SquareTrade seller, you probably won't have much need of protection. Fortunately, SquareTrade also offers dispute resolution services that can help you resolve a problem with a seller who is not SquareTrade-verified.

SQUARETRADE'S DISPUTE RESOLUTION

Your first step is to file a claim with SquareTrade. You can do that directly through its Web site, www.squaretrade.com. This identifies your problem and initiates the resolution process. SquareTrade will then notify the other party, providing him with instructions as to how to respond to the situation. The case data and all the related correspondence will appear on a password-protected page on SquareTrade's Web site. Once both parties have been made aware of all the issues spelled out between them, SquareTrade encourages them to work out their dispute directly. This process is contained completely on the Web site, and, at this writing, costs nothing for either party to participate. If you can't work things out between you, the parties can request that a SquareTrade mediator get involved. The mediator will not personally make a decision on behalf of either party. She will simply look over the facts of the dispute and work with the parties to come to an equitable solution. The fee for using a SquareTrade mediator is $29.95.

Should You Contact the Police?

Gulp. This seems like a serious step, and it is. It's probably one not worth taking if the item you bought cost less than $100. What if it's worth more? Then, if your seller lives in the United States, Officer Klink strongly encourages you to file a report with your local police. You've been the victim of a crime. Just because the criminal stole your money via online commerce doesn't mean he hasn't stolen from you. Your local police will contact the police department where the seller operates. Your police department may also work with other agencies to make

THIS REALLY HAPPENED!

And now, let's take a look at an actual transaction that went wrong and see if you can spot the ways this problem could have been avoided. Stephen Klink and Edward Klink included this story in their book, *Dawn of the eBay Deadbeats*. They granted us permission to share it with you.

> I ran into my first genuinely bad eBay experience while shopping for a *Star Trek* DVD set as a gift for my wife. I'm not a total space geek, but my wife is a bit of a "Trekkie." (Hey, as long as she keeps wearing the Lt. Uhura costume, I'm happy.)
>
> Anyway, after losing out on my first auction I found another seller with the DVD set I was looking for. The seller I found had no feedback, but I figured everyone has to start somewhere, right? So I bid $435.00 and won! I promptly paid the seller with PayPal and asked the seller to arrange shipment.
>
> The seller told me he'd ship that evening, but made sure to mention that he had 30 days to ship the item "per eBay rules." I thought this was odd as I was pretty sure 30 days was the deadline by which a person could file a complaint with PayPal. It turned out it was no coincidence after all, when I discovered the seller was now "no longer a registered user!" I immediately contacted eBay and PayPal.
>
> eBay wouldn't say much, but PayPal initiated an investigation. They said the seller provided them with a U.S. Postal Service tracking number as evidence of shipment. I tested the number on the USPS website, and it was bogus!
>
> Hope began to fade as I discovered that the seller's contact information on file with eBay was inconsistent with the information on the PayPal notification. I had been hopelessly duped!
>
> This was a particularly upsetting experience. I was very excited about giving this gift to my wife. So I never ended up receiving the DVD set. It was like Scotty beamed the cash right out of my pocket.

This story is filled with frustration and disappointment. This poor guy not only lost his money, but also found himself with no reliable recourse through either eBay or PayPal. Did you spot the mistake he made before he even made his bid? If you saw that he spent more than $400 on an item listed by someone with 0 feedback, give yourself a pat on the back. You wouldn't do that, now, would you?

things right again and catch the crook. With Internet commerce growing at such a fast rate, it may take some time to catch up with the online criminals, but your police department is definitely a good place to start.

What About Small Claims Court?

You may not have thought about taking your seller to court, but some eBay users we've spoken to have done just that. The process for filing a claim in small claims court varies from state to state. Check your local telephone book under the municipal, county, or state government listings for the small claims court office in your area. Ask the clerk how to initiate a claim. Visit the court to watch a case before you file a claim, so you can get a feel for how the process works. While the amount of money you can recover varies from state to state, for the most part the court procedures are simple, inexpensive, and quick. Many uncooperative sellers will decide to settle with you and get you out of their lives once you notify them that you're taking them to court. Also, many small claims courts have dispute resolution programs to help people settle their differences without going to trial.

STEVE KLINK LIVES IN A THREE-BEDROOM ranch home in suburban New Jersey. When he and his wife decided to remodel their basement, they wanted a bar that was in keeping with the Mexican theme they had chosen. Steve found a beautiful, handmade, solid teakwood bar on eBay, which he bought for $900.

The bar was made in Thailand, but the seller, like Steve, lived in New Jersey. It turns out the seller's son is still in Thailand, and he ships items to his mother for sale on eBay. To save what would have been hefty shipping costs, Steve picked up the bar himself, using a borrowed pickup truck.

When he got the bar home, he found that it was too large to get into his basement. In fact, to maneuver it into the room he had to literally tear down one of his basement walls! Then his wife came home. The story has a happy ending, though, because when she saw the bar, she said it was beautiful, and "didn't care what it took to get it into the basement."

They liked the bar so much that they worked the rest of the décor around it. Steve felt that he got a great deal, and that if he had bought the bar in a store it would have cost about $4,000. That's assuming, of course, he could have found such an unusual item. "The bar really works with our Mexican theme," Steve told us. "Where else could we have gotten such an item but on eBay?"

PowerSearch to PowerBuy: Advanced Searching Techniques

REMEMBER THE SCHEPP'S COCONUT LABEL and the old movie lobby card we showed you in chapter 1? Those are just two of the many great items we've bought on eBay over the years—items we could have spent years looking for if not for the online auction service. We hope that by now you've grown comfortable buying things on eBay, meaning that you've gone through the process a bit and had successful results. But browsing and even searching for items requires time and effort on your part, which you may not always have.

As you've seen, there are lots of things you can do to make shopping easier and more productive on eBay. You've probably already tried one of our favorites, sniping software, which we discussed in chapter 4. Now we'll show you how to set up automated searches and use eBay's Advanced Search options to zero in more precisely on those things you want. We'll also show you some tips and tricks for finding hidden bargains on eBay that will keep you one step ahead of other shoppers.

Advanced Searching

As you've seen, searching on eBay is simple. From just about any eBay page, you can begin a search by merely entering a word or two in the search box in the upper-right-hand corner. And searching that way is fine if you're looking for something unusual or have the time to check out lots of results. But with just a few more steps you can conduct a more targeted search. This will pull up the items you're looking for much sooner and without a lot of extraneous results you don't want.

Figure 9-1 shows eBay's Advanced Search screen, reachable by clicking the Advanced Search hyperlink that appears right below that search box we mentioned. Two of the most important features on the Advanced Search page are the Search Title and Description option and the Completed Listings Only option. You will use these options for different purposes, but you'll find both these methods of searching helpful.

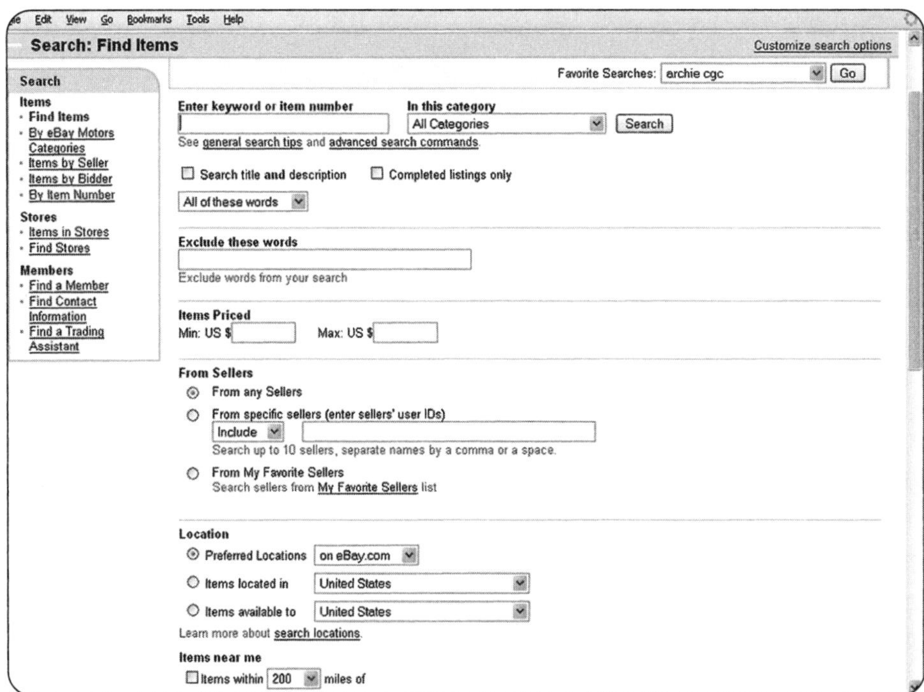

Figure 9-1: *eBay's Advanced Search screen.*

Searching by Title and Description

Searching by Title and Description will help if you're not getting enough items in your search results. By clicking this option you're telling eBay that your search terms don't have to appear in a title; they can also appear anywhere in the item description. Let's suppose you were shopping for a Charlie Brown lunchbox. When we searched for *Charlie Brown lunchbox* using a basic search, we got forty-four hits. When we used the same search phrase in a Title and Description search, we got more than twice that number: ninety-nine listings in all. They ranged in price from $3.99 to $24.00 for one that looked like Snoopy's doghouse. That's exactly the one we'd want if we were really shopping.

Be careful when using this search option, however, because this is an easy way to end up with too many results, or worse, off-target results. Some sellers load up their descriptions with irrelevant but popular keywords just to broaden the audience that sees their auctions. They shouldn't do that—eBay calls this *keyword spamming* and takes action against those sellers. But a lot of people still get away with it. eBay deals with the sellers they catch doing this by canceling the offending auction or suspending the accounts of repeat offenders.

Searching for Completed Listings

Using the Completed Listings Only search feature must become second nature to all eBay users—buyers and sellers alike. When you search using this option, you'll see auctions that ended on eBay within a designated time period. At the time of this writing, that time frame was up to within the last fifteen days. This search feature is important to buyers, because you can use it to see what the item you're interested in is currently selling for on eBay. Some buyers check this feature before every transaction to see whether the item they're thinking of buying is really a good bargain.

We searched for our Charlie Brown lunchbox after checking the Completed Listings Only box and saw that forty-eight had been put up for sale on eBay in the last fifteen days. Of those forty-eight lunchboxes, only twenty had sold. That shows us that supply of the lunchboxes is greater than demand on eBay. The sale prices of those that did sell ranged from $0.99 to $17.50, showing us that the one listed for $24.00 was probably not a good buy. Now we know how much we should reasonably expect to pay, and we know that quite a few Charlie Brown lunchboxes get listed on eBay and don't actually sell. That information will help us prepare for our bid, because we now know that we're not operating in a highly competitive market. We know that with time and patience, we'll be able to get just the lunchbox we'd most like to have. We'd also know if the competition were stronger and we were going to have to be more aggressive about bidding.

Other Ways to Tailor Your Search

As you scroll down the Advanced Search screen, you'll find lots of other ways to define your searches. You can specify that you want all results to be a certain distance from your zip code. That's especially useful if you're shopping for something large (say, furniture) that you'd like to pick up yourself rather than have shipped. You can choose the currency you want to use. You can specify the type of sale you want, such as Buy It Now, or just those items that you can pay for with PayPal. You can choose to exclude certain specific sellers. That's very useful if you come across a seller you don't want to buy from again, especially if that seller handles items you're still in the market for. Remember that every time you make your search more specific, you rule out possible search results. The best way to see which search terms and methods work best for you is to spend some time trying different things to see what results you get.

Luckily, eBay provides you with lots of tools to make searching for the things you want easier and more rewarding. No one wants you to be happy shopping on

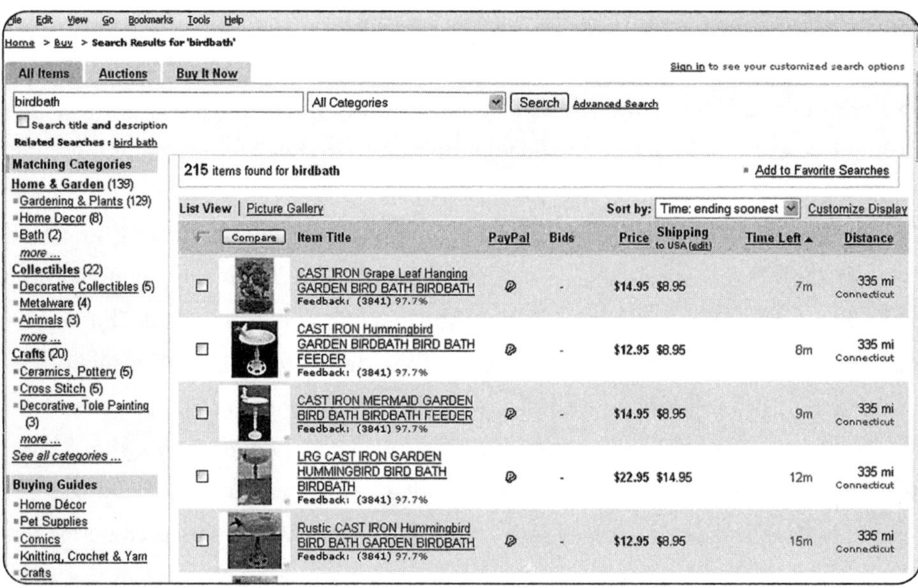

Figure 9-2: *The search results page from our birdbath search.*

eBay more than eBay does! Let's take a look at a typical search results page so that you can see all the options available to you for comparison-shopping. We'll start with a typical search page for a birdbath. Figure 9-2 shows the results page for the day we did this search. Starting from the far right of the page, you can see a link that allows you to customize your display. You can also sort your current results by time, price, distance, or payment options by using the drop-down menu. We've left the Time: ending soonest option showing in Figure 9-2. You can then move over to sort by price so that you either see the most expensive first or the least expensive first. Next, hop over to view those items that can be paid for with PayPal first. You can also specify these sort option options from the drop-down menu. At the far left of the screen, you'll see a button to activate the Compare feature. Just go down the list and click on all the birdbaths you might be interested in. Now click on the Compare button, and you'll get a new screen showing all your choices next to each other for quick and easy comparison-shopping.

You can also customize how your search results are displayed through the Customize Display hyperlink shown at the far right of Figure 9-2. Click on that link, and you'll get to a whole new page, shown in Figure 9-3, that allows you to set some of your own search options. We like to see the feedback of the sellers we shop with, so let's click that option box. Now when we do our searches, we'll also see the feedback rating of every seller listed.

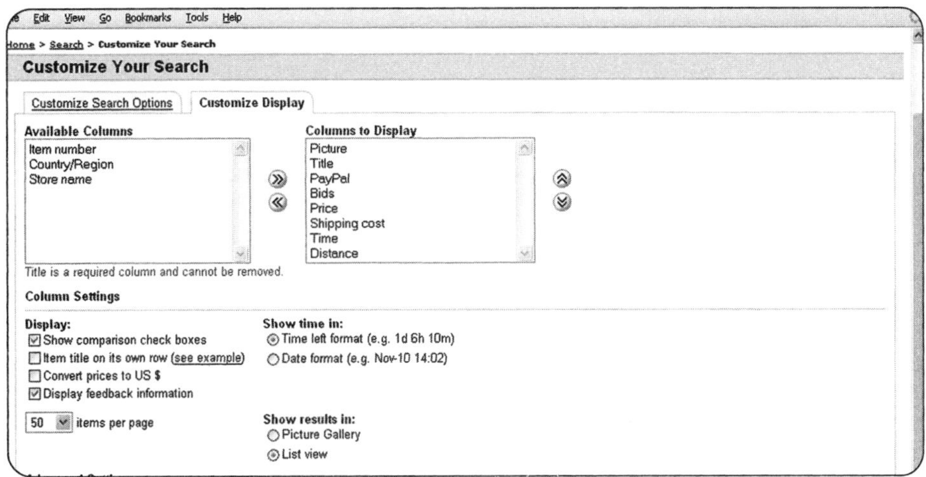

Figure 9-3: eBay's Customize Your Search page.

You can also choose to view your display as a list or in a Gallery view. (Gallery, a listing upgrade for which sellers pay an added fee, includes a photo of the item they're selling when search results are displayed.) It's simple to switch back and forth between these two options. Just click on the appropriate link at the upper-left-hand part of each search results page. Which view is best? If you are shopping for something that doesn't require you to make your decision based on an item's appearance, such as a cable modem, stick with the list view. That way you'll get all the available results, not just those that include the optional Gallery photo. If, on the other hand, you're shopping for something like emerald earrings, you might want to try the Gallery view. You'll lose a bit of information, such as the shipping cost, but you'll gain a clear view of every Gallery photo for all your choices. Sellers who list items like these generally pay for the Gallery photo option, so you aren't likely to eliminate too many items by choosing that view.

Favorite Searches

Okay, let's suppose that you've become an eBay Search Master (our highest level of eBay searcher). If you find that you regularly look for the same types of things (say, vintage Moonbeam clocks), once you've created an effective search, save it as a "favorite search." You do that by clicking on the Add to Favorite Searches hyperlink that's midway down the right-hand side of the results page. You can create up to one hundred of these searches, and they appear on your My eBay page, in the left-hand column under the All Favorites heading. Also, a Favorite Searches drop-down menu will appear whenever you click on the Advanced Search link. The drop-down menu shows the favorite searches you have created. You just click on the down arrow, select one of your favorite searches, and you can conduct that search right away.

eBay will also e-mail you the results of your favorite searches daily, for a period of anywhere from seven days to twelve months. From your My eBay page, you can manage these searches, edit them, and specify how often you wish to receive these e-mail notifications. Be sure to change these settings if you are no longer in the market for the item. Honestly, a potential problem with these e-mails is that they can entice you to buy more than your budget may allow, since each new e-mail is a personalized ad featuring your favorite things. It can take real willpower to resist these.

Other Favorites

You can also specify other favorites to show up on your My eBay page. You can designate your Favorite Categories and your Favorite Sellers. Although Favorite Categories may make it a little easier for you to jump to a specified category quickly, the more useful of these two choices is Favorite Sellers. On eBay, it's often difficult to distinguish one seller from another. Once you've found some sellers you like, you'll want to keep track of them. eBay is so large that you may have trouble finding a seller again when you want to do more shopping. Add that seller to your Favorite Sellers list and you won't have to worry about forgetting who did such a good job for you. You will easily be able to jump to that seller's auctions or his eBay store. You can also opt to receive any newsletters he offers.

Tips and Tricks

We all find the "right" way to shop on eBay. That's the way that seems to suit our own individual needs best. For example, one of us loves Favorite Searches and checks e-mail all the time to see what's new. The other hates Personalized Picks, discussed in chapter 2, because it feels creepy to be reminded that everything a person searches for gets noted and later commented on! You'll find the mix of tools that works for you, too. However, we did want to share with you some tips and tricks that veteran eBay users have developed over the years to make bargain hunting even more fun and profitable.

Use Aggregators to Find the Best Deal

eBay is a tremendous source for all kinds of things, but of course it shouldn't be the only place you look for stuff, especially in the case of commodity items, such as shoes, electronics, and DVDs. You may find a better deal elsewhere online or off. The price may be better, and the shipping and handling charges may be lower or even free.

There are Web sites, known as aggregators, that allow you to search a bunch of shopping sites at once for, say, the best deal on that new Disney DVD. These sites are popular and easy to use and will return a list of stores complete with prices (ranked) for just about any item you can think of. One, Shopping.com is owned by eBay, and when you search it you will retrieve results not just from Web sites like barnesandnoble.com, but from eBay auctions as well.

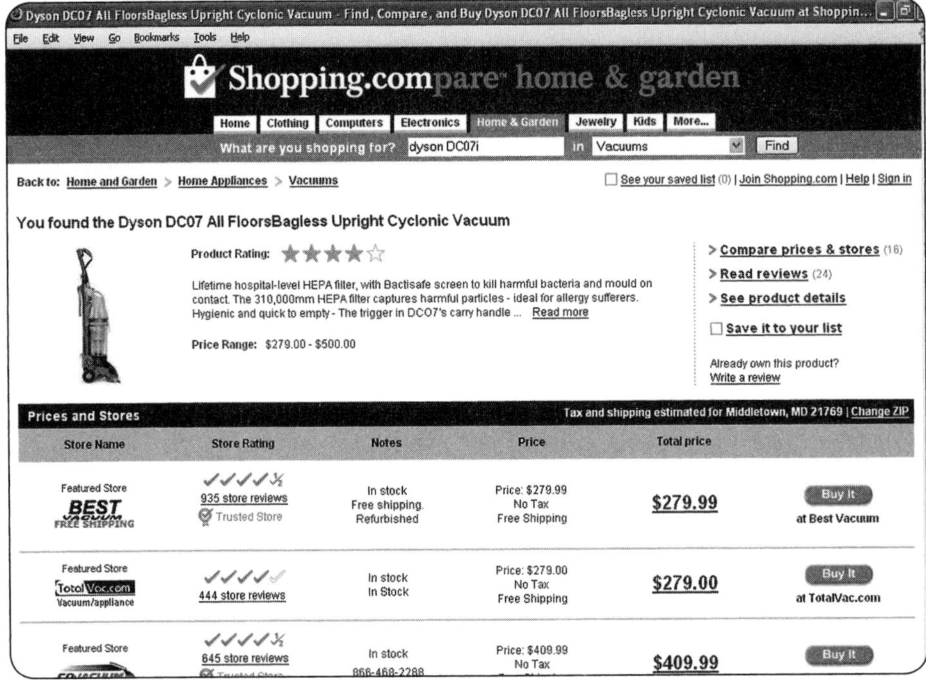

Figure 9-4: *The homepage for Shopping.com, one of many sites that aggregate product listings.*

AGGREGATORS

Here are just a few aggregators you might want to try:

Become.com
Froogle.com
MySimon.com
PriceGrabber.com
Shopping.com
Shopzilla.com
Smarter.com

Figure 9-4 shows the Shopping.com site. Here are the search results for a Dyson DC07 vacuum cleaner. As you can see, you can buy one and have it delivered to your home for free. When we did a comparable search on eBay, we found that we could come pretty close to the same sale price, but no eBay seller was offering it with free shipping, which instead averaged about $39. Of course, we didn't shop for any length of time on eBay, and we might ultimately have found a better price, but if what we wanted was a vacuum shipped to us, and soon, we might be better off purchasing it someplace besides eBay. So when you go to shop on eBay, make sure that's your best choice for the item you're trying to get. (As an aside, we conducted this search before eBay introduced eBay Express [see chapter 2], its new service designed to make just this kind of commodity-type shopping on eBay easier.)

Profiting from the Mistakes of Others

The most successful sellers on eBay are the ones who know how the marketplace works. They create careful titles for their listings, place their item in the correct category, write great descriptions that include clear pictures, and time their listings to end when there are most likely to be lots of people on eBay shopping and ready to buy. Those sellers do well, but they'll also tell you that you're more likely to get a bargain from other sellers who don't do all those things. eBay is loaded with listings that include mistakes. These may be spelling or typographical errors, but they may also be strategic mistakes. Whenever a listing goes up on the site with a mistake included, that seller is less likely to get a good price for his item, and he's also less likely to sell the item at all. That's because buyers can't buy what they can't find, and mistakes often lead to reduced traffic to an auction listing. That makes it ripe for smart eBayers like you, who can then swoop in and scoop up a bargain.

OOPS! IT'S SPELLED WRONG

The most common and likely mistake for you to profit from is a misspelling or typo in a title. As you remember, basic title searches are keyword searches. If the seller misspells a word in her title, her listing isn't going to get picked up in a keyword search that is spelled correctly. Let's take a common example. We searched for the term *dress shirt* and got more than 12,000 responses. When we searched for *dress shrit*, we found only one! That lonely little dress shirt is never going to sell, because it has so much competition that's actually spelled correctly and therefore turning up in search results. If we found we liked the shrit, we may have been able to snag it for its starting bid price of $0.99.

Now you're not always going to get lots of search results from misspellings, but here's an example of how you can put eBay's tools to work for you. Consider the most common misspellings likely to happen when hurried sellers create the titles for the items you most want to have. Test them out to see which seem to bring the most results. Now create some favorite searches and sit back while you wait for your desired items to turn up.

UH-OH, WRONG CATEGORY

Placing an item in the wrong category isn't quite as costly to a seller as misspelling a keyword in the title, but it does diminish the traffic to that listing and therefore limit its buyer pool. So don't limit yourself to the categories where the items you want are most likely to be found. This is another reason for you to become familiar with eBay's categories overall. The better you know the eBay categories, the more likely it is that you'll recognize which ones are candidates for misplaced items you may want. For example, suppose you collect Depression glass. You'll see thousands of listings on eBay for Depression glass of every variety. However, you'll only find seven listings in the Building & Hardware subcategory of Home & Garden. These sellers listed draw pulls and knobs, and, while they were accurate in thinking of them as Depression glass hardware, they'll still have fewer people finding their items here than they would if they were listed under Collectibles>Pottery & Glass>Depression.

NEW SELLERS' MISTAKES

In addition to making spelling mistakes in titles and placing items in the wrong category, new sellers are more likely than experienced ones to list the wrong things. New sellers need to build their feedback numbers before they can expect other eBayers to trust them enough to make expensive purchases from them. We'll talk a lot more about feedback from a seller's viewpoint in the next few chapters. For now, it's enough to say that if you have a feedback number of less than about 50, it may be challenging for you to get anyone on eBay to buy an expensive item, such as a designer handbag, from you. They just don't trust that you know enough about eBay to handle a bigger deal, and you don't have enough history on the site to prove that you're not a criminal.

At the same time, new sellers often turn to eBay because they have come into possession of something they don't want, but believe to be valuable. They want a large marketplace to convert that valuable into cash. Here's your opportunity. Don't automatically bid on a high-priced item listed by a new eBay member, but don't completely rule it out, either. You are also a new member, and, therefore, you can understand the challenges of maneuvering on eBay. Get in touch with the new member who has listed an expensive item. Talk to her on the phone and exchange multiple e-mails. After all this communication, you may end up trusting her enough to buy her higher-priced item when other eBayers may not. Of course, if you're simply too cautious at this point to pursue this strategy, we completely understand. Just tuck it away as a great method of scooping up a bargain that you can come back to when you're more experienced and more confident.

BAD PICTURES, BAD WRITING, BAD TIMING

Whether a seller is new to eBay or highly experienced, if he creates auctions with poor pictures and/or poor descriptions, he's going to have trouble attracting a large number of buyers to his listings. Everything listed on eBay has competition, and most things have lots of it. When you're shopping, you're likely to click out of any listing that seems to be poorly presented. Why bother trudging through an awful description when the next listing is probably better? Why squint at an out-of-focus photo when you know a little browsing will likely bring you a clearer image? People who don't take the time to do a competent job of creating their listings lessen their product's appeal. That's bad for their business, but it cuts down on your competition considerably if you happen to come across something you want.

Poor timing is another mistake sellers make when they post their auctions. When you get to the selling section of the book, we'll tell you how to time your auctions to maximize profits. For now, let's take a look at timing from a buyer's viewpoint. First, you need to know that when an auction ends, usually seven days after it begins, it does so at the exact same time at which it was posted. So if you post your auction at 6:00 a.m. on a Thursday, it will end at 6:00 a.m. the following Thursday. All auctions are set to Pacific Time, because that's where eBay's computers are. If you live in New York, you may post your auction at 6:00 a.m., because you're an early bird, and you like to get your work on eBay out of the way before you start your day. Unfortunately for you, the western section of the United States includes lots of buyers who would rather sleep at 3:00 in the morning than shop on eBay. You may be surprised to learn that many sellers overlook this point. As you search, watch for the listings that end at odd times, when fewer people are shopping. You can also look for auctions that end on holidays, when lots of eBay shoppers are distracted. We showed you in chapter 4 how to bid on items without being on eBay, by using sniping software. Keeping timing in mind is a good way to locate bargains.

Consider the Location

When you search on eBay, you can designate through the Advanced Search page that your results be limited to those items shipping from a range of ten miles from your zip code to two thousand miles away. Of course, leaving this option unchecked allows you to shop anywhere in the world. If you are looking for a large or heavy item, designate your search to be local, say within twenty-five miles. That way, you can simplify the sale and minimize or even eliminate shipping charges, should you opt to pick up the item from the seller. That will make you a more competitive buyer than someone who will require expensive or complicated shipping. When we searched within our own local area for bedroom furniture, we found not only a very nice set up for sale, but one also offered by a seller with a 0 feedback score! See what we mean? If we really wanted it, we could have scooped up that set for much less than it should rightfully have brought.

eBay started out as a place to buy collectibles, such as Pez dispensers and baseball cards. The founders never would have guessed that one day people would regularly buy cars and even houses through their site. Chapter 10 describes some of these big-ticket items available through eBay, and provides some savvy strategies for buying them.

YOU MAY KNOW BY NOW that Brad collects "Golden Age" comic books, defined as comics published between 1938 and 1955. For years, he scoured flea markets, comic conventions, comic book stores, and mail-order catalogs, hoping to add to his collection. While he found some comics here and there, it took many years for him to amass a modest collection. These comics are rare to begin with, and Brad found that without the time to travel from convention to convention, and the deep pockets to support that endeavor, he'd have to be satisfied with owning a dozen or so comics from this era.

Then eBay came along. Now it seems you can own any comic you ever wanted just by typing a few keystrokes on your computer. Even the most valuable comic book of all, Action Comics #1, is available on eBay! And if no one is selling it now, it's just a matter of time until someone is. As we write this, more than 33,000 Golden Age comics are listed for sale on eBay, ranging in price from $0.01 to $18,000.00!

Brad shared his passion for comics with Deb, who also developed a soft spot for Superman comics published during World War II. Those wildly patriotic covers showing Superman crushing our enemies, or in some other way helping the war effort, touched Deb's heart. That may be because her father served during that war, and while growing up she heard many stories about what life was like then.

Just a few months before this book was published Brad found a Golden Age Superman comic with one of those great World War II covers through a Favorite Search he uses. After only a little begging, he persuaded Deb to let him spend the $300 he needed to buy it (see Figure 9-5). Brad probably never would have owned this comic if not for eBay. You'll soon have similar stories of your own, if you don't already!

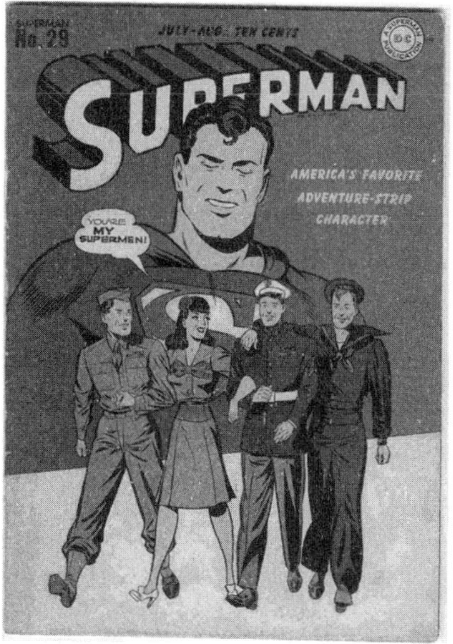

Figure 9-5: *The Golden Age comic Brad never would have acquired, were it not for eBay!*

Buying Motor Vehicles and Real Estate

NOW THAT YOU'VE REACHED the last chapter in the book about buying on eBay, we hope you've found a few treasures of your own, and that you feel empowered when you go onto eBay to shop. You've already learned enough to have moved up a few notches beyond the basic "Newbie" starting point. Be proud of yourself. At this point, maybe you'll want to learn a thing or two about buying your next car, or even some real estate through eBay. If you decide to give eBay a try for your next car, you won't be alone. More than 500,000 cars are sold on eBay each year!

When you shop on eBay Motors, which is the separate eBay area devoted to vehicles, you're still going to find auctions and Buy It Now listings. And a lot of the same kind of research that you've already learned to use will apply here, too. You'll sort through listings, reading each one completely and carefully. You'll research the seller, so that you'll know exactly what his history is, and how well he satisfies his customers. You'll find that listings on eBay Motors include a great many more photos than on eBay itself; you should expect numerous, varied, and detailed photos to be part of every listing you seriously consider when you shop for a motor vehicle.

Real estate on eBay is just another category accessible from the main eBay page. Believe it or not, you'll reach the real estate listings just as you would listings for antiques or stereo equipment. Unlike eBay Motors, real estate does not occupy its own specialty eBay site. It is also much smaller than eBay Motors, with a mere

1,700 listings available when we last checked. But you'll find that both eBay Motors and eBay's real estate categories have some special rules and protections in place to help you safely navigate and complete your transactions. We'll focus on eBay Motors, since that's where most of the action is, but we'll give you a glimpse at eBay's real estate market, too.

eBay Motors

In 2005, eBay Motors had sales of $13 billion. It is, by far, eBay's largest category. Estimates suggest that a vehicle is sold every minute through eBay Motors. It's easy to get to the eBay Motors site. It's a "Specialty Site" you reach through eBay's homepage. As you can see from the eBay Motors homepage, shown in Figure 10-1, you can buy much more than just passenger cars when you shop on eBay Motors. The last time we checked, there were more than thirty thousand passenger cars available, but you can also buy power-sports vehicles ranging from All

Figure 10-1: *The homepage of eBay Motors.*

Terrain Vehicles (ATVs) to snowmobiles and scooters. You'll find RVs and campers. You'll find auto parts, boats, and even airplanes—about two hundred of them when we checked. We even found a historic 1929 Ford Tri-Motor airplane, but since it was a BIN listing for $5 million, we let it go.

eBay Motors is also one of the largest auto parts stores in the world. We can personally attest to the great number of discounted auto parts you can find there. We've kept a couple of our old cars going by purchasing replacement parts on eBay at a fraction of their retail price. We've always had fast reliable service from the sellers we've found there. But, for the purpose of this chapter, we'll set aside auto parts, boats, and airplanes and turn our full attention to passenger cars.

Getting Started on the Road to Your New Car

The world seems divided into two camps: those who love shopping for a new car and those who loathe it. Shopping on eBay Motors can make things better for both groups. If you love car shopping, you can visit thousands of "showrooms" without ever stepping away from your home computer. If you loathe it, you can take your time, look around, and eliminate the salesperson peering over your shoulder and much of the haggling that intimidates so many of us. When you go to eBay Motors, you'll be able to shop for new and used cars from both dealers and individuals. You can zero in on the car of your dreams, whether that car is for sale down the road from your house or across several time zones. The variety of car-shopping opportunities is close to astounding. Perhaps the best reason for shopping on eBay Motors is that you can actually get the car you want for less money than you could by shopping in person.

To be fair, when you consider shopping at eBay Motors, you should keep in mind that car shopping in all venues has gotten easier these days. You can obtain a great deal of information about specific vehicle models through online sources like *Consumer Reports* and the *Kelley Blue Book*. You can also buy reports for individual vehicles through Carfax (http://carfax.com/), which details a car's title and accident history. So, overall, today's car shopper is potentially better equipped to make a good deal than she was ten years ago. And as an eBay Motors shopper, you can use these same services to educate yourself about the array of options available to you.

RISKY RIDES

Shopping for new and used cars has never been risk-free. Lemon Laws have helped protect consumers from the occasional faulty new car, but used car shopping is rife with risk. Buying a car the traditional way—from a dealer—is potentially as risky as ever, according to an article titled "Dodgy Dealing" by Bengt Halvorson, a writer for thecarconnection.com. Two of the top-ten categories of complaints that the Better Business Bureau receives are from transactions with used car dealers and new car dealers selling used cars. These are some of the dealers' common tricks, according to Halvorson:

- Clocking the odometer (turning it back so the car apparently has fewer miles on it).
- Disguising engine problems with additives. This refers to the tactic used by some unscrupulous dealers of introducing an additive to a problematic engine to quiet things down just long enough to make the sale.
- Covering up salvage and flood titles. This is the shady practice of selling cars that have been totaled for one reason or another by forging or failing to reveal key documents relating to past damage.
- Pushing overpriced extended warranties that, upon closer inspection, actually cover very little.
- Offering rustproofing and other add-ons. Unfortunately, some dealers take on tasks that only qualified body shops can handle and charge sky-high prices for these services.

We mention these things not to terrify you, but to show you that buying a used car offline isn't inherently any "safer" than buying one online. In fact, with all the safeguards and protections eBay Motors offers, and makes easily available through its site, offline buying of used cars may even be *less* safe!

Finding Your New Car

The mechanics of shopping for your next car aren't significantly different from the methods you used to shop for all the other things you've shopped for on eBay. Although eBay Motors is a specialty site, it looks and feels much like eBay. You can narrow your search geographically and use many of the same search parameters you've already become familiar with. But you'll also notice some differences, based on the items you're looking at. Within the subcategories, you'll find options you would not have had to consider when shopping for clothes or CDs. You can specify the make of car you're looking for and the type of transmission you want. When you specify the make you want, the model drop-down menu immediately changes to include the models available for that particular car.

Let's shop for a Lexus. Why not aim high? To get started, we'll go to eBay's homepage and click on eBay Motors, now the second link under Specialty Sites along the left-hand margin. Once we specify Lexus as the make, we'll jump to a page of Lexus listings. We found more than 650 to consider. Next, let's click on the drop-down menu, which enables us to choose from among any of the eight models of Lexus available. We can also specify the year range of cars we're interested in, the transmission type, and any particular search keywords we think are important. We'll shop for a Lexus RX 300, and we'll specify that we want a silver one, made between 2002 and 2006. We only found two items that exactly matched our search criteria, but eBay offers us a great tool to expand our search. As you can see

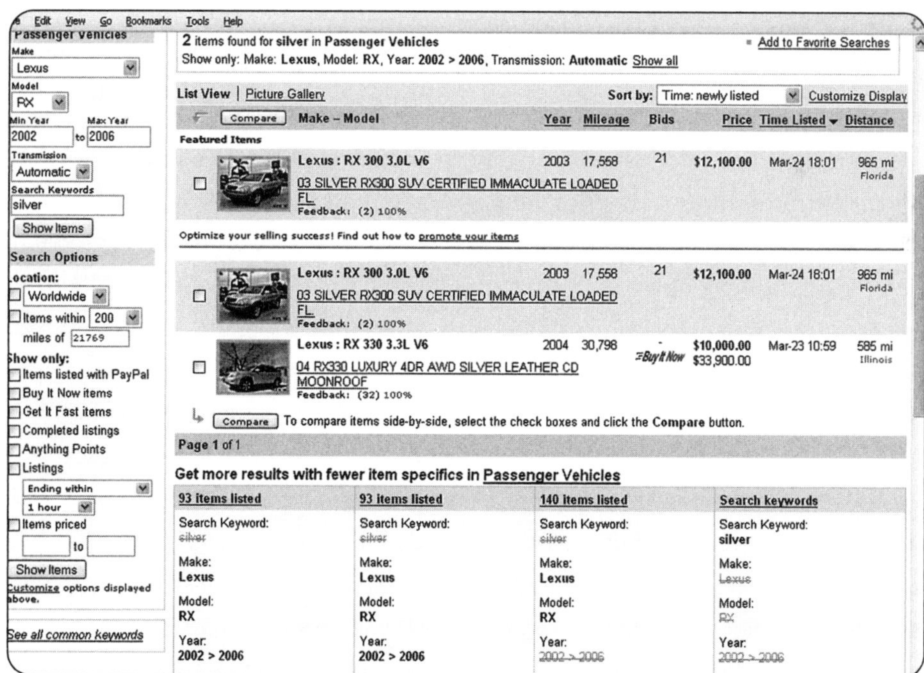

Figure 10-2: The results page from our Lexus search.

in Figure 10-2, eBay gives us some alternatives to consider. If we don't have our hearts set on a silver car, we'll have 93 listings to peruse. If we don't require a silver one built between 2002 and 2006, we'll expand our choices to 140 items.

This little exercise shows you how easy it is to get sidetracked once you've decided on what you'd like. Certainly, it makes sense to consider alternative colors, if you wouldn't mind another choice, but you have to be careful not to get swept away by the array of choices and end up with something you didn't really want in the first place. Of course, looking at alternatives can help you make a more considered decision, so you have to strike a balance here. Since we really wanted an RX 300, we'll stick with the two silver ones we found first. As you can see right on the search results page, both sellers have 100 percent positive feedback. One car has considerably less mileage than the other, even though it's a full year older. We've gathered this much information without ever looking at a single listing.

Reviewing the Listing

Next we'll move beyond the search page itself to review individual listings. By now, you're accustomed to working with listings as the first step in deciding about an eBay purchase. You'll use all those skills you've developed when you shop for cars, too. We probably don't have to tell you that you need to study the listings even more carefully and understand everything more completely when you're shopping for cars than for other, less pricey things. You're potentially risking $20,000 for a car rather than $20 for a DVD. Still, the skill set you use is very similar. Just remember: No impulse shopping in this corner of eBay!

Listings should be clear and filled with detailed information. You should read that listing and know everything about the condition of the vehicle, including any flaws or damage. Pictures are even more important for cars than they are for other types of items offered for sale. You should find enough pictures to make it feel as if you've actually seen the car in person. Those shots should include every angle, both exterior and interior. You should be able to look under the hood, and any flaws should be clearly photographed and featured. When viewing the photos, see if you can't get a glimpse of other cars in the background—or in the showroom, if the listing is from a dealer. This will help you learn a little more about the inventory your seller carries.

Most transactions on eBay Motors are "long-distance" sales, according to eBay. Don't be discouraged by this. Many buyers who travel to pick up their cars consider the trip a bit of an adventure. If that kind of adventure doesn't fit into your lifestyle, you can easily arrange to have the car shipped to you. We'll tell you more about that option in a minute.

Once you've found some listings that interest you, check them against other Internet sources. There are price guides and other online resources available to you throughout every step of the process. When you've narrowed your field to a few intriguing options, consider a Carfax report. All you need is the Vehicle Identification Number (VIN) in order to check the vehicle's history, including past accidents and other insurance claims, odometer readings, and ownership. The VIN is a standard element of every eBay Motors listing, so this information is easy to come by. You can also use True Market Value from Edmunds.com for information on what similar cars are now selling for. By clicking on the VIN link within an eBay Motors listing, you can immediately order a Vehicle History Report through AutoCheck, one of eBay's partners. You can learn whether the car's been damaged in a flood or an accident. You can also see if it's ever been used as a rental car, a police car, or a taxi. A report for one car costs $7.99, and ten reports cost $14.99. That's a great deal when you're seriously car shopping.

By the time you've finished this level of research, you should have a pretty good idea of which listings appeal to you, and you should have been able to eliminate a good number of vehicles that proved less attractive than you first thought. Now that you've found a few good candidates, it's time to turn your attention to evaluating the seller.

Evaluating the Seller

eBay reported to *BusinessWeek* that the ratio of individual sellers to dealers on eBay Motors runs just about 50:50. You are just as likely to come across a listing prepared by someone who has never sold a car on eBay as you are to find one from a dealer who sells dozens every quarter. Your own level of comfort will determine which type of seller you prefer to pursue.

Either way, once again, seller feedback is the place to start. Find out not only the seller's overall feedback rating, but how many transactions this seller has completed and how many of them were for vehicles. It doesn't tell you much if the seller has hundreds of feedback comments, but has never sold a car before. You'll know that this person is capable of handling an eBay sale successfully, but whether or not she's going to be a reliable partner to buy a car from is another question. The feedback the seller receives should be glowing, not lukewarm. It's one thing to be matter-of-fact about a seller who sent out the latest Nora Roberts novel on time and well packaged. But a person who has purchased a great car and had a smooth transaction is likely to be more effusive. Read the comments to learn just how pleased the buyers were.

You should also keep in mind that someone who sells cars will reach PowerSeller status much more quickly than someone who sells less-expensive items. To achieve PowerSeller status, you must maintain an average of four listings and an average of $1,000 in sales for three consecutive months. That earns you the lowest level of PowerSeller status, the Bronze PowerSeller. To achieve Platinum, the second-highest ranking (behind Titanium), you'll need to average $25,000 in sales in three consecutive months. Conceivably, someone could sell one car and keep three other listings going for three months, becoming a Platinum PowerSeller without actually completing many transactions. So the PowerSeller symbol, while still important, isn't an automatic guarantee of a great eBay seller.

On the other hand, a reliable car dealer may be a good risk, even if that dealer only has a few transactions to his name. A dealer delivers cars routinely and may only venture onto eBay from time to time. That doesn't mean he won't be trustworthy when he does business on eBay; rather, it may simply reflect his current business plan. (For instance, he may opt to offer hard-to-sell vehicles, such as vintage cars, on eBay, rather than on his lot.) If you are shopping with a dealer, you can check local and state sources, such as the Chamber of Commerce and the Better Business Bureau to explore the history of the dealership and whether or not there have been any claims against the business.

Once you've investigated the feedback history of the sellers you're interested in shopping with, call them on the phone. You should be able to reach a human being, talk to her about the car, and have all your questions answered. The seller should be willing to work with you to arrange mechanical inspections and put all your concerns to rest. If you're not getting that level of service when she's trying to sell the car to you, how reliable will she be when the real transaction begins?

Making an Offer

You've armed yourself with all the information you need about the car, the seller, and the deal itself. You even know exactly how much that car should cost, because you've done your research on pricing through the *Kelley Blue Book*. Next you'll need to factor in all your costs. That may include shipping or your expenses to travel to pick up the car. If you'll be picking up the car yourself, be sure to consider ancillary expenses, such as hotel charges and meals, in addition to the cost of a plane ticket. Now you know what you can afford to offer for the car. But first, stop at our yellow light before proceeding: You do not want to get into a bidding war in this eBay neighborhood. After you make your best offer, you must be willing to walk away from the deal if the price goes higher.

Beyond the amount you're willing to pay, you should be sure you've negotiated a way to change your mind. For example, your payment should be contingent on an inspector's report. eBay comes to the rescue here again, because you can arrange for an inspection right through eBay Motors. Just go to the eBay Motors Buy page and click on the Vehicle Inspection hyperlink. Most eBay Motor's inspection reports cost $99.50. As the buyer, you should expect to pay for this report, but some sellers are willing to pay for it in order to add to your level of comfort about the car. You can also arrange for one through Carfax.com. These inspectors are certified, and you should find one near the location of the vehicle in question. Your purchase should be contingent on this inspector's report. No reputable seller will insist on your completing the transaction if you don't like what you see at this stage.

Paying for the Car

When you've agreed to buy the car, you'll be expected to send the negotiated deposit to the seller very quickly, usually within seventy-two hours of the auction's closing. The deposit will reassure your seller that you're serious about completing the sale, and it will give you assurance that the seller can't sell the car to someone else while you're arranging financing and figuring out how to actually pick up the car. As with every other eBay purchase, make this deposit through a secure method. You can use your PayPal account to transfer the funds or charge your credit card. You'll find information right on eBay Motors about paying through PayPal. Just click on the Buyer Services & Protection hyperlink at the top of the eBay Motors homepage. You'll jump directly to a Web page that includes information on everything from making a bid to paying through PayPal and using an escrow service. Although you're already well acquainted with PayPal's services, review this information carefully; it will tell you a great deal about how PayPal can help you safeguard your money while you complete this kind of transaction. You'll also find information here about using escrow services. As we've said before, an escrow service is a very good idea when you're buying something as expensive as a car.

You can also go through eBay Motors to arrange financing for your new car, if that's what you'd like to do. You'll find the information you need about financing right on the same Buyer Services & Protection page. Once you've zeroed in on a particular car, you simply input the specifics of the deal and eBay will automatically connect you with lenders from all across the country who are willing to offer you a loan.

Getting Behind the Wheel

Well, now you've got a new car waiting for you. You just have to cover the miles between you and the vehicle. As we've already told you, many buyers travel to meet the new member of the family. If you do, the rest of the transaction won't be much different from buying a car from someone across town. You can even pay the balance due by certified check or bank check, if your seller agrees, because you're not going to give up the money until you're sure that you're satisfied with the car. If you go this route, you really don't have to pay the balance through an escrow service. As long as you've agreed with the seller that you have the right to refuse the car, you don't have much to risk.

You can also arrange to have the car shipped to you. That seems like a big deal, if you've never done it before, and we understand. But it really is very common and not that hard to do. Once more, you can start right on eBay Motors. On the listing page, shown in Figure 10-3, you can click on the hyperlink "Vehicle shipping quote is available." You'll go to a quote page from Dependable Auto Shipping (DAS). DAS will deliver your car to you at a price based on the distance between you and the vehicle. Prices range from $550 for a car that is 500 to 750 miles away to $950 for a car that is more than 2,500 miles away. By clicking on a button right on the site you can get an exact quote for your shipment. This is the easy way to make shipping arrangements, but it's not your only alternative. As you saw in chapter 3,

Hendrik Sharples located a transport service to ship his new car across the country from Florida to his home in the Pacific Northwest at a greatly reduced price.

Finally, complete the paperwork. Transfer the title, pay the taxes, and register the vehicle through your local state motor vehicle authority. You probably already know this drill from other cars you've bought, but it's simple to get help. Most states have Web sites now for their motor vehicle divisions, which provide all the details you might need. Enjoy your new wheels, and think about selling your old car through eBay! If you're interested, you'll find some information about that in Appendix A.

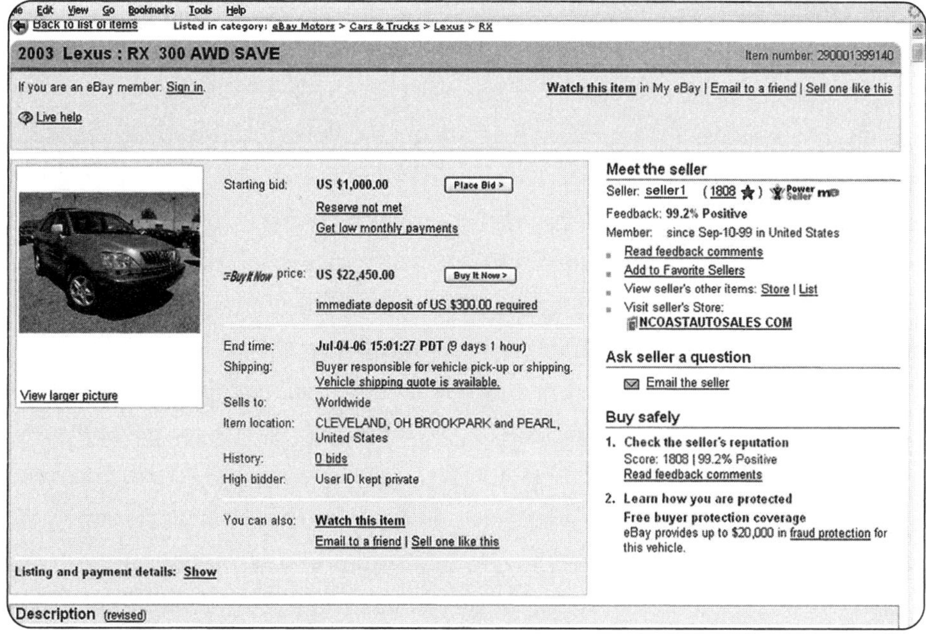

Figure 10-3: *From the listing page, click on the Vehicle Shipping Quote Is Available link (part of the shipping information appearing to the right of the picture) to view shipping details.*

Buying Real Estate on eBay

If you thought it was a bit of a stretch to buy a car on eBay, buying your next home or vacation property must seem completely zany. On eBay you can shop for land, time-shares, commercial properties, and residential homes. For the sake of this discussion, we'll concentrate on residential properties. There were more than 1,700 for sale when we looked.

Unlike eBay Motors, real estate on eBay doesn't occupy its own specialty site. As we said, it's an eBay category just like clothing and accessories or antiques and collectibles. (We must say we find this a bit odd, as real estate has its own set of rules, so it seems logical to break it out.) You'll reach the real estate listings directly from eBay's homepage. Another way in which this category differs from eBay Motors is that, rather than dominating its market online, it is actually dwarfed by its competitors, such as Realtor.com. While eBay Motors has no significant competitor in terms of volume and sales, eBay's real estate category is a tiny portion of the online real estate market. Still, at eBay's real estate category you can gain access to property sellers and buyers from all around the world.

The listings in the real estate category look much like the listings in other categories, but the rules for operating here are quite different. Unlike other items for sale on eBay, you aren't bidding on the actual property as much as you are bidding on the right to complete the negotiated contract to purchase the property. Sound confusing? Because the sale and purchase of real estate is subject to laws that vary widely from place to place, the auction listing you view is more of an advertisement for the property than it is an auction for it. Within those auction-style advertisements, you'll find two different types of listings: nonbinding and binding. It's difficult to distinguish which type of listing you're pursuing until you get to the bottom of the listing, where you'll find information about submitting a bid. There you will be told whether or not you are actively entering into negotiations for the property listed. Let's take a look at both types of auctions and explain how they work.

Nonbinding Auctions

When you consider a nonbinding auction, you're really just bidding on the right to pursue an advertised property that you find appealing. At the end of this type of auction, the seller will contact the highest bidder and the true discussion about purchasing the property will begin. The nonbinding auction is used in cases where binding auctions are not possible due to legal considerations or other restrictions. Just as you are not required to complete the purchase of the property, the seller is not required to complete the sale either. You've both just agreed to continue the discussion and consider the transaction. There will be no negative consequences for either party if the deal doesn't go through.

Binding Auctions

The term *binding auctions* doesn't mean that you are legally bound to complete the real estate purchase once the auction has ended. Instead, it means that, according to eBay's rules, when you win a binding auction, you are expected to complete the transaction for the listed property, subject to customary diligence and contingencies. A binding auction results in a good faith offer to follow through with the sale. If you don't complete the transaction and instead back out of the deal without pursuing it in good faith, you can and probably will receive negative feedback. But you are still not legally bound to complete the sale. The "binding" part of a binding auction relates strictly to the rules eBay has established.

Ad Format Items

In addition to the auction listings described, you'll find one more type of listing that doesn't appear in other parts of eBay—the Ad Format. When you complete a search and take a look at the search results page, you'll see that some listings include a little icon in the Bids column. The icon, which you can see Figure 10-4, represents a page from a newspaper's classifieds section with a red circle around an ad. This indicates that the item listing is strictly an ad for a property currently

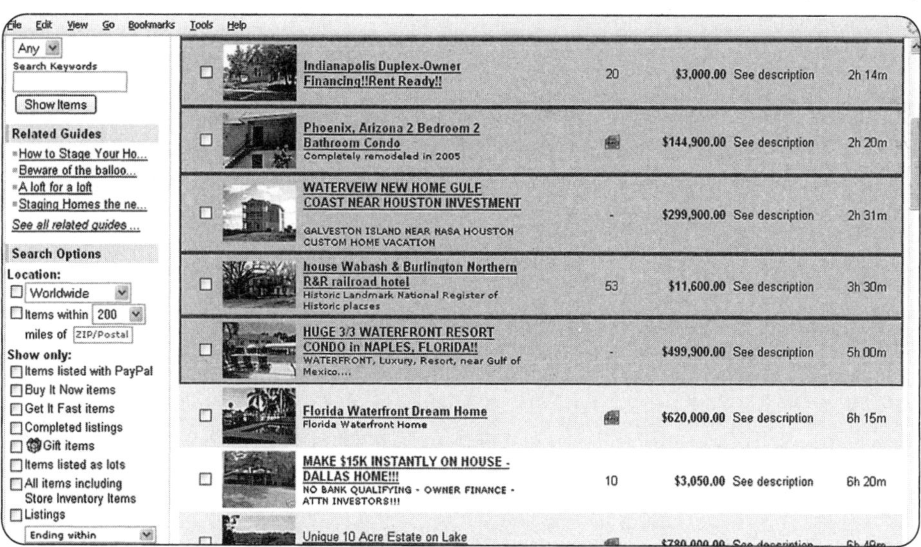

Figure 10-4: *The search results page for some real estate listings may include icons (see the column to the left of the prices) that indicate those particular listings are actually ads.*

available for purchase. The ad is a way for sellers and buyers to locate each other, but no bidding takes place on eBay. The price listed is simply the advertised price for the property.

What Can I Learn from Reading the Listing?

If you're thinking you couldn't possibly learn everything you need to know about the property in question by reading the description, you're right. Buying real estate is a complicated endeavor, even in person. But you can still gain a great deal of information about a prospective property, certainly enough to decide if you'd like to learn more.

In each listing, you'll find a hyperlink to a MapQuest map that will show you exactly where the property is located. That may not mean too much to you if you're not already familiar with the area in question, but it will give you an idea of how close the property is to main highways or bodies of water.

You can then click on Neighborhood Profile to jump to bestplaces.com for a complete demographic and statistical look at the surrounding area. Based on the zip code of the property, you'll see income statistics and average property values, population statistics such as median age and varying levels of education completed, and crime statistics. You'll also learn about the climate and the quality of air and water in this area. All these statistics are rated against national averages so you can get a better glimpse of how the area compares to the rest of the country.

The listings you consider should include lots of pictures, both of the property's interior and exterior, with an offer to e-mail even more photos to you, should you be interested. Some sellers also include shots of the neighborhood and views of the street where the property is located so you can see more clearly what the area surrounding the property looks like.

It's unlikely (and unadvisable) for you to view a real estate listing and decide unequivocally that you've fallen in love with that home and definitely want to move. You should come away, however, with a glimpse of the property's potential and a feel for the seller who is offering it. eBay is a place for you to *start* your search for the house of your dreams—not the final destination.

JENNIFER RIOJAS MOGAN AND HER HUSBAND are eBay PowerSellers with more than 3,400 feedbacks at the time of this writing. They operate on eBay with the user ID eauctiongurus. They've been building their eBay business selling an eclectic blend of goods for themselves and others since early 2000, and they are big fans of the site. When they were working to build their eBay inventory, they came upon a great way to generate some extra cash that they could reinvest directly into their business. Jennifer and her husband would shop on eBay for cars listed for sale close enough to their home location for them to conveniently drive to pick up.

They targeted cars being listed by new sellers with little or no feedback. They also looked for listings set to end late at night. They offered cash for the cars and drove them home prepared to get to work immediately reselling them. They completely detailed each car they bought to make it look shiny and clean. Then they put the car on the street in front of their home with a For Sale sign. "We almost always doubled our money," said Jennifer.

Of course, they did their research first. They always knew the street value of the car in question. They also phoned each seller to assess whether or not the person was legitimate and to learn more about the car than the listing could explain. "We were buying these cars so cheap, we knew if they had a few issues, we could always get our money back," explained Jennifer. "Plus, my husband is very mechanically inclined." Still Jennifer reported that they never had to do any repairs on the cars they bought. They only detailed them for cosmetic reasons. "It was a sweet operation!" noted Jennifer. Plus, it gave them a great boost in funding their budding eBay business.

Part II

SELLING

Quick Start Guide—

eBay Selling in 5 Steps

Ready to start making money on eBay? To get going immediately, follow the steps below. Since you've gotten this far in the book, we'll assume that you've bought a few things on eBay and have a feedback score of at least 10. That's important, because you'll need that to have some credibility with buyers.

1. Register as a Seller on eBay

- Click the Sell button at the top of any eBay page.
- Click the Sell Your Item button.
- Click the Create Seller's Account button.
- Fill in your credit card information.

2. Register for PayPal*

- Go to paypal.com and register as a seller*.
- Sign up for a Business Account.

3. Gather Items to Sell

- Start with items around your house.
- Try to find things that should bring at least $30.
- Stick with items that are new or in very saleable condition.

4. Research Completed Listings for Pricing and Positioning Ideas

- Click on Advanced Search on the top right of most eBay pages.
- Fill in a keyword or two that describes what you'd like to sell.
- Specify the most appropriate category.
- Fill in the Completed Listings Only box.
- Click on the Search button.

5. Complete the Sell Your Item Form

- Fill in the Sell Item at Online Auction option.
- Select a category.
- Select a subcategory, if applicable.
- Create a title and description for your item.
- Complete the Enter Picture and Item Details section.
- Enter payment and shipping information.
- Review and submit your listing.

*This will allow you to accept credit card payments. It's optional, but highly recommended, as many buyers will want to pay for their items through their PayPal accounts.

Start Selling on eBay

NOT ONLY IS THIS THE BEGINNING of a whole new section and chapter of this book, but it's also the beginning of a whole new chapter in your life on eBay. Until now, you've only had to consider eBay from the point of view of a shopper. You've been a shopper for most of your life, so you already had a set of skills you've tested and refined over all the years you've shopped for things. Relatively few of us have had the opportunity to be the seller as well. That's a whole different corner of the world, and although plenty of us earn our livelihoods through selling, many others never have the chance to do more than host the occasional yard sale.

If you're feeling a little intimidated by the thought of selling on eBay, you certainly are not alone. The great majority of eBay users never cross the line from buying to selling. In fact, according to a March 2006 article from *Time* Magazine, only 5 percent of eBay buyers also sell on the site. That's one reason why we're here. We don't want you to be put off by the thought of selling. Look how far you've already come as an eBay user. Not only have you learned how to find your way around the site and locate things to buy, but you've also learned how to do that safely, effectively, and with more savvy than most new buyers gain in months of eBay shopping. Besides, if selling on eBay were as hard as you fear, 300,000 people would not have become part-time or full-time eBay sellers in just the past year or so, and that's a fact, according to ACNielsen International Research. You'll see in this chapter and those that follow that eBay makes selling simple, with easy-to-use, fill-in forms and guides to walk you through the process. We'll make it even easier by sharing some insider tips and advice as you get started.

Selling: A Horse of a Different Color, but Still a Horse

If the thought of selling on Bay intimidates you, consider this: You've already learned a lot about how to be a good seller, because you've worked to become an educated and competent buyer. Selling is different from buying, and we don't want to downplay the importance of those differences. But knowing what to look for in a seller when you go to buy on eBay will help you understand the things that will make you a good seller yourself. The best advice is the simplest: To be a good seller on eBay, treat your customers the way you want to be treated when you're shopping on the site. Sound familiar? It's the same lesson we learned as children, and it's still the Golden Rule.

Keep in mind that selling something on eBay is just that—selling something. It isn't the same as making a life-changing commitment to pursue a whole new career. You can occasionally sell an item or two on eBay and never take that pursuit any further than a casual hobby. We've all read the stories about people who have created huge businesses on eBay, and those stories are fascinating. However, you never have to have one of those stories written about you, if you don't want to. You can keep your eBay selling small-scale and manageable. You aren't doing anything irrevocable here, so you can afford to lighten up a little bit. In this section of the book, we'll show you how and what to sell at very little risk, just to get your feet wet. And if you're intent on making selling on eBay your second—or your primary—career, we'll offer some insights for that kind of venture as well. Then you can decide for yourself what you want to do next.

We've talked to countless people who buy on eBay and never feel secure about selling anything. Remember Sharon Tendler from chapter 7? She buys memorabilia related to her grandfather, boxer Lew Tendler. She's been on the site for more than three years and has successfully completed dozens of transactions, yet she's always been too afraid to try selling. She even has the perfect item to sell: a $1,500 heater that she can't use in her home. It's slightly used, so she can't return it to the store, but she's too reluctant to turn it into cash by selling it on eBay. "My friends feel the same way I do," Sharon told us. "We are intimidated, afraid to do it wrong. Is it safe?" (People who remain uncomfortable with the idea of selling on eBay themselves can have an experienced seller do it for them, through an eBay drop-off store, for example. These are springing up all over and there's likely to be one close by you. Of course, we think there's no reason why you shouldn't sell your own things and save the cost of any commissions. These commissions are, on average, about 35 percent of the item's selling price.) So for Sharon and any others who might be afraid, come on along, we'll show you how to get started.

Thinking Like a Seller

Okay, so you've spent the first half of this book thinking like a buyer. Now you're going to switch gears. Step around to the other side of the sale counter and start thinking like a seller. It's not that hard, once you get the hang of it. Instead of thinking like a buyer, just broaden your point of view to include some things you may not have considered before. First and foremost, you're going to start out by being an honest trading partner, just as you were when you were strictly a buyer. Then you're going to work toward creating procedures and policies that will give your customers all the information they need to choose products that are exactly what you say they are. You'll add reasonable shipping rates and delivery times, and you'll offer great customer service. We'll look at some of the theoretical considerations involved in selling on eBay, and then we'll move on to the practical. We'll walk you through every bit of the process and then set you loose to learn as you go, gaining hands-on, practical experience. When you take it step by step, you'll see that the intimidation factor falls away and selling on eBay becomes fun.

Decide What You Want from Selling on eBay

Do you just want to sell off a few stray items that are cluttering up the house? Do you have kids who outgrow their toys and clothes almost before your very eyes? How about a hobby you no longer pursue or hand-me-downs you don't really want from a well-meaning relative? All these are items you can use to give eBay selling a try. If you just want to clean a few things out of your attic or closet every now and then, selling on eBay can be simple, and you don't have to spend too much time planning ahead.

If, on the other hand, you are considering launching an eBay business to contribute substantially to your household income, your foray into online selling requires more thought, right from the start. In that case, it's wise to create a business plan and prepare from the very beginning to track your sales and analyze everything you do in terms of profitability. We'll help you with all that in chapter 20, when you've gotten a better feel for selling. By the time you get there, you'll be better able to decide if this figures into your life plan as the part-time or full-time job for you. First, let's take a moment to consider a few of the issues that will crop up if you decide to sell on eBay as a profit-making venture rather than a hobby.

RECONSIDER YOUR USER ID

When we discussed choosing your eBay username in chapter 1, we were talking to you as a buyer. We suggested that you choose something pleasing to you, and told you not to use your complete name for security purposes. This advice is fine for buyers, but as a seller your username also becomes the name of your business. You want something memorable and fun, something that will help your customers relate you to the products you sell. For example, our son Ethan chose the username taketenguitars, because he envisioned having a business selling stuff related to guitars, and "Take 10" is a variation on "Take Five," a famous Dave Brubeck instrumental. You don't have to nail down your "permanent" business name before you get started, of course. But if you decide you like selling, you may want to consider changing your username, or opening up a separate "selling" account. If you change your user ID, your previous feedback score migrates to the new ID, and you'll have a little icon next to your name for thirty days that shows you've switched your ID. You may, instead, want to open a whole new user ID and start building your feedback score again. That's often a better option for sellers.

MAKE SURE YOU CAN CAPTURE THE IMAGE

We assume you already have a computer and a way to access the Internet or you probably wouldn't have reached this part of the book. The only other piece of equipment you need to start selling on eBay is a digital camera or scanner. Digital cameras are so common and popular now that capturing a digital image of what you want to sell should be simple for most of us. If you don't have a digital camera, you also have the option of using a flatbed scanner, either at home or at a copy center. In that case, choose as your first item something that can be laid flat enough to scan, such as a vintage postcard of old Atlantic City or a photograph of the Lone Ranger and Tonto from the film studio that produced the original *Lone Ranger* movies. A scanner will get you through your first few sales, but before long you'll wish you had a digital camera, so consider buying one now if you don't have one already.

Be sure you're comfortable with the mechanics of using your digital camera, because taking photos of whatever you sell will be a vital part of selling on eBay. Finally, if you don't have a good way to capture an image yet, consider selling a book, DVD, or video. eBay makes it simple to sell these items, because it has a large file of stock photos that you can automatically add to your listing. We'll tell you how that happens later on.

GET YOUR SHIPPING MATERIALS TOGETHER

You must be thinking we've lost our minds! Here you haven't even chosen a single thing to sell, but we're telling you to organize your shipping materials. Well, come on now, admit it, you already have a few ideas about what you might sell. Before you list a single item for sale on eBay, consider how you're going to package and ship it. That's part of deciding what to sell, especially when you're new at it. Choose something that won't be complicated to pack or expensive to ship. Find something that isn't easily broken. Make sure you have the packing materials in mind, and preferably in place, to create the finished package and get the item out your door for shipping. That will help you when you create your listing, because the shipping materials you plan to use will have to be figured into your shipping costs and, therefore, the fees you'll be charging your customer.

So far, we've talked about theories and given you some specific advice as you prepare to sell on eBay. By the time you're done with this chapter, you'll have some clear ideas about what your first sale will be, and you'll be ready to move on to creating a great listing. Nothing too scary or intimidating has happened yet, has it? Let's switch gears from the theoretical to the practical, and get started.

A HOBBY THAT CHANGED A LIFE

PowerSeller Robert Sachs operates under the username *rosachs.* Here's a little story to show you how his eBay business took off and led him to the full-time job he made for himself on eBay.

> I started in 1997 by registering on eBay and selling odds and ends, just to get the feel for it. It wasn't too long afterwards that I found some collectible Pepsi bottles, produced locally for the opening of Elvis Presley's Graceland Restaurant on Beale Street in Memphis. The bottles that were not used at the grand opening were being sold at Exxon stations and Wal-Mart stores in Shelby County only—nowhere else. I bought a couple for myself, since I collect Pepsi stuff, and a couple for my parents who are Elvis fans. When I got home, I looked them up on this new eBay site and found out that the bottles I was buying for $.99 were selling for $10.00 to $15.00, PLUS SHIPPING!!!!! I ended up with four cases of bottles in all. I sold one case to pay for all four. My devotion to eBay selling has grown ever since.

Bob moved on to selling computers and computer components, and today he sells shoes. He also operates as a Trading Assistant.

Register Yourself in the Eyes of eBay

You're already a registered eBay user, but if you're going to sell, you need to register again, this time as an eBay seller. Registering as an eBay seller is a ten-minute process that is as easy as can be. You'll need to furnish some financial information, and make a decision or two. Because you are already registered as a buyer, it's likely you've supplied eBay with much of the information needed for you to register as a seller.

To begin, click the Sell button at the top of most eBay pages. The page shown in Figure 11-1 will appear. Guess what? This page tells you what you already know: You need to set up a seller's account before you can actually sell anything on eBay.

eBay asks you to supply credit card or debit card information, as well as checking account details. Why? Unlike buying, selling involves fees that you'll need to pay to eBay. There are fees when you first list an item (whether it sells or not) and additional fees to pay when you sell the item. We'll have much more to say about those fees in subsequent chapters. eBay wants to know how you'll be paying these fees. Also, providing this information to eBay helps prove to their computers that you are who you say you are.

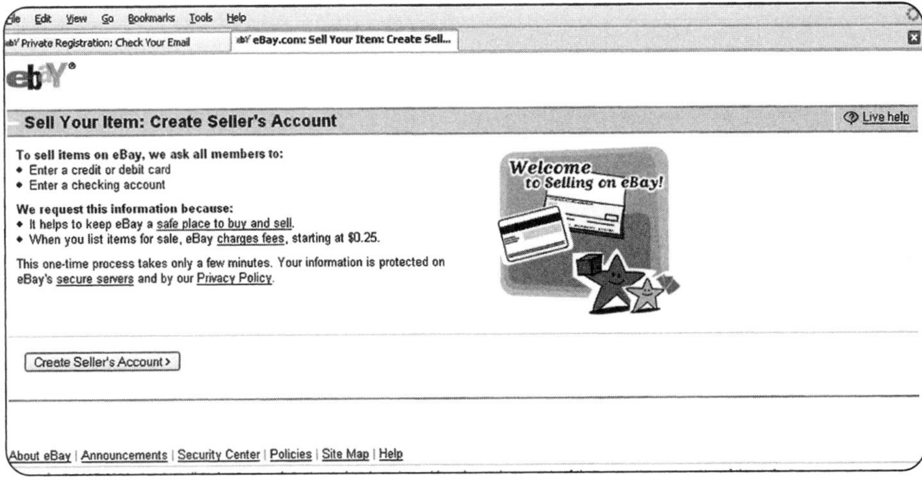

Figure 11-1: *eBay's instructions for new sellers. This page appears when you click on the Sell button.*

Done? Click on Create Seller's Account at the bottom of the page. The page that's shown in Figure 11-2 appears, and from there you'll need to start providing the financial information mentioned in the last screen. Note that, as a registered buyer, you should already have a credit card or debit card on file with eBay. You can use that same card for your seller's account, or use a different one if you want to keep your buying and selling activities accounting separate. When you're done entering that information, click the Continue button, where you'll be taken to a screen to fill in your checking account information (Figure 11-3). If all this is starting to feel a bit intrusive, we understand, but please realize that you'll never have to furnish this information again—it's truly a one-time process. After you fill in the information regarding your checking account, click Continue.

On the next screen (Figure 11-4) you'll specify how you would like to pay your

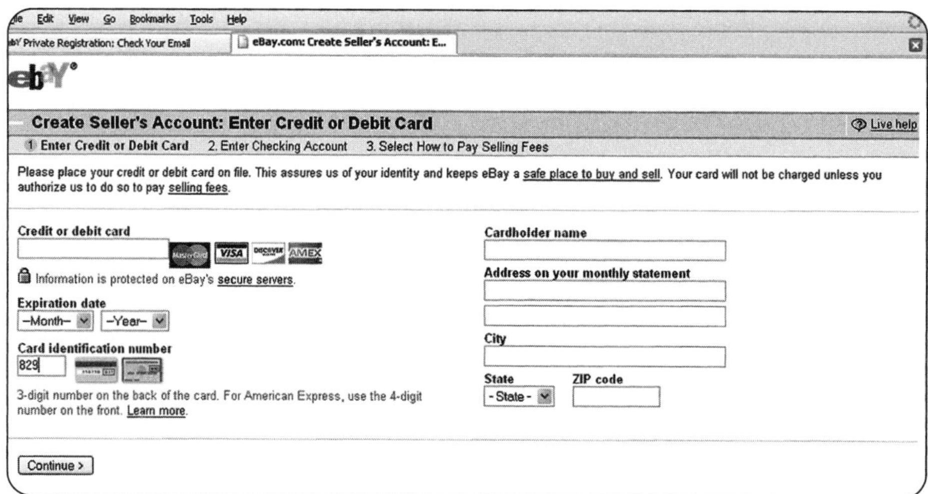

Figure 11-2: eBay's Create Seller's Account page.

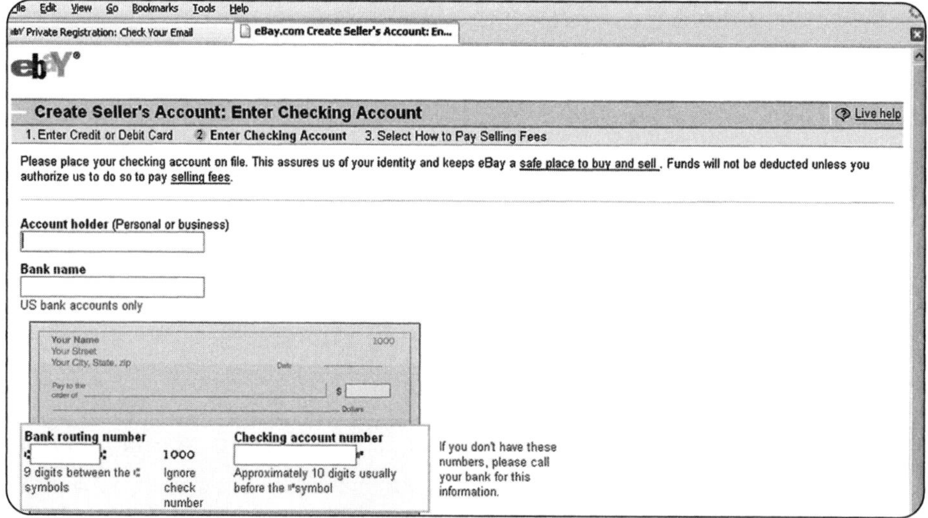

Figure 11-3: From here you'll enter your checking account information when setting up your seller's account.

seller fees, which eBay will collect automatically each month. You can specify how you will pay these fees by clicking on either Checking Account or Credit or Debit Card. Checking Account is the default option, already filled in by eBay. eBay suggests that you pay by checking account because you'll save interest charges. Of course, eBay then also saves the merchant fees it must pay the credit card companies! We think a credit or debit card is your best choice for paying your eBay fees, because these fees can vary widely depending on what and how much you sell. You don't want to be caught short. Also, eBay has been known to make invoice mistakes, and you don't want to have to pay for their errors, even temporarily. Don't worry too much about having to make the "right" decision now—you can always change your mind. You can change your payment method any time (for example, you may decide to pay your fees through your PayPal account), by going to the Seller Account section on your My eBay page.

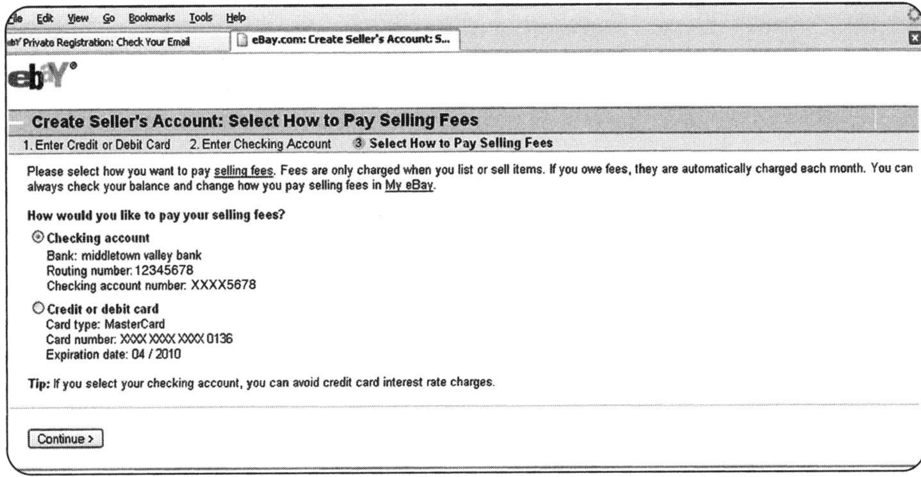

Figure 11-4 *From this page you'll specify how you want to pay any seller fees you incur.*

That's it. You're ready to sell. You've hung out your shingle. You're officially a seller. Soon after you complete your registration, you'll get a friendly e-mail from eBay, welcoming you as a seller and offering you step-by-step guidance as you prepare for your first sale. See, that wasn't so painful after all.

Choosing an Item for Your First Sale

You can make your introduction as an eBay seller easier and less stressful if you choose the first item you list for sale carefully. Most of the sellers we've spoken with remember their first eBay sale just as you remember the person who taught you how to ride a bike. It's a milestone. We agree with their advice here. You should choose to sell something you already own, and you should sell something for which you can accurately determine the value. Here's why. Remember when we told you how to shop for bargains by scooping up valuable things sold by new sellers? Well, see, you've already learned from those sellers, and you're ready to avoid their mistakes.

You want your first sale to be as problem-free as possible. You can increase the chances of having everything go smoothly by choosing the right item to start with, so you can devote all your energy to the mechanics of listing and completing the sale. That way you won't have to worry about the challenges of accurately describing something that may not be in great shape. You want these first few sales to result in uncomplicated transactions with totally satisfied customers.

The first place to look is in your own home. Your closets and cabinets, your family room and basement—all are probably filled with things you could live without. The average American home has about $2,200 in "unused goods," according to that same *Time* Magazine article we mentioned earlier in this chapter. And you thought it was just junk! So the first place to look for that first sale item is right under your nose. If you get your first few sales under your belt by cleaning out the clutter, you're gaining experience, earning some cash, and it's not costing you anything. Even the shipping materials we already told you to get won't really cost you, because you'll factor those into the shipping and handling fees you'll charge your customer. So step away from the computer and go find something that you don't need or want.

Know What It's Worth

Now that you're back online, you'll start your selling life by doing some research on eBay. Do a search of Completed Listings (see chapter 9 for a refresher on how to do this). Your goal is to determine what other people have been able to earn from selling items similar to the one you've chosen. Just as a lawyer never asks a question she doesn't know the answer to, a smart eBay seller never lists an item he doesn't know has already sold and for about how much. That's not to say you should price your item according to the final sales price of other auctions. We'll tell you a lot more about pricing strategies a few chapters down the road, but, as you consider what to sell for your first sale, you should have an idea of what price you can expect to earn. Remember, since you already own the item, you're looking at pure profit.

You will give yourself a confidence boost if you choose your first sale item from a category that you already know. You don't want the added the stress of having to learn the history and value of an item in order to write a good description when you're producing your first listing. This should be as simple as possible, so stick with an item you already know something about. Then you can devote all your energies to creating the best listing you can without having to worry that you're missing important details.

Is It New or Used?

You can certainly use eBay to clear out used, outgrown, or unwanted items. It happens all the time. But you can also consider using the site to move along any new items you may have that you don't really want. eBay can be a perfect alternative to the old regifting game. If it's new and unopened, you'll likely have an easier time selling it. Writing the item description can be a cinch if the box is still factory sealed and you know it's complete.

On the other hand, eBay wouldn't exist if it weren't for the secondhand market, so if you've chosen a used item, don't despair. For your first sale, you'll need to be especially careful that what you've chosen is clean and usable. If you smoke, or live with a smoker, be sure you're choosing something that doesn't hold odors, such as stuffed toys, dolls, or clothes. The same applies if you have pets. Make sure that there are no significant flaws in the item. Some damaged and even broken collectibles do sell on eBay, but you don't want these kinds of issues to complicate your first sale. Remember the goal here: to get some experience under your belt and keep the transaction as simple as possible. Now, with your chosen item in hand, we'll move on to helping you create the best listing possible. First, here's some advice from PowerSellers who all once stood in exactly the same spot you occupy today.

NUGGETS FOR NEWBIES

We've sold countless things on eBay, but we've also spoken with hundreds of PowerSellers who have sold many tens of thousands of things on the site. These are among the most creative, clever, successful businesspeople you'll ever meet. We asked them what advice they'd give to someone just starting out selling on eBay. Here, in their own voices, are some of their responses:

Research, Research, Research! For eBay sellers, this is just like real estate's mantra "Location, Location, Location." No matter what you sell, if you don't research it on eBay, you've just violated the cardinal rule of selling." —Stephen Ganus, eagleauctionsusa

Build feedback. Shoot for 20 to 25 before you sell. There's no magic number, but that's a good range. —Stephanie Inge, stephintexas

Get a good camera. The better the pictures, the more natural looking the object. Get the best camera you can for taking still pictures. —John Wade, john_wade

Take baby steps and watch your business grow. Don't invest a huge amount of money to start. —Jenny Loomis, socaltrends

You have to consider the other person's position. It's all about other people. The Golden Rule is still true. —Nick Boyd, tradernick

Don't wait till tomorrow to list. Be prepared to work hard, deal with disappointment, be endlessly frustrated, and meet some of the most interesting people in the world. —Robert Sachs, rosachs

Learn how to list and take pictures. Don't ask me any questions until you've listed and sold 10 items. Go through the whole process, and you'll get every bit of experience you need. —Marcia Cooper and Harvey Levine, generalent

Honesty. Customers can respect that. —Cindy Walker, superiormats

Take one thing in your house and sell it. Keep doing this until you've got multiple listings up and running. Learn from your mistakes before you've spent any money. —Jody Rogers and Asad Bangash, beachcombers!

Look at everyone else's stuff, especially those with experience. Emulate them, but don't cut and paste from their listings. —Bob Kitchener, bobkitchener

Stick to the categories you know. If you try to sell everything to everybody you are going to lose. —Drew Friedman, whitemountaintrading

MY BEST eBAY SALE

HERE'S A STORY FROM POWERSELLER stephintexas, also known as Stephanie Inge. She's built a complete business, not only selling on eBay, but also working as an eBay Education Specialist to help others follow along her path.

I have always favored old books, and found a box of vintage children's books at a local yard sale in the summer of 2004. After digging through them for a couple of minutes, I knew they were from the 1940s–1950s and in pretty good shape, so I asked the young lady how much she wanted if I bought the whole box.

"How about a quarter each?"

I whipped out $5 and hauled the box to my car. I got home that afternoon, fired up the computer, dragged my box over next to my chair, and started thumbing through the books. Then I ran across *See Dick Run.* Being a child of the '50s, I knew I had something special, since I learned to read with the *Dick and Jane* books.

After digging through my box, I discovered four hardcover *Dick and Jane books* that cost me a total of $1. Seven days later, I was about $2,500 richer. No, it didn't land me on *Antiques Roadshow,* but it certainly put a big 'ol Texas smile on my face!

Creating Winning Listings

IF YOU FOLLOWED OUR ADVICE in the last chapter, you now have something sitting near your computer that you'd like to sell on eBay. You've selected your item carefully to help ensure that your first sale will go smoothly, and you can easily see how you'll package and ship it once it sells. Now let's get to work creating a listing that will help you turn that item into cash.

The first listing you create can easily take you an hour or more to complete. But, just like everything else in life, it gets easier with experience. We'll walk you through the whole process and help you make those first critical decisions. After that first listing is up and running, the others won't be nearly as difficult, scary, or confusing. Once you get the hang of it, you may just find that selling on eBay is at least as much fun as buying is!

We'll start by walking you through a couple of different types of listings so you can get a feel for how the process works. We'll tell you which optional listing features might be best for you and which are probably not worth the expense. We'll help you with the pricing, the shipping, the photos, and all the other details. When we're finished, we hope to have listed (and sold) a couple of things we have hanging around here, too. Then, once you see how the whole thing works, we'll introduce you to some software that will automate the listing process and help you manage your auctions. That's just in case you like eBay selling so much that you want to keep doing it again and again and again.

You may be surprised to learn that, for many people we've met, that first eBay listing became the cornerstone of a whole new chapter in their lives; the chapter in which they became professional eBay sellers. If you decide you'd like to try your hand at eBay selling as a professional venture, too, you're going to need to know about auction automation software. Once you consistently list about ten items a week or more, it's important to get some help keeping track of all the details. We'll show you how such software works before we send you off into the next chapter to discuss some savvy pricing strategies.

Creating a Listing

By now you've viewed dozens, if not hundreds, of listings. You probably already have a feel for what makes one listing good and another not quite as good. But as you begin creating your own listings, we want to be sure you completely understand the anatomy of a listing. That knowledge can help you perfect your listing skills so that each element of the listings you create encourages your customer to become a bidder. All listings have four essential components.

1. **The Title:** The title of a book might entice a reader to open the book and give it a try, but the title of a listing has a different function. Sure, it should appeal to your prospective customers, but here's the key: The title should be so keyword-rich that your item pops up every time someone on eBay searches for the thing you're selling. Don't despair; we'll help.
2. **The Description:** Your description makes it possible for shoppers to feel as though they know everything they need to know about what you're selling. That way they can make a good decision about whether or not they want to buy it. At the same time, your description must be honest, accurate, and complete. Remember how you felt when you were the buyer. Give your customers the same consideration when you write your description.
3. **The Photos:** If you could, you'd let a prospective buyer pick up your item and look at it, turning it over in her hand and feeling its weight. But since you can't, be sure you include photos that will let your buyer feel as if she's actually seen the item for sale with her own eyes.

4. **The Policies:** Your listing should include all the details your buyer needs to know in order to decide whether or not you're someone he wants to do business with. That means you should completely describe the payment options you'll accept, your shipping and handling policies, and how you handle returns.

Now you can see why that first listing takes such a long time and is so challenging to create. The first time you list something, you have to make all the decisions about payment options, policies, and shipping procedures. Once you've done this one time, eBay will store your preferences for you, and they will become defaults for future listings. You may well have to alter and adapt them to other items you plan to sell, but you'll never again have to create them from scratch.

In addition to completing all these elements of your listing, you'll also have to decide which type of sale you want to use, an auction or a Fixed Price listing, for example. For the sake of this exercise, we're going to work with a regular auction format. You'll also have to choose the category and subcategories where your listing will be best placed. This is a vital decision you have to make at the very start of the process. Placing your listing in the wrong category will diminish your chances of selling your item. Relax. We'll help.

Do Your Research

We've decided to sell an old puzzle from the 1940s we bought cheaply at a yard sale years ago. It's collectible, compact, light, and easy to package and ship. Our first step in creating this auction listing is to search on eBay for completed listings for the same type of item. Knowing what such items have sold for previously is at least as important when you sell on eBay as it is when you buy. So whatever it is that you're selling, go to eBay and search for it in Completed Listings, using the Advanced Search feature. (If you need some help with advanced searching, refer to chapter 9.)

You'll learn a great deal about how to proceed with your listing from this simple exercise. Take a look at what price others have gotten for items like yours, as well as which categories and subcategories worked for the other sellers. Notice which titles were successful, and consider the language other sellers use to describe this kind of item. Compare listings that brought more money to the listings that didn't fare as well. Now you'll have some models for how you want your listings to look.

Please note that you should never cut and paste other peoples' work into your own listings, but you don't have to start completely from scratch, either. You can use other listings to inspire you as you decide how to create your own.

In searching Completed Listings, we saw that thirty-eight auctions for other puzzles from the 1940s ended recently. Of those thirty-eight auctions, only seventeen sold, and all of those went for less than $20. So now we know that we'll have to price our puzzle competitively if we really want to make the sale. We also see that selling this puzzle will be a good exercise for a first sale. We're probably not going to earn a fortune, but we won't be risking much if we make some mistakes. Remember, we bought this at a yard sale years ago, so recovering our initial investment won't be difficult! So we can proceed with very little stress while we get some experience in creating a listing.

Start Your Listing

Our research also showed us which category and subcategories will be right for this puzzle. We can simply write those down on a scrap of paper, and now we're ready to go to the Sell Your Item form on eBay and get started. Click on the Sell button at the top of most eBay screens, and you'll reach the Sell Your Item form shown in Figure 12-1. eBay occasionally refines its Sell Your Item form. When you

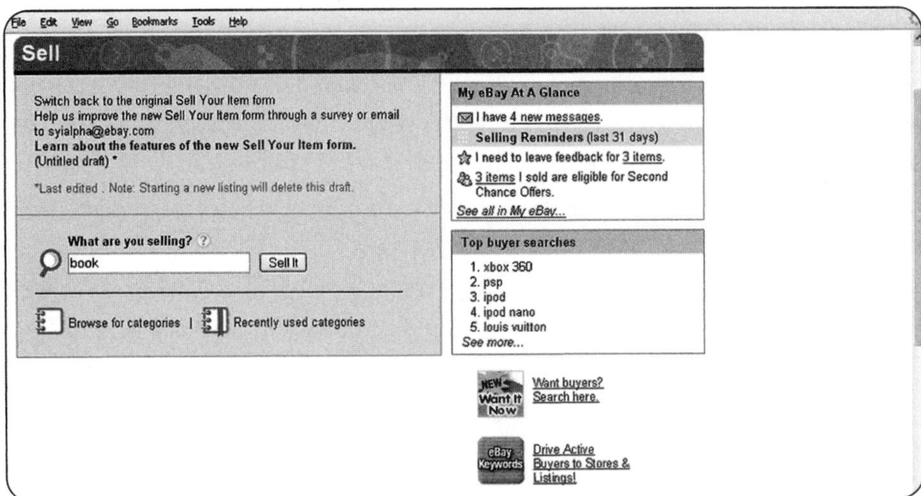

Figure 12-1: *eBay's new Sell Your Item form, in development as we write this, makes listing an item easier than ever.*

go to create your listing, the form may look somewhat different from the ones we're using as we write this book. That's actually good news for you. Every time eBay changes the form, it gets easier to use. eBay adds features or simplifies steps to make listing as simple as possible. Nobody wants you to have an easier time listing than eBay does. So the process keeps getting increasingly simple. On the other hand, simpler forms streamline the process for everyone, which allows your competition to also create listings that look great. So you'll have to work a little harder to make your listings stand out from the crowd. But, for our first listing, that's not something we'll worry too much about.

Now all you have to do is answer the question, "What are you selling?" Type in a few words that describe your item. We'll put in *vintage puzzle.* Click Sell It and you're off. Now it's time to choose our category and subcategories. As you can see in Figure 12-2, eBay gives us a lot of help in this area. Luckily for us, the first choice on the menu is perfect for what we're selling. *Toys & Hobbies>Puzzles>Vintage (Pre-1970)>Jigsaw>Under 1000 Pieces* not only describes our puzzle perfectly, but it was exactly the category we found when we searched Completed Listings. There really was no guesswork involved in this decision at all! Sometimes the right category won't be so clear, so your research will really pay off if you've spent some time familiarizing yourself with the choices that might be right for your item. We'll click the Save and Continue button and move on.

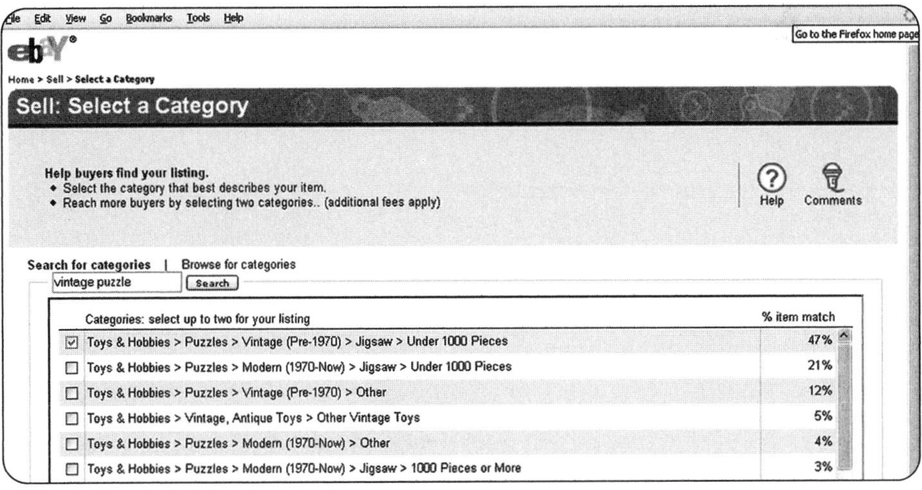

Figure 12-2: *eBay's category suggestions are right on target.*

YOUR TITLE, PHOTO, AND DESCRIPTION

The next screen is where we really get down to the nitty-gritty. In Figure 12-3, you can see that now that we've chosen our categories, we've reached a screen where we'll actually construct the listing itself. First we'll be asked to create a title. We're going to use every one of the fifty-five characters (including spaces) available to us, but we're going to be careful to make sure that each word or phrase counts as a potential search term. We decided on "1940s USA Map Jigsaw Puzzle Complete E.E. Fairchild Co." We wanted to include terms for collectors of puzzles, but also for collectors of USA memorabilia, maps, and puzzles made by the E.E. Fairchild Corporation. Notice we didn't waste any of our characters with words like *vintage*. Even though we used that term to describe our puzzle when we placed it in a category, we didn't choose it for a keyword in our title. Since the puzzle is from the 1940s, collectors realize that it's vintage. We also didn't try cutesy things like *L@@K!* Nobody on eBay searches for anything by the keyword *L@@K!* Remember, we're constructing a keyword search with every title, not just a description of what we're selling. So choose your title characters as if they were precious, because they are. You don't get enough of them to waste a single one.

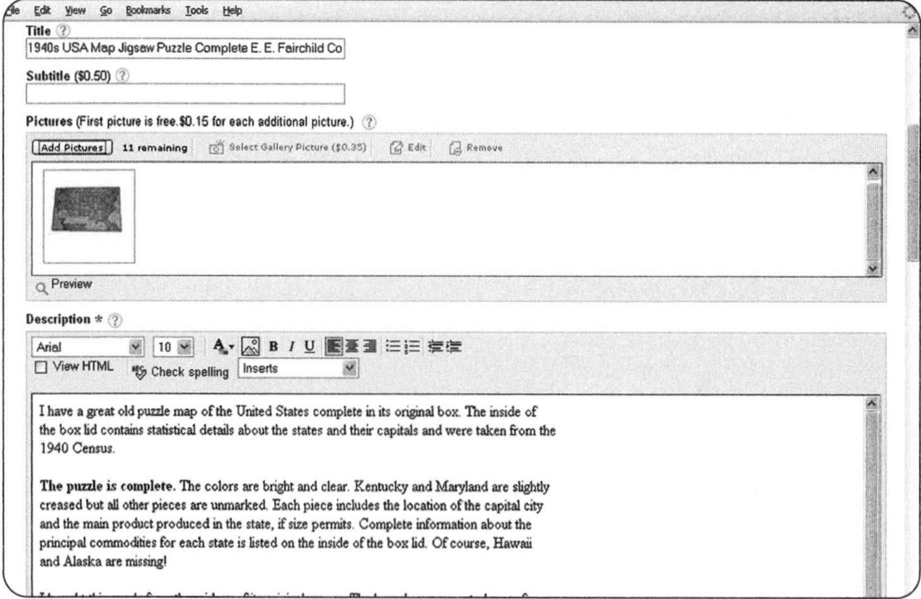

Figure 12-3: *You'll provide many details about your listing from this page.*

When you create your title, be very careful not to engage in *keyword spamming.* Keyword spamming means you include a word in your title or description that doesn't apply directly to the item you're selling but will entice buyers to come take a look. Suppose you're planning to sell a pocketbook you don't want anymore. Now suppose you bought that bag because it looked to you like a Coach purse. You can't list it with the word *Coach* anywhere in the listing. You can't even say, "Looks like Coach, but it's not." Similarly, we could only include the name of the puzzle manufacturer in our example because that name was clearly stamped on the box. It's authentic. Any use of a brand name other than one specifically authenticated on your item constitutes keyword spamming. eBay takes trademark violations very seriously. Your listing will be shut down. So keep it legitimate. For more information about eBay's intellectual rights protection program, check out the Verified Rights Owners (VeRO) program at http://pages.ebay.com/help/tp/programs-vero-ov.html.

The next step will be to upload a picture of our item. eBay makes that no more complicated than clicking a button. Click on Add Pictures, and you'll get a box that allows you to locate an image stored on your computer for uploading. Specify where that file is located and click the button. It will take just a little while for eBay's computers to get the image file. (We'll talk more about your photos when we've completed this little exercise.) Your image will appear in the box directly below the Add Pictures button.

Now we'll move on to the box below to write a description of the puzzle. We want to give our customers as much information about the condition of the puzzle and the design as we can. Think about how you feel as a buyer when you're shopping on eBay, and try to answer all the questions your customer may have. You can add color to your words or boldface, italicize, or underline them for emphasis, simply by clicking on the toolbar, much as you do in your own word processing software. Be sure to be upbeat and encouraging in your description; it's a bit like smiling at a potential customer as he walks through the door to view your wares. We tried to include plenty of information about this puzzle, and we specifically pointed out the flaws, noting that two of the pieces are slightly creased and the box has been taped. We don't want someone to buy our product and feel as if we weren't completely honest about it; that's why we make sure to call out what's not perfect about it. It's more than sixty years old, so someone who really likes old puzzles won't mind this normal wear and tear. When your description is complete, be sure to take a second and run the spell check. It's important to catch any typos or misspellings before the listing goes live. Typos mark you as a beginner, or strictly a hobbyist seller, and while that may be true, you certainly want to appear professional!

PRICING AND SHIPPING

Moving down the listing form, we'll be able to choose a template design to frame our listing at a cost of $0.10. We're not going to opt for this extra feature, because we know our puzzle isn't going to bring much money at auction, and we want to keep our listing fees as low as possible to maximize our profits. Besides, every eBay seller has access to these same templates, and they're all over eBay. So they don't really enhance your listing all that much. Scrolling a little further down the screen brings us to the pricing box. First we'll choose between an auction and a Fixed Price sale. We definitely want to try the auction format. Now it's time to pick a starting price. We'll spend the whole next chapter talking about pricing strategies, but we're going to start this puzzle at only $0.99. Our search of Completed Listings proved that we're not too likely to earn much from the puzzle. By starting the pricing low, we'll offer a bargain and hope to attract some buyers who think this would be a cool item to scoop up at a great price. Since you've also completed your research of Completed Listings featuring items like the one you're selling, you know already what you can expect to earn if your item sells. Just remember that listing fees increase as your starting price increases, and decide where you'll be comfortable starting your auction. If you feel stumped, skip ahead to the next chapter then come back and join us as we complete the listing.

With your price input in the appropriate box, it's time to choose your payment options. We've decided to check the boxes for PayPal, money orders/cashier's checks, and personal checks. We think it's best to offer shoppers as many payment options as possible, and these selections will give us adequate security while still being considerate of our customers' needs.

Moving on to shipping costs can seem a little intimidating, but remember that shipping was one of the things you had in mind when you chose your first item to offer for sale. If you have a good idea of how much your item weighs, you'll be able to estimate a reasonable shipping cost. Don't forget to add the weight of the packing materials and the box you'll ship the item in to the total weight when you figure the costs. You can specify a flat rate for all customers no matter their location, or you can decide to add eBay's shipping calculator to your listing. This calculator enables buyers to input their zip codes and get a price for shipping the item from your location to theirs. To do this, you'll be prompted to designate which types of shipping methods you'll offer. Give your customers a few reasonable choices to let them control how quickly they receive the item. You'll also be asked to include a handling fee. Don't feel shy about adding this on. You are entitled to a reasonable fee for your labor and the materials required to create the package. This handling fee won't be visible to your customers when they calculate their shipping costs, but the total shipping fee will be increased by the amount you designate for handling. We'll tell you much more about this in chapter 16.

You'll see that the item location is automatically filled in for you because your address is on file with eBay. Next you can choose which countries you're willing to ship your item to. Since this is your first time as an eBay seller, we'd advise you to sell only in the United States. If you decide you love selling on eBay and want to pursue it as a money-making venture, our opinion would be different about that, but for now, we want your first sale to be simple and smooth all the way, which means keeping your customers domestic. Complete the shipping information and click on Save and Continue.

LISTING EXTRAS

You'll get to the next screen, which is where eBay tries to earn a little extra money from you for listing extras. We're not going to enhance our listing with anything special, but we will spend $0.35 for a Gallery picture (see page 184 for an explanation of this feature). You already know from shopping on eBay that listings that include photos stand out better in the search results lists than auctions without them. We want prospective shoppers to see how cool our puzzle is and open our listing, so the Gallery photo is worth this small investment. Any other extras would be diminishing our profits on such an inexpensive item.

Before we go much further, let's define the most common listing upgrades:

- **Bold.** Makes your item stand out on a search results page by "bolding" your item's title.
- **Border.** Adds a colored border around your listing, so it really pops out.
- **Buy It Now.** Gives buyers the option of buying your item immediately, thus ending your auction.
- **eBay Picture Services.** Gives your photographs added emphasis by making them larger and allowing them to be viewed in a slideshow format.
- **Featured Plus.** Boosts your item's visibility by placing it in your category's "Featured Items" section, as well as at the top of the page where the "regular" search results are displayed.
- **Gallery.** Adds a small photo of your item, which appears next to the item listing on the search results page.
- **Gallery Featured.** Places your item in a special promotional area above the general picture gallery, and nearly doubles the size of the picture.
- **Gift Services.** Adds a gift icon next to your listing, to suggest it would make a good gift item.
- **Highlight.** Showcases your listing with a colored band.
- **Home Page Featured.** Places your listing on eBay's Featured Items page. It also rotates on eBay's homepage in the featured section.
- **Item Subtitle.** Allows you to add a subtitle to your listing, which appears right under its title on search results pages.
- **Listing Designer.** Allows you to use a variety of themes and layouts to customize your listing's appearance and boost its aesthetic appeal.
- **Listing in Two Categories.** Enables you to list your item in two categories, instead of just one, thus increasing its exposure.
- **Picture Show.** Places multiples pictures in your listing. These pictures can be viewed in a slideshow format.

UPGRADES: ARE THEY WORTH THE MONEY?

Are listing upgrades "worth it"? Should you pay the extra money, which ranges from $0.10 for a scheduled listing, to $39.95 for a listing that's featured on eBay's homepage? There's no clear-cut answer to that question. Even eBay provides contradictory information. Depending on where you look on the site, eBay notes that adding Gallery to your listing increases the average price by either 11 percent or 12 percent. Fair enough—that's only one percentage point difference, so perhaps you can use eBay data there to make a decision. However, the answer is much murkier when you are weighing whether or not to use Bold. In one place on its site eBay says Bold will add 25 percent to the average sale price; in another it says this feature boosts the average sale price by 39 percent! Which is it? Can we count on either figure being up-to-the-minute? eBay says its data is from a study done by a consulting firm called the Parthenon Group; however, there's no date given for the study.

What to do? To help sort things out we looked at data provided by Terapeak, a company specializing in eBay data. We checked out thirty days' worth of listing data for three very popular items: white-gold diamond rings, baby strollers, and iPod Nano MP3 players. We looked at the sell-through rates (that is, the percentage of auctions resulting in a sale). Then we checked how the sell-through rates compared if the seller used some type of listing upgrade, such as Bold. While the data didn't show the effect an option had on *price*, it did show its effect on sell-through rates. Still with us? In sum, across the board we found that the following features significantly boosted sell-through rates: Bold, eBay Picture Services, and including a Buy It Now price. Gallery also was important, since it either kept you at the average sell-through rate, or placed you above the average.

Therefore, to increase your chances of making a sale, you should always consider using these particular upgrades. For diamond rings, by the way, springing for Featured Plus significantly boosted the chances of a sale.

Of course, if you're listing an item that will likely sell for under $5, it may not pay to spend extra for any type of listing upgrade. When you get above $10 or so, and especially when you sell in very competitive areas, listing upgrades seem increasingly important.

eBAY'S LISTING FEES, FINAL VALUE FEES, AND UPGRADE FEES

There's no way around it: once you sell on eBay you've got to deal with listing fees. How much you pay eBay for listing your item depends on several factors, including the starting price you choose, the extra features you want, the number of pictures you include in the listing, and the final value of the item you sell. As an occasional eBay seller, these fees won't cause you much worry, but professional sellers watch their fees very carefully. Every penny they can save is a penny they can keep in their profit column. eBay's fees change from time to time, usually in February, but here's a quick look at what they were as we wrote this book. For more complete information about eBay listing and final value fees, go to http://pages.ebay.com/help/sell/fees.html.

Starting or Reserve Price	Insertion Fee
$0.01 to $0.99	$0.20
$1.00 to $9.99	$0.35
$10.00 to $24.99	$0.60
$25.00 to $49.99	$1.20
$50.00 to $199.99	$2.40
$200.00 to $499.99	$3.60
$500.00 or more	$4.80

Closing Price	Final Value Fee
Item not sold	No fee
$0.01 to $25.00	5.25% of closing value
$25.01 to $1,000.00	5.25% of initial $25.00 ($1.31), plus 3% of remaining closing value balance ($25.01 to $1,000.00)
$1,000.01 or more	5.25% of initial $25.00 ($1.31), plus 3% of initial $25.00 up to $1,000.00 ($29.25), plus 1.50% of the remaining closing value balance

Buy It Now Price	Buy It Now Fee
$0.01 to $9.99	$0.05
$10.00 to $24.99	$0.10
$25.00 to $49.99	$0.20
$50.00 or more	$0.25

Listing Extra	Listing Extra Fee
Listing Designer	$0.10
Scheduled Listing	$0.10
Gift Services Available	$0.25
Gallery Picture	$0.35
Ten-day Duration	$0.40
Subtitle	$0.50
Value Pack	$0.65
Bold	$1.00
Border	$3.00
Highlight	$5.00
Featured Plus!	$19.95
Gallery Featured	$19.95
Pro Pack	$29.95
Home Page Featured	$39.95
For listing in second category	Fees doubled

Picture Extras	Picture Fees
First picture	Free
Each additional picture	$0.15
Preview picture	Free
Picture show	Free
Supersized pictures	$0.75
Up to 6 pictures	$1.00
7 to 12 picture Picture Pack	$1.50

Note that eBay also offers certain features in specially priced "bundles":

- **Pro Pack.** A package deal combining bold, border, highlight, gallery featured, and featured plus.
- **Value Pack.** A package deal combining gallery, subtitle, and listing designer.

Satisfied that we've purchased everything we need for this listing, we can scroll down to the bottom of the page where we'll get a preview of the listing as it will look on the site and a list of our current charges for listing the auction as we've designed it. In our case, we were charged $0.20 for listing an item that costs less than a dollar and $0.35 for the Gallery picture. We're ready to sell at a total fee of only $0.55. Let's hope we'll earn enough to make our investment worthwhile!

We still have time to change and edit anything we're not satisfied with. If we feel that everything is satisfactory, we can click on List Item for Sale, and there you have it. Not only is your first listing up and running on eBay, but you can choose to save the details of this listing as a template for the next one you create. That makes it simple to list again—just be sure you double-check your new listing to change any details that might apply to this item only.

Your next screen is a message from eBay congratulating you on having listed your item for sale. In that screen, you'll get a link to hop directly to your listing so you can see it live for yourself (actually there's a short delay before your listing will be live and searchable). You'll also get an e-mail from eBay confirming your listing; that e-mail will contain a link to your auction as well. Now you can take a deep breath and savor your achievement.

Don't be too worried if you feel that you'd like to make a change, or you've made a mistake in your listing. You can easily keep track of anything you've listed through your My eBay page. The items you're selling will appear in the left-hand column under Selling. As long as you've not yet received any bids or the listing is not ending within the next twelve hours, you're free to edit what you've submitted. To revise your item, click your way to it through My eBay. Then click on the Revise Your Item link in your listing. Revisions are free, unless you add special features. Nothing in your listing is cast in stone, so enjoy the feeling of having become an eBay seller! As further reassurance, if your item doesn't sell, and you relist it, eBay will waive the relisting fee if your item sells the second time around.

Using Pre-Filled Information to List Qualifying Items Quickly

Now that you've successfully created an auction listing, we're going to show you a great shortcut eBay has come up with to help you quickly and easily list books, DVDs, CDs, video games, cell phones, PDAs, and digital cameras. eBay calls the shortcut *Pre-Filled Item Information.* If you have something to sell in a category that's compatible with this feature (and eBay adds categories regularly), you may only need to input an identifying number or title. Once you do that, a stock photo and the manufacturer's standard product information are automatically inserted into your listing! This can save quite a lot of keystrokes, and provide a much more complete description than you might be able to whip up yourself.

Most of us have some items that work with this feature that we don't need to keep around anymore. Selling these things is a great way to gain experience, build feedback, and clean house at the same time.

Let's use a book as our example. You'll start the same way, by clicking on the Sell button and getting to the Sell Your Item form. Once there, answer the question, What Do You Want to Sell? with the answer, "book." Now you'll get to choose the subcategories. We've got a children's book that we received as a gift. Since we already owned the title, we decided to sell it, so we selected Books>Children's Books>Picture Books as our category. We clicked the Save and Continue button and the next screen is where all the fun happens.

A new form appears, shown in Figure 12-4, asking for the ISBN (that is, the International Standard Book Number), the title, or the author. We input the ISBN from the bar code box on the book's back cover, and click Save Selection. The next screen appears complete with all the specific information necessary for completing the listing form for this book, including a great picture from eBay's own collection of images. We also have the author, publisher, format, publication year, and links to some reviews of the book, as you can see in Figure 12-5. We could just add our pricing and shipping information and call this listing done!

But we want to add some specifics about our particular book, so we include a description of the condition the book is in (new) and mention that, because it was a gift, the inside flap of the dust jacket has been neatly cut to eliminate the original retail price. We input the price at $5.99, which we think is a bargain.

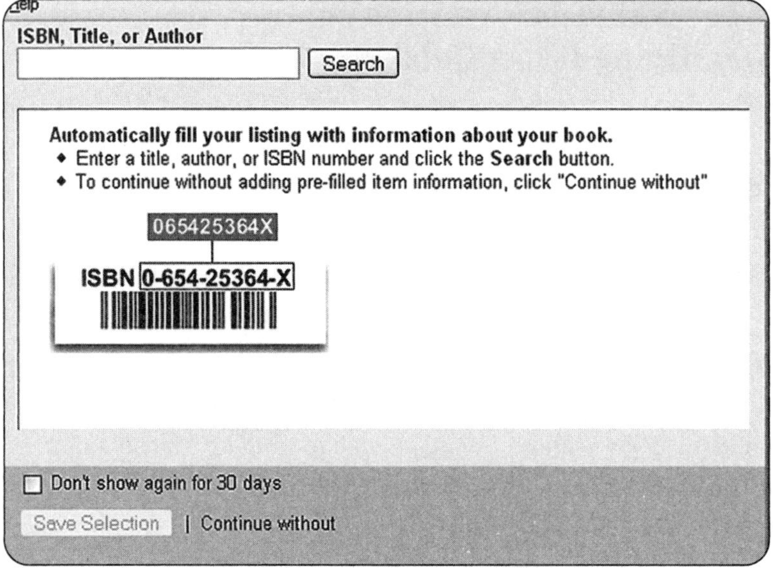

Figure 12-4: *Listing an item with eBay's Pre-filled Information form is fast and simple.*

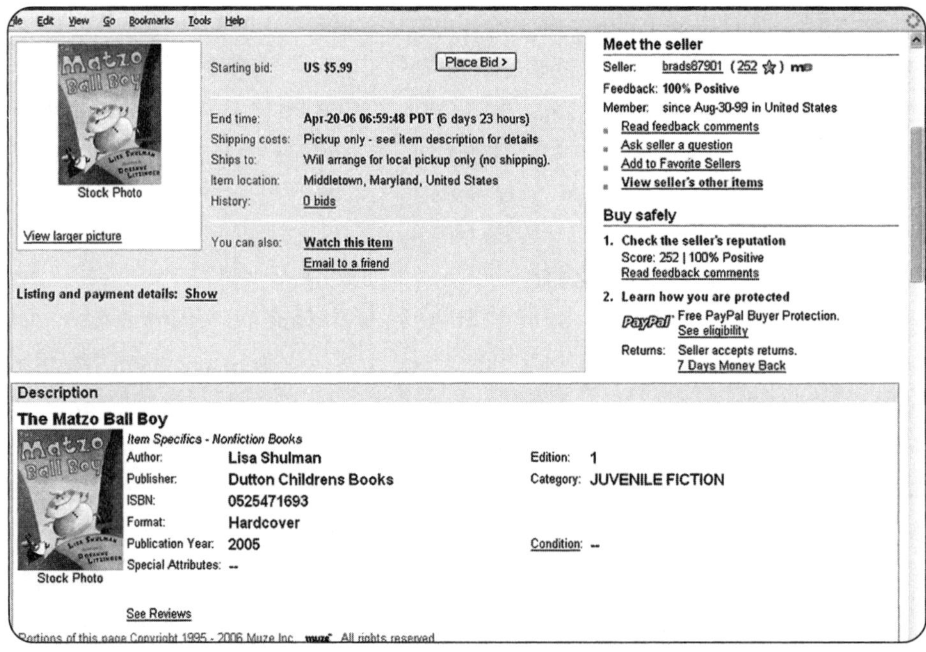

Figure 12-5: *When you list with eBay's Pre-filled Information option, you can quickly retrieve from eBay many details for your item, and even a picture, just by entering an ISBN or similar identifying number.*

If you've listed something previously, when you get around to trying this shortcut, you'll see that shipping and payment options are already completed on the form, too. We're going to change the shipping information and offer this as a flat-rate item to all customers, and we're going to select Media Mail as our preferred shipment option. Offered by USPS, this method is inexpensive and a good (but slow) option for books, CDs, and other media items. Media Mail may take up to three weeks for a package to go cross-country, but within the same state or from one state to a neighboring state it may not take nearly as long. We're also going to offer Parcel Post to those customers who might want faster delivery. Double-check everything, especially any text you've typed in, and click the Submit Your Listing button. Congratulations! Now you have two items listed for sale on eBay.

Make Your Listings POP!

Now that you have a couple of listings under your belt and have begun to get a feel for the mechanics of listing on eBay, we'll turn our attention to helping you get the most from your listings. Creating listings is one thing; creating listings that result in sales at good prices is quite another. We want to help you find the best ways to increase the chances that the items you list will turn into items you sell. Let's take a look at some of the specific features of your listing and see what experienced eBay sellers have to say.

There are many different ways to enhance the look of your auctions. You can choose a variety of standard templates right from eBay's Sell Your Item form. If you decide that you'd like to try making your listing look a little fancier, you can also buy templates from many different sources, including other eBay sellers. These are files that include all the fancy codes (HTML in Web-speak) for you to customize the look of your listing. Once you get some experience, you may want to try making everything look a little fancier by using templates. They're so simple, and they make it completely unnecessary for you to know anything more about HTML than you do right now!

Title and Description

We're not going to belabor the point about creating keyword-rich titles. We told you about how titles work in chapter 2 and again at the beginning of this chapter.

THE SELLER SOURCEBOOK

PowerSeller Stephintexas is a big fan of the Seller Sourcebook (http://www.sellersourcebook.com/), a Web site that offers many easy-to-use eBay tools all in one place. The site includes a library of more than 850 auction templates, which you can use to make your listings stand out from the great majority of eBay listings. A subscription (which is only $8 a month) also entitles you to use its Automatic Listing Generator, a nifty tool that takes the pain out of creating listings with fancy fonts and colors. To use it, you just enter the item title and details, and then choose your image(s). While the software will not actually go onto the eBay site and post listings, it's compatible with eBay's own automated listing tool, Turbo Lister, and together they pack a powerful, but inexpensive one-two punch for making your listings look more professional. They'll also be quicker to create and post.

We'll just reiterate that you should make every character count. You will be better able to choose your titling terms than we are, because you'll know the features of your item that will most likely appeal to your prospective customers. Think long and hard about each title, and include as many important key features as possible. The title will be the thing that entices your customer to check out your listing, so make it a real "grabber," as a PowerSeller once advised us. Take a minute to review the chart in chapter 2 that explains commonly used acronyms to help you put more details in the small space allotted for your title.

Your description gives you a little more freedom and opportunity for convincing your shopper to buy your item. The first thing you should consider is the tone. "Keep your copy friendly, fun, and dependable," says PowerSeller Bob Kitchener of bobkitchener. "You want good vibes all the way." Remember when you were the buyer? Didn't you prefer shopping with sellers who were friendly, cheerful, and easy to shop with? Did you find any sellers who said things like "If I don't receive payment within 7 days, I will file a Non-Paying Bidder (NPB) claim against you"? How did you feel about them? It's easy to understand that a new seller might have some anxiety about the act of selling, but your customers shouldn't detect that anxiety. Sure, you'll file an NPB claim if the buyer doesn't pay you. (Don't worry, we'll show you how in chapter 15.) But, you don't need to threaten anyone with that now. You want your customers to feel good about you and not be afraid to do business with you. Here are some other points to consider as you compose your description:

- Accuracy counts above all. Be sure your description is an accurate, detailed look at the item you're selling. Include all the details, flaws, and good features too. "We underrate our auctions so our customers will always be pleased," said PowerSeller Bob Buchanan of avforsale. "Our goal is to underpromise and overdeliver."
- Make it thorough. "New sellers often are not thorough enough in their descriptions," says PowerSeller and eBay Education Specialist Stephanie Inge of stephintexas. Don't be afraid of saying too much, as long as you stick to the item at hand. You may not want to tell the story about how your grandma had one just like it and how much she loved it, but if the information you're conveying is going to give your buyer a clearer picture of what you have, then include it. Don't hesitate to suggest uses for the item, especially if you've come up with a clever way to use something that might not be obvious to others (a hand-painted ceramic pitcher that makes a terrific vase, for instance). Your goal is to make your shopper really want what you're selling.
- Tailor your description to the item you're selling. This is another way of reminding you to consider your audience. If you're selling a computer part, a tool, or some leftover brackets from your latest shelving project, you don't need to wax poetic in your description. Make it complete, but keep it short and strictly factual. If, on the other hand you're selling clothing, remember that you'll need to include all the measurements of the piece so shoppers can determine fit. Be sure to specify fabric types, since prospective buyers can't touch what you've got. If you're selling a collectible, make sure to include details about how the item was used and what its value is. You'll know what things will appeal to your shoppers, because you'll know enough about your item to understand its selling points. If you don't know that yet, you're not ready to sell it!
- Make your description easy to read and attractive. If you have a lot of specifications for your item, consider a bulleted list. It will make it easier for your customer to pull out the important details. Don't hesitate to add some color or

design features. eBay's selling form makes that as easy as pushing a button. But strike a reasonable balance. Use some of these features to call attention to the best things about your item, but don't overdo it. That will diminish their power.

Your Photos

By now you've seen enough eBay listings to fully understand the importance of great photos. Maybe you've also been surprised to find listings without any photos at all or with photos of such poor quality that they really weren't helpful to you in making a decision about whether or not to buy. You know firsthand that listings without pictures or with really bad pictures discourage potential shoppers. Fortunately, taking great pictures for eBay listings gets easier with each new generation of digital camera. Since the first photo you include in your listing is free, why would you not include at least one?

You don't need a very sophisticated digital camera to get a great shot of your item. Actually, for Web-publishing purposes, a two- or three-megapixel camera will be all that you need to get a photo of the right size and resolution to do justice to your item. If you are shopping for a new camera, consider one that allows you to turn off the flash and that also has a macro feature for giving you great close-ups of your items' smallest details.

Here are some things to keep in mind when you're shooting photos for your eBay listings:

- Lighting. It's best if you can take your photos in natural light. It will give you the truest image without artificially changing the colors of your item. Avoid bright, direct sunlight, which can wash out your item, but try to get the lighting as natural as possible. Placing your item in a north-facing window is a good idea, because the light from the north is softer and more diffused than the stronger southern light. If you use artificial lighting, try using two different sources of light to reduce strong shadows.
- Background. You want your item to stand out—not the flowered wallpaper behind it. Every extraneous detail that appears in your photo detracts from the impact of the item itself. So use a neutral, but contrasting, drape behind your item to highlight it. Avoid using a white drape, because white reflects light. Consider having on hand two separate drapes, one light and one dark, so that

you can choose the one you think highlights the details of each item best. Remnants from the local fabric store often make great backdrops. If you decide you really like selling, you may want to invest in a great product called the D-Flector. It comes in several sizes, and it's shaped like an oversized briefcase or portfolio. It's light, portable, and very easy to use. Simply pop it open and place your item on the white screen. As you can see from Figure 12-6, your photo will feature your item as though it were suspended in midair. D-Flectors are available in four different sizes and range in price from $89.99 to $199.99. Some of the more expensive ones come with additional tools, such as a tripod for your camera. For more information about the D-Flector, go to www.sharpics.com.

Figure 12-6: *When you photograph items like this ceramic pitcher against the D-Flector's background, you come up with a professional-looking photograph that blends in well with an eBay item page.*

- Shoot your item from several different angles. Include as many photos as you think will be necessary to highlight the best features of your item. For our puzzle example, we chose to include only one photo, because we were only listing the item for $0.99 and each photo after the first one costs money. The top of the box clearly showed the puzzle and the bottom of the box is blank. We could have shot an image of the completed puzzle too, but we were not convinced it would have added anything to the listing, since it's identical to the box top. If we'd been selling a more valuable collectible, we would have taken several shots of the front, the back, the bottom, and the inside of the item. We would have used the macro feature on our camera to get close-ups of any flaws or special features. We would have done everything possible to make it seem as if our customers were actually turning the item over in their hands and examining it from every angle. If you're going to add listing fees to your item, extra pictures are a great investment.

Timing Your Auctions

When you just start out selling on eBay, you don't have to worry too much about timing your auction listings. If you are just trying to get some experience and clear out the clutter, timing won't make too great a difference in how you proceed. If you want to maximize your profits, or if you're considering selling as a real moneymaking enterprise, you'll have to be much more concerned about timing. When we talk about timing, we mean two things: the duration of your auction and the time your auction ends.

Your Auction's Duration

The default length of an eBay auction is seven days, and seven-day auctions are the most popular ones by far. You can also choose to list your auctions for one-, three-, five-, or ten-day periods. A one-day auction won't give you much time to build interest in the item before your auction ends. A three-day or five-day listing may be useful in selling particular items, and many sellers like them, too. Sellers say that the two most important days of the listing are the first and the last. With a three-day auction, those two are only separated by a single day, helping sellers to move their inventories quickly. Five-day listings can be staggered among seven-day ones to alter the day on which you create your listings and help you balance your workload. If you want all your auctions to end on a Sunday, for example, you can run half of them as seven-day listings you create the Sunday before and half of them as five-day listings you create on Tuesday. Of course, this is only helpful to you once you're listing in enough volume to require spreading out your workload throughout the week. A ten-day listing is often used for more expensive items. Adding a few extra days to the auction helps increase the odds that you'll attract more buyers. If you start a ten-day listing on a Thursday, you'll actually be able to have it span two weekends, and weekends are when eBay traffic is generally heaviest. Only the ten-day auctions carry additional listing fees, so you can try the others to see which you like without risking too much.

Ending Time

The other factor in considering timing is when your auction will end. As you saw in chapter 9, an auction ends at the exact moment it began, however many days later the auction format calls for. Sellers have spent a lot of time and effort tinkering with their auctions to determine the best time of day and the best day of the week for their auctions to close. The best answer is to end your auctions when there are the most people on eBay who would want to bid on your item. If only it were that simple! Many people swear by Sunday night as the best time to end an auction, and it is a time when lots of people are cruising around on eBay. Still others say lunchtime on Monday is good, because people at work have had the morning to catch up on e-mail and meetings and are looking to reward themselves with some time spent shopping on eBay. Just remember not to end your auction on a Sunday night during a three-day weekend. People are distracted during holiday weekends and are less likely to be paying attention. Also, don't list when the endtime will be during special events of national interest like the Super Bowl or the Academy Awards. Anything that distracts potential bidders also cuts down on potential profits. Finally, consider the needs of your customers. If you sell items most likely purchased by stay-at-home parents, then afternoon naptime might be your best bet.

Managing Your Auctions

Here we are, having just completed your first couple of auction listings, and we're ready to tell you about how to manage once you're running dozens of listings at the same time! See how much confidence we have in you? Once you get the hang of listing on eBay, you may just find yourself craving more and more. Many people do. If you do fall into that category, you'll need some help managing all the details. Anyone who runs more than ten or fifteen auctions a week will soon lose track of the details without some outside help. On the next page we review different auction management programs and how they can help you once you become a high-volume seller.

Now it's time for you to take a deep breath and let some of this information sink in for a bit. We really didn't mean to overwhelm you, but there are many different considerations when you start creating listings on eBay. Don't worry. Every listing you create will go a long way toward building your confidence and teaching you your own special preferences and techniques. We'll move on now to a more complete discussion of pricing your item. That's a subject worthy of its own chapter.

AUCTION MANAGEMENT PROGRAMS (HEY, BIG SELLERS!)

It doesn't take too many sessions of creating and posting eBay auctions before you wonder to yourself if there isn't an easier, faster way to do all this. We admit it—selling on eBay takes a lot of work, and unless you're selling items that go for a lot of money, we wouldn't recommend your figuring out, on a per-hour basis, how much you're actually making. You'd be shocked (or maybe not).

Fortunately, a lot of innovative people within eBay and outside the company have come to your rescue by developing auction management software. This is a seller's dream come true, and we highly recommend using it if you sell more than ten items a week. We suggest that you start with eBay's own programs(go to http://pages.ebay.com/help/sell/advanced_selling_tool.html). Here's a quick rundown.

- Turbo Lister. This is a free program for creating listings offline (when you are not connected to eBay), and then quickly posting them. With Turbo Lister, you can easily save information you use repeatedly, organize your listings offline, and then upload them to eBay's computers all at once. There's no charge to download and use Turbo Lister. So definitely check it out when your selling progresses beyond the beginner level.
- Blackthorne Basic. Blackthorne allows you to easily create and post professional-looking listings, as well as quickly track your listings and handle e-mail correspondence. So it's a tremendous timesaver. A free thirty-day trial is available, and after that it's $9.99 a month. Blackthorne was formerly known as Seller's Assistant Basic.
- Blackthorne Pro. This is for big-time sellers who post more than one hundred listings a month. It does everything that the Basic version does but it also handles inventory management, and the creation of reports that provide important data on your sales, profitability, and even your customers. In addition, you can use it for bulk printing of shipping labels, and other things sellers running a fairly large eBay business need. It's $24.99 a month to use, but, as with Blackthorne Basic, you can try it out at no charge for thirty days. Blackthorne Pro was previously called Seller's Assistant.

For the sake of completeness, we also want to mention eBay's other selling tools: Selling Manager and Selling Manager Pro. These handle many of the same functions as do the Blackthorne programs. Unlike the Blackthorne programs, however, which you download to your computer and which can only be used on that computer, Selling Manager and Selling Manager Pro are Web-based. That means you don't have to use them from your own computer—you can access them through any computer with an Internet connection. If you have a very fast and reliable Internet connection, you may prefer a Web-based program.

As we mentioned, there are other companies that produce auction management software. If you'd like to explore some of them, check out the *Auction Software Review* newsletter at http://www.auctionsoftwarereview.com/.

MY BEST eBAY SALE

MARGUERITE SWOPE IS A POWERSELLER who lives in Pennsylvania. She turned her eBay hobby into her job more than five years ago when her youngest son came into her life. She's also an eBay Education Specialist and a Trading Assistant. For many years, Marguerite has enjoyed browsing around thrift stores and secondhand shops as a hobby. She's also a seamstress with a great eye for good-quality ladies' clothing. She now specializes in ladies' gently worn clothing that she buys at her usual haunts and sells on eBay. She has also begun to design and produce her own line of clothing. She shared her favorite selling story with us:

> I sell mostly women's clothing. I tried children's clothing, too, but I have the most success with the women's clothes. I try to find name-brand items for resale, because people come to eBay looking for a particular brand. It's easier to sell a "Liz Claiborne Red Shirt" than it is to sell a "Red Shirt." But that doesn't mean I won't buy something I think will sell well. I'm always open to new things.
>
> I bought a whole boxful of vintage "stuff" at a thrift store. It cost $25. At the very bottom of the box were two small pairs of moccasins. As it turned out, they were authentic and each pair sold for $500! With the rest of the contents of the box included, I earned $1,250 from my little box of stuff.

Chapter 13

Making Sure Your Price Is Right

WELL, NOW THAT YOU'VE CONQUERED the task of creating great listings, it's time for a reality check. The sad fact is that most of the items put up for sale on eBay don't sell. According to Medved's Auction Counts, the online auction branch of Medved Quote Tracker, a financial research site, somewhere between 30 percent and 45 percent of the items listed on eBay sold during the first few months of 2006. That means that far more than half of them didn't. Buy It Now (BIN) items sold somewhat better, with an average sell-through rate that bottomed out at about 25 percent, but also touched 60 percent several times. For up-to-the-minute figures, visit Medved's Web site at www.medved.net. The company monitors eBay 24 hours a day, 7 days a week, at 1.5-hour intervals, so you know the statistics are current. The figures are largely based on eBay's U.S. site only, but some numbers for eBay's UK site are also included.

So why are we telling you this discouraging bit of news? Because we promised that if you read this book, we'd tell you the truth. You won't get hype from us. Sure, people earn money selling on eBay, and some even earn their livings there. But you might as well know going in that many of the things you list won't sell. Our job is to help you create great listings, develop sound business practices, and enhance the likelihood that you will sell what you list. That includes deciding what price to list your items for to increase the chances that they'll sell.

We honestly don't have a magic formula. (Don't we wish we did!) We have had varying success ourselves selling on eBay, although we think we've increased the odds in our favor. We've also gotten a range of advice from other experienced sellers, but here's the bottom line: Pricing your items is part art and part science. You'll need to strike the balance that makes you feel comfortable about selling your things and good about the prices you get for them. Nothing we say here is cast in stone. We recommend experimentation, since eBay is always changing. If you keep a close eye on what you spend to buy your items, you'll know how much you need to earn when you sell them.

Here's to More Research

By now you must think we sing only one note, but it turns out that the best way for you to determine how much your item is worth is to research what other items just like it have sold for in the past. And, of course the best place to start your research is with the Completed Listings searches right on eBay itself. We won't belabor that point. By now, you know all about it. But Completed Listings is not the only place for you to gather great information about pricing and sell-through rates.

eBay Sales Reports

eBay now offers free sales reports to all eBay sellers. You can either choose the basic Sales Reports or Sales Reports Plus. Signing up for them is as simple as clicking a couple of buttons on your My eBay page. Along the left-hand column of that page, you'll see Subscriptions, the last choice under the My Account heading. Click that and you'll go directly to the page of all possible eBay-related subscriptions. Near the bottom of that page is the link to the Sales Reports.

Basic Sales Reports track information about your total sales, your ended listings, your sell-through percentage, the average selling price for your items, and the total amounts of your eBay and PayPal fees. Once you subscribe, eBay will automatically send a message to your registered e-mail address, notifying you that a new report is ready for you. All you have to do then is log onto eBay, check your My eBay page, and click on Sales Reports, now under the My Subscriptions heading. In order to qualify for the free reports, you must have a feedback score of 10 or more and at least one sale within the previous four months. eBay recommends the basic Sales Reports for small- to medium-sized sellers.

Sales Reports Plus include all the information listed above for the basic reports, but they also cover a lot more ground. eBay designed these for the larger sellers who need more data to manage their businesses properly. With these reports, you'll also get data about your sales by category and format (such as Buy It Now listings or regular auction listings). You can also track the sales of your store inventory (more about eBay stores in chapter 19). The details about your fees include your store referral credits (credits eBay offers sellers who successfully route customers to their stores from Internet locations outside of eBay) and the unpaid item credits you've requested (the fees refunded to you when the buyer doesn't pay for the item sold). To keep your reports active, you must sign on to check them at least once every ninety days. If you let them lapse, the reports will be deleted.

Other Sources of Research Information

We've already introduced you to Medved's free information and also to eBay's free Sales Reports. As you can tell, we're fans of free information! To stay current with all the eBay trends, you can also subscribe to AuctionBytes, a free online newsletter devoted to online auction information. You'll find information about other selling venues through the AuctionBytes newsletter, but, of course, when it comes to online auctions, eBay is like King Kong! It definitely gets the most attention. Ina and David Steiner are the editors of the newsletter, and they are greatly respected by the online auction world. To subscribe, simply go to www.AuctionBytes.com. We're quite certain you'll be glad you did.

Of course, there are other sources of eBay market research data that you can tap for a fee. Whole industries have grown up around the site to support sellers and help buyers make better purchasing decisions. We've found great information through Terapeak. We mentioned this company previously, but if you decide you really want to pursue your eBay selling, you won't find a better source of information about what sells, for how much, and when than you will through Terapeak's online site. The company provides item information that includes:

- Average Final Sale Price
- Average Start Price
- Total Listings
- Total Bids
- Percentage of Successful Listings

As you can see, Terapeak offers plenty of valuable information. Terapeak has two levels of subscriptions, which the company calls Research Lite and Research Complete. Research Lite, at $9.95 a month, will probably provide all the information you need as your business gets off the ground, and it would certainly give you a huge leg up over the average eBay seller. When you're ready for more, Research Complete is available for $16.95 a month. More information about these plans is available at http://www.terapeak.com/. We don't think you should worry about this now, but we wanted you to know this kind of help is out there, just in case you decide to move from beginner to professional. This way you can keep Terapeak in mind for up-to-the-minute data about what sells on eBay and for how much.

Pricing Strategies for Your Auctions

Now you know how to get lots of information about what items sell for and how to figure out what you can reasonably expect to get for any item you list. At this point, let's turn to the philosophies that drive pricing decisions. As you just learned, the majority of items listed for sale on eBay don't sell. So what can you do to increase the likelihood that yours will? So glad you asked. The answer, of course, depends more on you than it does on anything else.

Just as investors must decide how they will approach investing, you'll have to decide which type of seller you want to be. Do you want to be aggressive or conservative? You'll also have to consider how much the item cost you to acquire, since that will be the one factor that has the greatest impact on your profit when you sell it. Then you'll have to consider what the item actually means to you. If you own something you simply can't stand (and don't we all?), you'll be willing to get what you can for it and let it go. But if the item has some intrinsic value to you, you're going to need more before you're willing to part with it. So you see, after you've done your research, you're ready to ask yourself these questions and answer them. We're here to show you two very different approaches to pricing your items, and to give you some tips about what you should do—and what you shouldn't—as you get ready to sell. Let's first consider the standard auction format.

Price It Low and Let It Go!

Here we separate the bold eBay sellers from the ones who do their best to avoid risk. We're not judging either type, just laying out the facts. Many sellers advise that when you set your opening price you "start it low, and let it go." We've spoken with many big sellers, even those who sell fine jewelry and watches, who start every auction at $0.99! They claim they've never sold an item at a price that disappointed them. Here's how it works.

eBay is very much a self-monitoring system. Items have a way of finding their own value on eBay, and that value equals the amount someone else is willing to pay for them. "List lower," advises PowerSeller Bob Buchanan of avforsale. "Trust eBay to do what it does well, which is sell things. We were selling between 60 and 70 percent of the items we listed. We decided to lower our starting price, because our percentage of unsold items was too high. We cut the listing price in half, and within a month we discovered our sell-through rate was 85 percent! If you list a $100.00 item for $9.99, you won't sell it for that. If you do, it wasn't really worth $100.00."

Okay, you say, but Bob is an experienced seller who, with his partner, Greg Scheuer, handles hundreds of transactions a month. Why should you take this risk? There are several very good reasons.

LOWER LISTING FEES

As you saw in the last chapter, your listing fees increase with your starting price. So suppose you have an item you believe to be worth $35.00. Do you list it for $35.00 and pay $1.20 for your auction? Or do you list it for $24.99 and pay just $0.60? Or maybe you list it for $9.99 and pay only $0.35. It won't make much difference if you only sell one item every now and again, but if you sell several items a week, your listing fees will quickly eat into your profits, and that's before you choose any special features like Gallery photos, Bold, or Highlight. So you earn some immediate benefits by starting at a lower price.

BUILD INTEREST IN YOUR ITEM

Suppose you have a bicycle to sell, and you know that your bike is worth about $400.00. Look what happens when you list that bike for $9.99. Anyone who comes to eBay looking for a bike will see your auction in her search results and be compelled to take a look. As you already know, many buyers sort their search results by lowest price first. Your bike will be at the top of the list every single time. Sure, no reasonable buyer will realistically expect to scoop up a valuable bike like yours for $9.99, but they'll all be tempted to see what you've got. Then eBay psychology takes hold. If you were shopping on eBay for a bike, you'd realize that you couldn't get a $400.00 bike for $9.99, but who knows, maybe you could scoop it up for $50.00 or even $150.00. You'd still get a bargain. So with little to risk, you'd probably go ahead and place a bid, hoping for the best. That's the stuff eBay dreams are made of! You wouldn't be alone. Others would do the same, each bid driving up the price of the bike. Now when your listing pops up in the search results, you may not be at the top anymore, because the price has gone up. You'll have multiple bids on your item, however, and that will make even more shoppers curious about what you have and why so many others have already decided to vie for it. That's only human nature. We tend to want what others want. So by pricing your item low, you increase the traffic to your auction and the chance for bids right from the start. That enthusiasm is likely to carry through the entire listing period.

IF YOU'RE GOING TO DO IT, DO IT RIGHT

So now you see the strategy and philosophy behind this aggressive pricing policy. If you think you've got the stomach for the roller-coaster ride, give it a try. But here's a solid warning. Before you do, make sure your listing is as clear and well-designed as you can possibly make it. That means make sure you've placed your item in the proper category and subcategories, and make sure your title is complete and keyword-rich. This strategy won't work if no one can find you. Make sure your listing also has great photos, and plenty of them, if they'll add value. Check that your description is complete, accurate, and every word is spelled correctly, and that you've chosen any special listing upgrades that you think will enhance your listing. Prepare your listing carefully, and then sit back and let eBay do what it does best.

Conservative Pricing

If you decide you simply don't want to take the risk of starting it low and letting it go, we do understand. Then you have no alternative but to do your research and set a price that you will be comfortable with. You can still lower your listing fees by setting your starting price below the level that bumps them up. In our example above, if you believe your item is worth $35.00, listing it for $24.99 will still start it lower than your expected value, and you'll save 50 percent on your listing fees.

So decide what the lowest price is that you're willing to take for the item. Then consider the line at which your listing fees increase, and start your item just below that. Of course, if you're only going to sell an occasional item, those listing fees may not matter to you, and you may be willing to swap the money for the security you'll get from knowing your item won't sell for anything less than you'd be willing to take. Of course, keep in mind that your item may also not sell at all. In that case, you can relist it one time for no additional insertion fee (as long as the item sells the second time around). This benefit applies only to the insertion fee, not to any fees you may owe for listing upgrades. After the second attempt, you'll have to pay the insertion fee and all listing upgrade fees whether or not the item sells. Also, keep in mind that you won't be selling terribly valuable items for a while yet. Remember those low feedback numbers, and how they translate into bidders willing to risk buying from you. So you'll have some time to try both methods before you're risking things that are worth a great deal.

Reserve Reservations

Why not start your item at a lower price, but list it with a reserve? As you know by now, a reserve establishes a bottom price below which you aren't going to sell the item. Isn't that the best of both worlds, a lower starting price and the security of knowing you can't risk a loss? Well, no, not exactly. First of all, adding a reserve carries its own fee. If you add a reserve for an item priced below $50.00, you'll pay a $1.00 fee. From $50.00 to $199.99, you'll pay $2.00, and for any item you list with a reserve above $200.00, you'll pay 1 percent of the reserve price up to $50.00. So, as you see, you're already paying for your security.

But, beyond the cost, the fact is that reserves often turn buyers away. They work against the concept that buyers can actually have what they want on eBay. It's a psychological fact of life, and it's backed up by eBay data, that listings with a reserve price see fewer bids than those that don't include a reserve. Many buyers get discouraged about being able to meet the reserve and go shopping for listings that don't have them. In fact, some sellers will even trumpet the fact that their listing does not include a reserve by stating that right in the title.

So does that mean you should never use a reserve? No, of course not. Sometimes a reserve is entirely appropriate, especially if you're selling something for someone else, and you don't want to risk letting it go for below its value. But we recommend that if you do set a reserve price, state that price clearly in your listing. What's the big secret? That way shoppers can see right away whether they are likely to be able to approach the price you want for the item. They'll find it encouraging to know that your lowest acceptable price is pretty close to their highest one. They'll be more likely to bump it up a bit and place a bid that meets your reserve.

Best Offer

You can also decide to include a Best Offer option in your auction listings. This tells buyers that you're willing to consider an offer as an alternative to the price you're setting for your item. You are under no obligation to accept any offer you receive, but you may just entice someone to offer enough money to prompt you to end the listing and sell the item. If you do select the Best Offer feature, you'll have a little icon appear in your listing where the Buy It Now button would be. Selecting the Best Offer choice is no trouble at all. It's simply a box choice you select when you're completing the Pricing and Duration section of the Sell Your Item form.

Let's take a look at how Best Offer can work for you. Suppose you have a major league baseball game-worn batting helmet that was worn by infielder Jeff Kent that you believe to be worth $45.00, but you only paid $15.00 for it and you'd be happy to get $35.00 for it. You could list the helmet with a starting price of $24.99 to control your listing fees and add the Best Offer feature. Now you can entertain any offer that gets close to the $35.00 you'd like to get for your item. You may not end up with the $45.00 you'd ideally like to get, but you might just entice a buyer who would offer you enough to satisfy you while feeling like he got a bargain, too.

Best Offer is available at no charge to the seller, although you do have to have a feedback rating of 10 or more to use it. Using it also varies depending on the category you're listing in, so if you decide to give it a try, check on eBay's Help pages for specifics.

Fixed Price Listings

Pricing your Fixed Price listings doesn't require quite the psychological considerations your auction listings entail. They're not auctions at all, but items you place for sale at a specific price. Of course, you'll still do all your research and clearly understand what similar items have previously sold for, and then you'll consider what price you would be satisfied with if you were to sell what you have. Keep in mind that your particular item may actually be worth more than some of those that have sold previously. Maybe the quality is somewhat higher, the color more sought-after, or the condition finer, but those things don't always translate to better sale prices, so you'll have to be realistic in your expectations. Keep in mind that, once again, the cost of your acquisition of the item might be the tipping point for you. If you bought it for less, you can afford to let it go for a little less, too. Just remember: You want to guard against wasting both your time and your listing fees by setting your price too high.

Buy It Now Prices

As you've already seen, Buy It Now prices are great incentives for shoppers who have definitely found what they want and want to buy it immediately, without having to wait for an auction to close. This is certainly a great alternative to running a listing strictly as an auction. If you decide to use the BIN feature, you'll set your starting price at the lowest price you'd be willing to accept and then determine your BIN price, perhaps somewhere near 10 percent higher than that starting price. You can still use BIN with an eye toward reducing your listing fees by setting the starting price carefully, but remember that it does cost between $0.05 and

$0.25 to include the BIN feature. Still, that's a modest investment if your BIN option will allow a shopper to find exactly what she wants and buy it immediately, so by all means give it a try and see how it goes.

eBay Express

eBay Express offers you the opportunity to list new items, such as electronics, shoes, or vacuum cleaners, for sale at a fixed price. eBay introduced this new service in 2006 to compete with other online shopping sites. You won't be ready to list on eBay Express (see the homepage in Figure 13-1), until you've built up your feedback number to 100 and you have a feedback rating of at least 98 percent positives. But professional sellers have high hopes for this new service, which, at the time of this writing, was just really getting underway. Pricing your items for eBay Express requires you to consider all the fixed-price issues we've already discussed, but you also have to make sure to price your items even more competitively. Since all the sellers you compete against on eBay Express have to meet the same requirements for customer service and satisfaction, you'll be competing only with other successful sellers. That means you won't be able to distinguish yourself based on

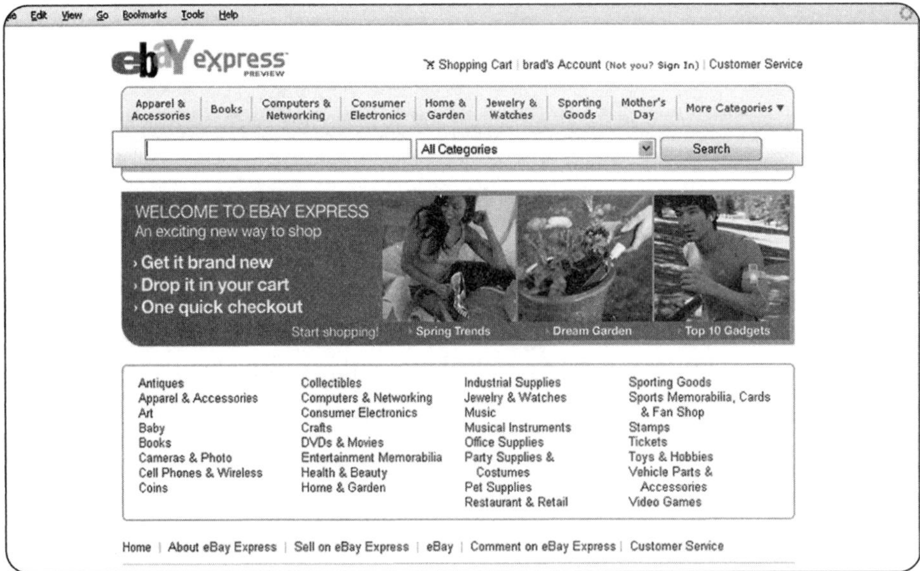

Figure 13-1: *eBay Express is a specialty area within eBay, catering to buyers looking to buy new items at fixed prices.*

your professionalism as easily as you can on the general eBay site. You'll have to depend on competitive pricing and shipping rates to make yourself stand out in this crowd.

Specials and Discount Pricing

At some point, you may decide you're selling successfully enough to offer discounts and incentives to your customers. ACNielsen surveyed eBay PowerSellers at the end of 2005 to see how they'd prepared for the holiday shopping season. According to the Nielsen report, 40 percent of these sellers offered some type of "seasonal special," defined as free shipping or merchandise discounts. If your volume increases substantially, you might want to consider offering such incentives to your customers, too. Free shipping is one popular choice that makes good sense. You can't afford to offer it routinely, but for a special offer, it may help push customers into your shopping cart instead of your competitors'.

POWERSELLER JOHN WADE sells mostly books and paper ephemera under the user ID john_wade. He buys lots of his items at house sales, estate sales, and auctions. He was visiting a house sale one day and found a beat-up old brass horn just displayed on a couch. All the other shoppers were walking past it without a second look, since it was so battered and dented. He bought it for under $10 and put it up on eBay with a starting price of $75. As it turns out, it was a brass horn from the Civil War and highly collectible. The bidding grew so intense for the horn, that John had twelve to fifteen people trying to get it! A Civil War reenactor finally won the auction and had the horn carefully restored, even replacing a piece that was missing. The closing price for this one was $3,800!

Chapter 14

Customer Service Without the Smile

ISN'T IT NICE TO ENCOUNTER A FRIENDLY, helpful salesperson when you go shopping? Doesn't it make a big difference in your shopping experience if the person working in the store knows her merchandise, helps you with great advice, and cheerfully rings up your order, wraps it, and sends you on your way? For those of us who love shopping, that kind of experience can really brighten a day. (Not so much for Brad, who'd rather stay home!) We're much more likely to return to a store where we've had a great experience.

eBay buyers should be able to feel that same glow of satisfaction. In fact, the attention and respect you show your customers matter even more on eBay than they do offline. When a customer walks into a store, the merchandise can be well ordered and attractive, pleasant music may be playing, or there may be a distinctive and pleasant fragrance to the air. Top that off with a friendly, helpful sales staff, and you've got yourself a nice little business—a place that tells your customers just how important it is to you that they feel welcome and special. On eBay, you're reduced to the very bare bones of shopping. "You only have service and price to sell for you," says Michael Kolman who operates Parrothead and is one of eBay's top sellers.

As an eBay seller, you can't actually smile at your customer and ask if you can help him. But there are things you can do that will still make your customer sure that you're happy to have him shopping with you, instead of with your competition. eBay may appear to be a vast anonymous universe, where one seller is the same as the next, but, of course, that's not so. It's vast, yes. But there are as many types of sellers as there are types of snowflakes; each one is different. By the tone you set and the language you use in your listings, and by your policies and how you follow through on those policies, you can project a warm, professional, and caring tone that will set you apart from your competitors.

You're Already Thinking about Great Customer Service

You've already begun to think about great customer service. You did that in chapter 12 when you worked on creating your first listing. All the things you do to make your listings clear, accurate, and complete are steps on the journey to providing great customer service. When you choose the tone you are going to use in writing your listing, that's customer service. When you decide what your policies are going to be for payment options, shipping, and returns, that's customer service, too. So, you see, you don't have too much to fear from taking on this role. Just remember those childhood lessons about treating others as we wish to be treated, and you'll be on your way.

If you operate your eBay business with integrity and look toward making your customers feel comfortable dealing with you, your customer service practices should run smoothly most of the time. You can maximize that likelihood, especially when you're just starting out, by sticking with less expensive items as you build your selling savvy. If you know you're not risking much with any one sale, you can afford to make good on an item damaged in transit or one that the customer just doesn't like as a way to cultivate customer goodwill. You can put any missteps or mishaps in the column of "lessons learned."

Customer service gets to be a lot more challenging when things aren't going smoothly. There's no doubt that, as one seller told us, customer service is a "test of character." It's challenging to maintain a pleasant and polite demeanor when a buyer is making unreasonable demands and treating you badly. Yet we agree with seller Stephanie Inge, who shared with us the policy that guides her eBay business:

"Customer service is a test of character. When solving a problem, give your customers more than they expect."

Communication Is the Key, and That Means E-mail!

It's true. Your first chance to put out the welcome mat is when you create your listing. If you don't accomplish that, no other customer service practice will matter, because your customer will be getting her service from the next eBay seller on the search results list, and you won't get a second chance to make a first impression.

The next opportunity you have to shine is when you get an e-mail from an interested shopper, asking for more information. That's the same thing as feeling a fish nibbling on your bait, and it's exciting! It's also the time to jump into action. Here's some advice that we'd like to cast in stone:

Check your e-mail and your auctions several times a day!

If you have something listed on eBay, you owe it to your customers and to yourself to keep track of your e-mail very carefully. You owe it to your customers, because it's the only way they can reach you for more information or guidance about the item you're selling. You owe it to yourself, because eBay makes customers impatient. If you really want to sell, you can't keep them waiting more than a few hours for a response from you. Unless what you're selling is very rare, they won't wait. They'll simply buy the same thing from someone else. A delayed response tells your customers that you're not that interested in them. If they can't get your attention when they're potentially waving money in your face, why should they believe you'll be responsive if something goes wrong between you?

Your e-mail responses should be friendly but professional. Remember, you're not talking to a friend. You're trying to make a sale. Your customer will judge you based on how you respond. A quick, complete, friendly answer assures an eBay buyer that you're on top of your work and ready to do business. Once again, remember how you felt when you were the buyer. Keep that in mind and you'll know what to do when you're serving other buyers yourself.

At the same time, it's good to personalize your correspondence. eBay can seem huge, cold, and impersonal. The real fun happens when people start to connect to each other. That's why successful seller Stephanie Inge of Stephintexas believes in calling her customers by their names when she answers e-mail, for example. She also believes that you should "thank them for viewing your auction and wish them luck." It's her little way of putting a big, friendly, Texas smile into her eBay business. It's especially important to do this because messages are likely to come through eBay's Ask the Seller a Question link. While that's a convenient and safe way for customers to reach you, it also means that when you answer them through the eBay form you receive, the communications will seem more like they came from eBay than from a real person.

Once you have a winner, eBay will send out an invoice for you as soon as the auction ends. Don't send out your own invoice unless, for some reason, the auction management software you use does that automatically. From a buyer's viewpoint, a second invoice feels pushy. Trust that your customers will pay you on time. There is always time to follow up later if you have to. Chapter 15 covers invoicing in detail.

It's hard to be nonchalant when you're making those first few sales. It's all pretty exciting. And we're not recommending that you be naïve about payment. We recommend instead that you save electronic copies of all the e-mails you send and receive for each transaction, just in case problems should occur later on. But don't jump on your customer as though you believed he were about to steal the family treasures. Assume that all is well, until you know better, and then be prepared to act if you must.

Reach Out and Touch Your Customer

Of course, you'll respond quickly to all e-mail queries, but that's not the only time you should communicate with your customer. There are other reasons to stay in close touch with your buyer as well. You will certainly correspond with the winning bidder when the item is sold. The invoice eBay sends out may serve as that first contact with your buyer, if she hasn't asked any questions during the auction. If your buyer pays by check or money order, be sure to send an e-mail thanking her and notifying her that you've received her payment. That's just common courtesy. In that e-mail, you can reiterate that you'll be holding off on shipping the item until the funds clear your bank. Again, do so in a friendly manner, because it's not a note of personal distrust, it's just a common-sense business practice. A quick note to your customers who used PayPal also adds a personal touch, even though PayPal will confirm their payments automatically. You'll send another e-mail once you've shipped the item. This one will include the date you shipped it, the method you used to ship the item, and any tracking numbers you may have for the package. Your customer will really appreciate having that information, and it will allow her to track the package's progress to its destination, eliminating the need for you to do it. You'll also send a message to your buyer in the package in which you ship her item (we include an example later in the chapter). And finally, your feedback comment to your customer will be the last time you communicate—until she buys from you again! We'll discuss feedback from the seller's point of view in chapter 17.

Good Customer Service Equals Good Business for You

The subject of this chapter is good customer service, but customer service is also a matter of good business practice. You can't have a business selling on eBay if you don't have any customers who are willing to take a chance buying from you. Everything you do by way of customer service is meant to increase the level of comfort your customers associate with your business and their willingness to risk their money on the items you sell.

As shoppers, we all know that queasy feeling deep in the stomach that comes from the realization that what you've bought isn't what you had hoped it would be. You wonder if what lies ahead is mere inconvenience or ultimate torture as you make your way from unhappy camper to satisfied customer. Will your friendly shopkeeper suddenly treat you with all the pleasantness of a prison guard? Or will the store manager cheerfully offer to assist you and make things right? You know that the outcome of this encounter will determine whether or not you ever shop there again, but it may not have occurred to you that when you sell on eBay, you are the store manager. How your customer feels at the end of a transaction falls squarely on you.

The Customer You Please May Just Come Back

Now you may say that you don't really care about repeat customers. You may say that you're not interested in making a career out of selling on eBay. You just want to clear out some stuff that's been collecting dust in the corners of your house. Fair enough, but pleasing your customers is still important. Remember that all-important feedback score. Don't you want every interaction you have on eBay to improve that number, keep it clean, and make you more competitive as a buyer and a seller? Of course you do. Besides, just because this is strictly a hobby now doesn't mean you'll feel that same way six months from now. Please every customer, and if you decide you want to sell seriously, you'll already have a base of people willing to buy from you, to go along with your glowing feedback score.

Unfortunately, repeat business on eBay is pretty rare. So if you've had a particularly good experience with a buyer, invite him to add you to his list of favorite sellers in the last e-mail you send to him. There's no guarantee you'll soon list another item he's interested in buying, but you might. Once you're signed up as a Favorite Seller, eBay will send him e-mail links to your new auctions, as you post them. Keeping customers is so much easier than finding new ones, especially when you practice great customer service!

Return Policies

The first thing we need to do now is remind you of a simple fact. We are always on your side. Even when we're giving you advice you don't want to hear, we're doing it with your best interests at heart. With that in mind, we're here to say that you need to offer your customers a 100 percent satisfaction guarantee for every item you sell. Okay, okay, we hear all your protests! We can even make a list for you.

- *I'm selling used goods. How can I possibly guarantee them?* You can guarantee that they are just the way you've described them. Then you can describe them with all their flaws, creaks, and cracks. You can resist making any grandiose claims you can't support. You can guarantee that they will be just as you say they are, or you'll refund your customer's money.

- *I'm just starting out, and I only sell a couple of things a month. How can I afford to offer a money-back guarantee?* Especially if you're only selling a few things, you can't afford not to. You need those customers! You will attract customers who are willing to take a chance on a small, nonprofessional seller if you offer them a money-back guarantee. eBay's own research shows that 21 percent of nonbuyers report the lack of a return policy as the reason why they didn't buy a given item. We've passed on auctions ourselves if the return policy wasn't stated or seemed too stringent. Admit it. So have you.
- *How will I know a buyer isn't going to take advantage of my kind offer?* You don't know that, but it's not likely. Seller Jack Walters has had such a return policy for years now, and it hasn't failed him yet: "In my listings I have a 100 percent money-back guarantee. I don't care why the item is returned; I would rather have my customer be happy with his purchase." In our experience, and the experience of the hundreds of sellers we've communicated with, you're not likely to be cheated on returns. Our friend Jack, for example, has sold about a thousand items and has had perhaps three people take advantage of his return policy.

We could go on, but you've gotten the point by now. So if we've done our job, you're now planning for 100 percent customer satisfaction, and that means you will accept returns. That doesn't mean you have to roll over and show your belly, as a friend of ours from the South used to so colorfully put it. You can set some parameters. For example, it's perfectly acceptable for you to set a time limit, say, within seven days, for you to receive a returned item. You don't have to provide your buyers with lifetime guarantees. It is also perfectly acceptable to say that the item must be returned in the condition in which it was sent. We know of one jewelry seller who sold a ruby ring, only to have it returned with a cough drop instead of a ruby as the stone! Finally, insist that the buyer notify you before sending the item back. That gives you notice to watch for its return, it allows you to have it shipped back to you according to your wishes (insured, return receipt requested, FedEx), and it gives you the opportunity to better understand what the problem actually is, according to PowerSeller Bob Sachs. So one last time with gusto! Accept returns and don't make your customers feel squeamish about asking to return something. Aside from it being good customer service, you minimize your own aggravation down the road. Nothing takes the steam out of a disgruntled, dissatisfied customer quite like the phrase, "I'll be happy to refund your money." You may actually turn your disgruntled customer into a favorite shopper, or at least avoid a negative feedback comment and earn a positive!

Show Them the Real You!

Selling on eBay gives you a great deal of freedom to express yourself. Yes, your listings must be carefully crafted and neatly produced with accurate information. But as long as you abide by eBay's rules, you can list almost anything you want for sale on the site, and that gives you plenty of opportunities to put your own personality on display. You can also use your customer communications as a way to let the real you shine through and, as a matter of fact, you should. When you craft your correspondence, let your personality come through. Stephintexas likes to "flash" her big Texas smile, but maybe you'd rather show your Midwestern calm or your California cool. Whoever you are, you have the freedom to share that with your customers and fellow travelers on eBay.

Your About Me Page

Nowhere is your personality more apparent than in your About Me page. Remember way back in chapter 3 when we were explaining to you how to check out trustworthy sellers? One of the ways was to visit a seller's About Me page and see what the person had to say about himself. Maybe you haven't gotten around to creating your own About Me page yet. We understand, what with all the new and exciting stuff to explore on eBay. But now that you're going to be selling, the time is right.

As you saw in chapter 3, the best About Me pages leave visitors a little better connected with the people who created them. Perhaps you never thought of yourself as having your own page on the Web, but that's what you'll be creating when you finish your About Me page, so here's your chance to make the most of it. Reward your customer's curiosity with some friendly tidbits about who you are. Go ahead: Talk about your favorite hobbies or your pets. Mention your family. Give some information about the merchandise you like to sell and why you like to sell it. Spotlight your favorite charity (you can even include a link to that charity's Web site). Think about all the little details you consider when you create a profile of yourself in your mind, and then share some of them with your customers. Of course, you don't want to give away so many specifics about yourself that you leave yourself vulnerable to identity theft, but you'll know what's important to share and what's important to safeguard as you write your profile.

It's also a great idea to spell out in detail your shipping and return policies right there on your About Me page. That helps confirm and clarify them in your customer's mind, and it increases the chances that your customer will remember them when he goes back to your listing. You can also include a number of your most recent feedback comments on your About Me page, but don't let that list overwhelm the page. That information is easily available on the feedback page; you don't need to let it be the focus of your About Me page, too. It would be a better use of the space to make yourself a real person in your customers' minds. Remember what you looked for when you were visiting the pages of prospective trading partners, and you'll know what's right for your own page.

Thank-You Notes

We'll tell you more about including your "thank you" when we talk about shipping practices in chapter 16, but no customer service discussion would be complete without a brief mention of this all-important way of showing gratitude. Don't you hate it when the salesperson tosses your change at you and doesn't even look up when he hands you the bag? In our opinion, anyone who has chosen to spend money with you deserves a "thank you." So when you correspond with your customers, remember to be gracious.

It's simple to include a thank-you note with each package you send. If you decide you really like selling on eBay, you'll want to build a client list. The right thank-you note can help with that process. To illustrate how to be mindful of your audience when constructing any message or correspondence, we'll show you two types of thank-you notes, sent by two different PowerSellers. The first one is from preferreddiscounts, a seller of cigar and pipe accessories. The second is from harleyglasses, who specializes in all types of sunglasses.

PREFERREDDISCOUNTS' THANK-YOU NOTE

Preferred Discounts
PO Box 1924
Snoqualmie, WA 98065
www.preferreddiscounts.net

Hello {Customer First Name},

Thank you once again for your purchase! The Humminbird Legend 2005 Deep is a terrific fish finder, and I just know you will love it!

If there are any problems, please let me know right away. I have left great feedback for you, and if all is as expected, please leave great feedback for me as well. Thank you.

If you would like to be notified of our occasional specials, please send an e-mail to preferreddiscounts@comcast.net and in the subject line, type "Specials." Be assured we will never share your information, and you can request to be removed at any time, for any reason.

Now let's both relax and go fishing!

Best wishes,

{Kevin - Handwritten Signature}

Kevin W. Boyd
Preferred Discounts, LLC
eBay Store: www.preferreddiscounts.net
e-mail: preferreddiscounts@comcast.net

Some of Kevin's customers are from what you might call the "clenched teeth and brandy set"; others are not so highfalutin, but you get our point.

HARLEYGLASSES' THANK-YOU NOTE

Greetings,

Your item has been gently taken from our shelves with sterilized, contamination-free gloves and placed onto a satin pillow.

A team of 50 employees inspected your product and polished it to make sure it was in the best possible condition before mailing.

Our packing specialist from Japan lit a candle and a hush fell over the crowd as he put your product into the finest cardboard box that money can buy.

We all had a wonderful celebration afterwards and the whole party is set to march down the street to the post office where the entire town of Locust Grove will wave "Bon Voyage!!" to your package.

I hope you had a wonderful time shopping with us on eBay. We sure did. Your picture is on our wall as "Customer of the Year." We're all exhausted, but can't wait for you to come back to us soon.

Thank you for your business.

Gary
HarleyGlasses
www.harleyglasses.com

Gary's tongue-in-cheek approach really resonates with his no-pretense clientele. In fact, he says his thank-you notes are so popular that buyers send copies to their friends and families!

There's No Beginning and No End in Sight

We hope you've seen that providing great customer service doesn't have to be scary or intimidating. It can even be fun. It's the people connection that makes it so rewarding. At the same time, customer service doesn't really have a beginning, middle, and end. You'll consider your customer when you decide what to list for sale on eBay, and you can still learn from your customers even after they've posted feedback. When your feedback starts rolling in, closely analyze what your customers are saying. Although you may have earned a positive, perhaps your shipping took too long to suit one person, or your packaging didn't hold up as well as you thought it would for another. The point is to operate knowing that you can always improve your customer service. Your buyers will appreciate it! Now let's go on to the part of this you'll really appreciate, "Chapter 15: Making Sure You're Paid."

YOU'VE ALREADY MET STEPHANIE INGE, known as Stephintexas, throughout the pages of this book, but she is so full of personality, we thought you'd like to hear one more of her great stories about her favorite eBay sales.

Stephanie found a vintage golf book at a yard sale and bought it for $1. She went back home, checked for Completed Listings, and discovered that a similar item had recently sold for $200! She had to admit that hers wasn't in such great condition, so she decided to list it with a starting price of $1, "and let 'em fight for it!" And fight they did! She sold it for $128. When she heard from her buyer, she saw that his e-mail address ended with tampabaybucs.com. Since her son is a huge fan of the Tampa Bay Buccaneers, she couldn't resist asking about the e-mail address. As it turns out, her buyer was the head pro scout for the football team! When Stephanie told him about her son's devotion to the team, he asked her if the boy would like an official Tampa Bay Bucs jersey. It took her less than a second to respond with a hearty, "YES!!!" It seems her buyer was pretty impressed to have discovered a fan from the heart of Dallas Cowboys country! To sum up a great story: a profit of $127 and one jersey later, Stephanie had confirmed for herself first-hand the eBay philosophy that "People are basically good."

Making Sure You're Paid!

WITH THE VERY FIRST LISTING you put up on eBay, you entered the world of international commerce. No, you're not ready for lunch with Donald Trump just yet, but you do have a small business operating on the World Wide Web. Congratulations! eBay has made it possible for the average person to start a business with less effort and less capital investment than ever before in the history of humankind! We're not exaggerating. You may never move beyond the occasional eBay sale, or you may end up as a Titanium PowerSeller, but either way, when you list on eBay, you enter a new world of Internet commerce. Now we'll help ensure that you get paid for your efforts. Selling something on eBay and being certain you've been paid for it are two different things. Until you are certain that you've been paid, we encourage you to hold onto the item you've sold, and not ship it to your buyer. And as you step into the international world of commerce, the first and last word in safe payment is PayPal.

So you're having a little trouble thinking of yourself as a major-league business mogul? Well, consider all you've done to prepare for selling to a potential market of nearly 200 million people. Now add PayPal to the equation. When you sign on as a seller with PayPal, you step into the same arena as the Wal-Marts and Home Depots of the world. After all, your business, just like theirs, can now offer customers the easiest, most secure way to pay—with credit cards. As an eBay seller, you don't need to go to the trouble and continuing expense of opening a merchant account with a credit card company. As a beginning, small-time seller, you simply couldn't afford the time or trouble. You'll be reading even more about PayPal in the pages that follow, but you already know we consider it to be an eBay seller's best friend. Along with PayPal, we'll discuss other ways your buyers may pay you. It's all about the money, which makes this chapter perhaps the most important one in the book. eBay is great fun, sure, but we haven't encountered a seller yet who doesn't hope to make a profit.

The Payment Mechanics

In previous chapters we discussed the importance of accommodating your buyers, and being flexible about the forms of payment you'll accept. Such flexibility helps attract customers and gives the impression that you are a sophisticated, competent seller. So whichever method of payment your buyer chooses to use, you need to be ready to get that money from his hands to yours. Before that can happen, he'll need an invoice.

The Invoice Is Automatic

eBay automatically takes care of invoicing your winning bidder if you use eBay Checkout. And it's likely that you will use it, since the setting for it in your Selling Preferences is "on" by default. Checkout neatly tallies up the winning bid and the shipping and handling costs you specified, or those determined through eBay's shipping calculator. Checkout also provides a Pay Now button right on your listing page at the end of a successful auction. Your buyers can start the payment process by clicking on the Pay Now button there or the one in the e-mailed invoice from eBay. Of course, you can always send your buyer a separate invoice if there's anything to be clarified, but routinely, one should be sufficient. You don't want to seem too pushy about payments. So as soon as your listing ends with a successful bid, your winning bidder will get all the information necessary to complete the checkout process without your having to do anything at all.

It's PayPal Above All

When it comes to paying for things on eBay, there's PayPal and then there's everything else. PayPal allows buyers to pay for things via the credit card or debit card on file with the company, without revealing account details to the sellers. In fact, eBay says that "75 percent of buyers prefer to pay for their items with PayPal," so as an aspiring seller you simply have to accept this preference. Not that you'll mind—sellers love PayPal, too, because PayPal transfers funds immediately from the buyer's account to their own—there's no waiting for anything to arrive by mail or to clear the bank.

In order to be able to accept credit card payments through PayPal you must be a Premier PayPal member. That's why in chapter 6 we encouraged you to sign up as a Premier member when you established your PayPal account. We were hoping you'd want to sell one day! But if you didn't sign up as a Premier member, just log on to PayPal and upgrade your account now. There's no charge to do so. We'll wait right here for you.

Once you're set up to accept all types of PayPal payments, let your buyers know about it. They will be looking for evidence that you accept it, so why not make it easy for them by including the PayPal logo prominently in your listings? To do

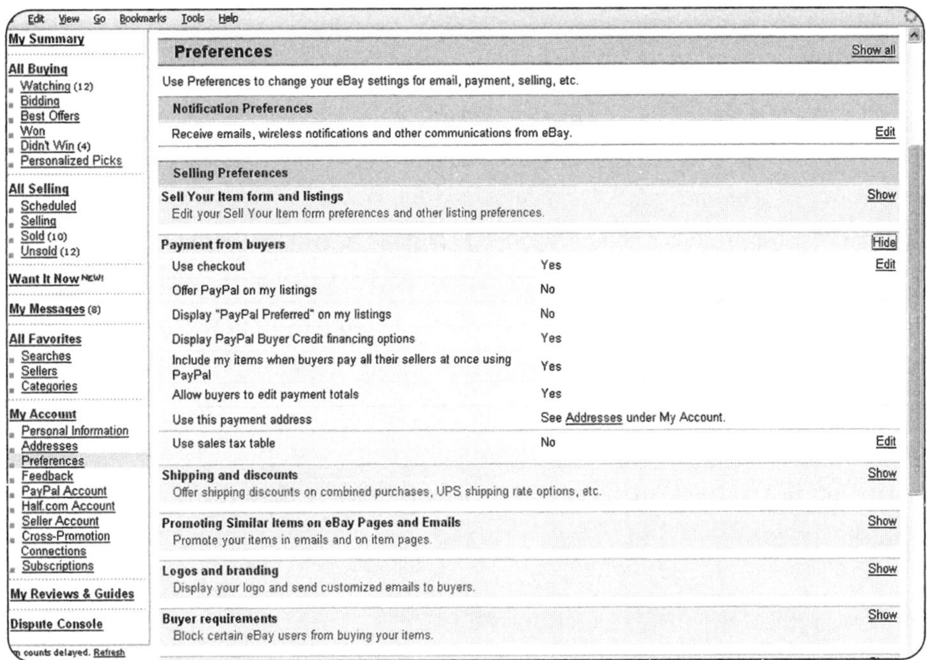

Figure 15-1: *From this page you can set all your selling preferences, including whether or not you'll accept PayPal.*

this, go to My eBay>My Account>Preferences>Selling Preferences>Payment from Buyers. Edit these preferences as needed to indicate that you want to offer PayPal as a payment method in your auctions (see Figure 15-1). That way, all your listings will automatically include the PayPal icon. eBay also encourages you to edit your preferences to tell buyers that you prefer PayPal. But since we feel you should accommodate your buyers rather than have it the other way around, we don't encourage the use of this language.

Because PayPal is owned by eBay, it's well integrated into the site. So, for example, you can easily get to PayPal right from your My eBay page. Aside from being well integrated, PayPal also facilitates communication between buyers and sellers and simplifies the shipping process, as you'll see in the next chapter. Perhaps the best things about PayPal are the speed with which you can be paid and the message PayPal sends to you as soon as your buyer has paid.

PAYPAL'S FEES

PayPal is great, but remember that as a seller (unlike for buyers), you will incur fees for using the service. The standard fee is now 2.9 percent of your selling price plus a flat $0.30 per transaction. That percentage drops and becomes performance-based as sales volume increases above $3,000 a month. Should you find yourself in that pot of jam, apply for a PayPal Merchant Account, so you can take advantage of the lower transaction rates you'll be eligible to receive. Don't fret about paying your PayPal fees. Remember that without PayPal you would have to search for and open a merchant account with a credit card company in order to accept credit card payments from your customers. That would be way more expensive, and most likely would discourage you from accepting credit cards at all. Of course, you could choose not to use PayPal, but your potential customers would find that a reason not to shop with you, and you'd lose much more than you'd gain by saving the PayPal fees.

PAYPAL'S SELLER PROTECTION POLICY

We've discussed how buyers can use PayPal's Resolution Center if they have a dispute. But sellers can also use it to help mediate disputes. In addition, as part of its Seller Protection Policy, PayPal covers you for up to $5,000 a year in the event of fraud. Suppose someone pays you with a stolen credit card. You process the order, send the item, and then PayPal discovers that the buyer was using a stolen card. You've now lost your item, but your payment will still be covered. PayPal will take the loss rather than to sending it on to you. To qualify for this protection, you must follow "good selling practices," as defined by PayPal. For details, we suggest you read your PayPal User Agreement (just the thing to snuggle up with in front of a cozy fire on a cold winter's night).

The Seller Protection Policy will not protect you if your buyer requests a chargeback, alleging that the item he received is not as you described it. (A chargeback is when a dissatisfied buyer requests to have a charge removed from his credit card bill.) It's your responsibility as a good seller to ensure that your description matches what you're selling. If your customer returns the item and demands a chargeback, in a case like this where the customer is right, PayPal will comply with the buyer.

While the Seller Protection Policy carries with it a lot of ifs, ands, and buts, the mediation process is a lot more straightforward. That's good, because as a seller you're likely to get into disputes, and if you do, chargebacks can follow. Like you, PayPal doesn't want things to get to this point, so PayPal representatives will work with you and your buyer to resolve any disputes. During this process, however, PayPal will place a hold for the amount of the requested chargeback on your PayPal account, meaning you can't draw on that money.

One thing you can do to help protect yourself from the costs of dealing with bad bidders is to make it a policy to ship only to PayPal-confirmed addresses. Address confirmation, as you may remember, means PayPal has received additional documentation proving a buyer's address is as she stated. We encouraged you early in this book to confirm your address with PayPal, as a means of reassuring your trading partners and helping sellers feel secure about doing business with you. PayPal will only offer its Seller Protection Policy if the item in question was shipped to a confirmed address. So why would a buyer request that you send an item to an unconfirmed address?

First of all, not all buyers, especially new ones, know about confirming their address through PayPal. Your buyer may simply not realize that this detail is missing. Another reason could be that the buyer is purchasing a gift, say, for a child away at college or a friend in another state. That buyer may be completely legitimate and simply be asking you to ship her package to an address other than her own to save her the extra shipping charge. Or the buyer may be trying to scam you. If that's the case, she knows that by shipping to an unconfirmed address, you'll lose your PayPal seller protection. For this reason, many professional eBay sellers refuse to ship to any address that is not confirmed through PayPal. They may process hundreds of orders a week, and they can easily set their automation parameters to ship only to a confirmed address. However, as a new seller you'll have to decide on your own comfort level. You may be risk-averse, and willing to refuse shipment to unconfirmed addresses, or you may want to be a bit more lenient at first to keep your pool of customers as large as possible. We've told you how professional eBay sellers feel, but we can also speak from our own experience. With hundreds of PayPal transactions, we've never had any problem when shipping to an unconfirmed address.

Accepting Cash

While eBay has always discouraged cash payments, in 2005 it formalized its stance when it issued its Safe Payments Policy. There eBay made its position quite clear: "Sellers may not solicit buyers to mail cash." In fact, sellers who do solicit cash payments within their listings may have those listings removed from the site. Of course, the policy prohibits you from soliciting cash, not from accepting it. If a buyer decides, on her own, to send you cash, no one is saying you should turn it away. Cash payments may also come into play if a buyer comes to your house to pick up an item. In that case, paying with cash may just be a lot more convenient for her. But we agree that you shouldn't advertise that you accept cash. It's just too easy for it to get "lost" in the mail. In that case, no one is happy.

Personal Checks

You can guess what we're going to advise here. While from a seller's viewpoint checks are less convenient than PayPal payments, for example, you have to suck it up and accept them anyway. As a newer seller you should definitely wait for the check to clear before shipping an item. As you become more experienced, you may choose to decide on a case-by-case basis whether you'll follow that practice. For example, if a buyer has a sterling feedback record and the amount in question is relatively small, you may just want to go ahead and ship the item. One caveat about checks: A scam that's occurring with greater frequency involves buyers ordering items, paying by check, and then stopping payment on the check soon after they receive the item. Longtime PowerSellers recommend that you be especially careful with low number checks, which may indicate that an account has just been opened, and checks for large amounts.

Money Orders

Money Orders used to be as good as cash, but, alas, things have changed. We've never had a problem ourselves, but our seller friends tell us that fake money orders are "out there." If you get a money order that was purchased from the U.S. Postal Service, you can count on it being valid. If it was bought somewhere else, you may want to take a closer look at it and consider the source. If you have any doubts at all, hold the item, and don't ship it until you're sure the funds have cleared the bank. In time you'll become more familiar with money orders and be better able to spot a fake. For now, if you suspect a fake, protect yourself. Hold off shipment, and notify your buyer that you're holding the item until the money order clears. You can also take it to your bank for advice or even show it to the police, if you think it might be counterfeit.

Cashier's Checks

Our advice here is the same as it was for money orders—you just can't automatically accept them at face value. In the case of certified or cashier's checks, your bank can help if you suspect a counterfeit.

Wire Transfers

We think as a matter of policy that sellers shouldn't ask to be paid via a wire transfer outside of PayPal. Educated buyers will become suspicious if you do, and rightly so. That's a red flag. Of course, if you are selling a large item, like a car, you and the buyer can work with a verified escrow service to make a safe wire transfer. Just be aware that wire transfers are a payment option positively fragrant with fraud, so protect yourself and your buyers by using PayPal or an escrow service whenever you consider them.

International Payments

We haven't spoken much about international sales up until now for one simple reason. We think you should cut your seller's teeth on domestic sales first, and then (when you're ready) graduate to international selling. Despite what you may have been led to believe, international sales are more work, even though that added work may be as simple as filling out a customs form. Every step involves more thought, from payment to shipping. Not only that, because of the prevalence of fraud, there are also some countries you shouldn't sell to at all, because they are known sources of credit card and Internet fraud. For information on current scams check eBay's International Trading Discussion Board (just click on the Community link and then Discussion Boards to reach it). When you're ready, know that PayPal will allow you to accept international funds, and you can also use international money orders.

When Something Goes Wrong

Notice we said *when* something goes wrong, not *if.* It's happened to us, it's happened to all the others sellers we know, and if you decide to sell routinely on eBay, it will eventually happen to you.

Unpaid Items/Nonpaying Bidders/FVF refunds

The number-one question members have when they search eBay for help is this: "What if my item sold and the winner didn't pay for it?" While no seller likes to think about that, it's just a matter of time before you're faced with what, in the language of eBay, is called a *nonpaying bidder.* It's a fact of eBay life that some people don't follow the rules because they don't take their commitment to pay for items they win seriously. There are also new people coming on the site all the time, and some may just not know the rules. Before we go any further, we want to emphasize again that dishonest trading partners are rare on eBay, with the exception of buyers in certain categories of items, such as fine art and name-brand accessories. Here are the steps you should take if you haven't received payment or heard from your winner with an explanation as to why you've not been paid.

- If you haven't received payment or heard from your buyer after about seven business days, send him another invoice, or an e-mail message asking him if you can provide any further information about the transaction.
- After that, give it another week and, if there's still no response, file an Unpaid Item Dispute (see Figure 15-2). You only have forty-five days after a listing closes to do this, so don't delay. To start the process click on the Security & Resolution Center link at the bottom of most eBay pages, or click on the Dispute Console link on your My eBay page. Once you file a dispute, eBay will e-mail your buyer to "encourage him to complete the transaction." The buyer will also receive a pop-up message, reminding him to pay if he signs on to eBay within fourteen days of your filing.
- If the buyer still doesn't pay, you should end the dispute. You'll then be eligible to receive a refund for the final value fee (FVF) eBay charged you after the auction ended. Your buyer will then receive an Unpaid Item strike against his account. If a buyer receives too many of these, he'll be banned from the site.

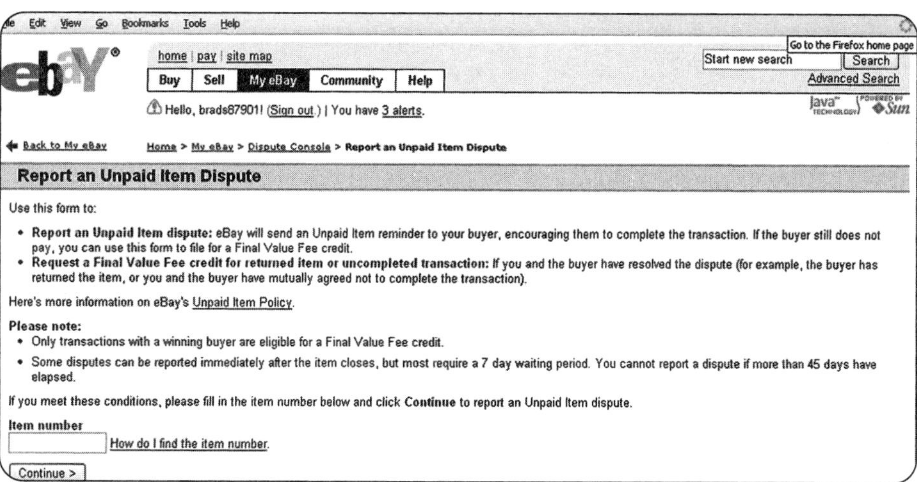

Figure 15-2: *From this page you can file an Unpaid Item Dispute.*

You'll still be responsible for your listing fees; however, if you relist the item, and it sells the second time, you won't have to pay for the second listing. For details about relisting an item, see http://pages.ebay.com/help/sell/insertion-fee-credit.html.

You may feel that going to all this trouble may, in some cases, not be worth the bother. If the item only sold for a few dollars or so, what's the point in filing a Nonpaying Bidder claim and then going to the added trouble of tracking its status? But even in the case of a very small loss, we urge you to file a claim anyway. It's good for you, and it's good for the eBay community as a whole. The system only works if people who don't play by the rules are reported and stopped.

MANAGING WHO BIDS ON YOUR AUCTIONS

The idea of restricting who may bid on your auction seems contrary to your goal as an eBay seller: to make money! After all, the more bidders, the higher the likely final price of your item will be. However, as you can see, some bidders bring more calamity than cash. In cases like that it's best to head them off at the pass.

As we mentioned in chapter 3, eBay allows you to create a list of bidders who are blocked from bidding on your auctions. As you encounter nonpaying bidders, for example, you simply go to the Blocking a Bidder/Buyer page at http://cgi1.ebay.com/ws/eBayISAPI.dll?BidderBlockLogin and enter their user IDs in the box shown. You may also want to add bidders who are troublesome in other ways—for example, they leave negative feedback for you when it's truly undeserved. You can add or delete bidders whenever you'd like, and enter as many as one thousand user IDs (although we hope things never get *that* bad for you)!

Another way to manage your bidders is to create lists of pre-approved bidders/buyers, restricting who can bid on your item to only those names on the list. If someone who is not on your list wants to bid on one of your items, eBay will ask them to first contact you by e-mail. Lists of pre-approved bidders can only apply to one of your items at a time, so you can leave your other items open to everyone. Go to http://offer.ebay.com/ws/eBayISAPI.dll?PreApproveBidders for details.

Finally, you can cancel a bid if a bidder backs out, or if you're unable to verify a bidder's identity. The details can be found at http://offer.ebay.com/ws/eBayISAPI.dll?CancelBidShow. As you might expect, eBay asks that you cancel a bid only if you have a good reason to do so. (Quick question: Why would you cancel a bid, thus losing a sale, unless you had a good reason to do so?)

Once you know you've been legitimately paid for an item, ship it as soon as possible. Aside from that being just a part of good customer service, it helps head off buyer's remorse, which may start to set in just a short time after the auction ends. For more on shipping, turn to chapter 16.

AS WE MENTIONED IN CHAPTER 1, Adam Hersh was a college student when he started selling on eBay. Today the twenty-seven-year-old is one of eBay's top sellers, specializing in movie posters and generating millions of dollars in revenue each year. He employs dozens of people in two states. He is also a consultant to others who want to build their eBay businesses. This young tycoon for the new millennium told us about his favorite type of sales. Surprisingly, they're not the ones where he collected the most money. Adam is one of the large eBay sellers working with the concept *strategic philanthropy.* That means strategically working toward raising money for charities while also earning a profit on eBay. Adam's favorite sales are the ones he does for charities.

Adam recently participated in a series of auctions for the New York Public Library. He wanted to help the library raise money, but the organization had nothing to sell. Instead he created a partnership with New York's restaurants to sell meals in honor of the library. Together they gained a great deal of exposure, and they earned close to $30,000. Adam has also conducted charity auctions for Big Brothers and Big Sisters of New York. So even though Adam lists tens of thousands of items a month, his favorites are the ones he posts to help others. When you ask Adam what he likes best about eBay he responds, "It's so much fun!"

Chapter 16

Packing and Shipping Without Schlepping

AS ANY JOB HUNTER KNOWS, you only get one chance to make a great first impression. If you slip up, you may never get another opportunity. The same is true for eBay sellers. The packages you send out into the world are your emissaries, and through them you get only one chance to impress your buyer. Think of this for a moment from your customer's viewpoint. We're sure you remember what it was like as a child to know you're "getting something in the mail." It's very much like expecting a present! eBay buyers often view the packages they receive in the same way. It doesn't matter that it's from a stranger and that they themselves paid for it. It still feels like a present.

As longtime eBay buyers, we've received hundreds of packages, and the ones that really stand out arrived in deplorable, disappointing condition. For example, we once received a collectible in an old, unwrapped, Blockbuster video box! The name of the movie and a lot of the other printing from the box was just scratched out hastily with a pen! There was barely room for the address label in all this mess. We're sure this seller thought he was being clever and saving money, but we were appalled! Another time we received an item that reeked of cigarette smoke. Since we're not smokers ourselves, the smell hit us smack in the face as soon as we opened the package. We left it in front of an open window for a few days, but the smell (and the memory) lingered. Other times we've received items that were wrapped in dirty paper, or in packing material that scattered all over as soon as we opened the envelope. As you can imagine, we never bought anything from any of those sellers again.

The goal of this chapter is to show you how to avoid making these bad first impressions. We don't want you to spend a fortune in packaging or endless time wrapping, because that can eat into profits (and satisfaction) from your eBay business. Instead, we'll give you some simple advice about creating professional-grade packages efficiently. We want you to ship quickly and cost-effectively, and in a way that increases the chance of your item arriving intact. We want your customers to be glad they did business with you, and willing to give you a try again.

We can't overemphasize how important proper packaging and shipping is to buyers. It's one of the most direct and important ways you have of communicating with your customer, and, as you know, good communication is key to a successful life on eBay. When customers have a good experience, it's something they'll often mention in their feedback. If you'll pardon our horn tooting for a moment, here are some of our favorites among feedback comments we've received:

> Great item—fantastic packing, and very fast. Thanks
> Awesome deal! Fast shipping!! A ++++++++++
> Lightning-fast delivery; book in perfect shape, outstanding eBayer.
> Safe, fast shipping.
> Well packaged and shipped. AAAAAAAAAAAA+++++++ seller

Get Organized

It's one thing to have a single item to pack. You're bound to have a spare box around the house and probably some packing tape, too. Throw in some paper for packing material, and you're done. Even if it takes some time to find the supplies, that doesn't matter. You're only talking about an occasional chore that takes no more than ten or fifteen minutes. It's when you consistently have a few items or more to get out that shipping becomes strategic. There are two keys to starting off right: organizing your space and organizing your supplies.

Keep Your Space Ready to Pack

You'll need to dedicate part of your eBay workspace just for your shipping supplies and package preparation. Once you start preparing packages routinely and consistently, make sure everything is accessible and within easy reach. With everything ready to go, you can prepare your packages with a minimum of effort and as quickly as possible. You'll dread fulfilling your orders if, every time you go to package something, you have to scrounge around the house for packing tape, scissors, markers, and padding. (Not that we have anyone around here who takes stuff and doesn't put it back!) Having all your supplies on hand, within easy reach, makes it possible for you to package and ship quickly once the auction ends. That leads to satisfied customers and positive feedback!

Shipping Supplies

As a small shipper, you don't need a lot of materials. And the items you do need will not be mysterious or alien to you. Boxes, envelopes, bubble wrap and/or packing peanuts, and a digital postage scale are basically all you'll usually need. We admit that you may not have a postage scale lying around the house, and that's understandable. What isn't understandable, though, is why you wouldn't shell out the $20 or so to buy one once you start selling on eBay. A postage scale can pay for itself very quickly, depending on how much shipping you do. You just can't expect to estimate weights accurately every time, and carrying stuff to the bathroom scale wears thin very quickly.

NEW SUPPLIES

Some sellers will only ship in new boxes, and it's difficult to argue with their reasoning. Bob Sachs is one such seller. In his opinion, used boxes, because of the condition they are sometimes in, just don't make the kind of first impression he wants to make on his buyers. "That box is the first part of my business they can touch," he told us. "I want it to give the best impression possible. It's the same with the materials inside—I always use clean packing peanuts, new bubble wrap, and quality sealing tape. For all intents and purposes, that box and its contents are *me*, as far as my online buyers are concerned."

When buying your supplies, your goal should be to buy in the largest quantities possible that make sense for your business and wallet. This is easiest to do if you customarily send out things that are approximately the same size (say, books and DVDs). Bob Sachs buys single-size boxes in quantity and finds this saves money and cuts down on confusion when it's time to pack. When you're buying new shipping supplies, don't forget about eBay! It's one of the best sources for shipping supplies.

RECYCLED (AND OTHER FREE) SUPPLIES

We've done it, too. A book arrives from Barnes & Noble in a perfectly reusable box. So we remove the old address label and reuse the box. Sounds smart, right? Isn't recycling always a good thing? Well, it is, mostly, but not always. Before you reuse a box, you obviously need to make sure the box hasn't been damaged. Also be aware that once you remove a label from a box you're weakening it by removing some of its paper along with the label. So be careful!

When recycling in this manner, you're not just limited to your own hand-me-downs. Local stores and businesses can be a tremendous supply of boxes, bubble wrap, packing peanuts, and more. We've found that sellers develop their own favorite sources over time. Seller Catherine Yeats of 4-a-little-lady has a "secret weapon": bars. They have plenty of boxes, and they can be easily cut down to the size you need. Most are made to be strong enough to transport beer bottles. You can also check with your local gift shop. If the owner doesn't already sell on eBay, he likely receives far more boxes and packing material than he can possibly use. You can arrange with him to stop by routinely and take the leftovers off his hands. He avoids having to haul these things to the trash, you get free packing materials, and the landfill avoids overflowing too. Or get creative about how you pad your items. Save clean plastic bags from the newspaper, the dry cleaners, or the grocery store. Blow them up and tie them off to make free bubble-packing to surround your item and cushion it. Just be sure, of course, that any recycled material you use is clean and presentable. You don't want to save money at the cost of customer satisfaction.

A great source for free, new, and good-quality boxes is the U.S. Postal Service. As long as you are shipping via Priority Mail, they are yours for the taking. The

USPS even has an arrangement with eBay to provide sellers with Priority Mail boxes preprinted with the eBay logo. They can be ordered online by going to http://ebaysupplies.usps.com/. We think it's fine that eBay and the USPS have this arrangement, but we're not so sure that it's wise to announce so prominently that a package contains something from eBay. Remember: That package may well be sitting on someone's porch, for example, for the entire world to see until the buyer arrives home. Sometimes it's better to be discreet—and, really, does including the eBay logo benefit you, or does it benefit eBay? You can also order all the free Priority Mail supplies you'd like, sans eBay logo, directly from the USPS Web site (www.usps.com).

Your sources of supplies will change over time as you begin to sell more varied things. And you should always be on the lookout for better-priced supplies, no matter what you're selling. Consider Australia-based PowerSeller Phil Leahy, who sells a lot of DVDs. When he first started out, he used rather large padded envelopes. He learned from experience though that they made his product too bulky, and in his post office's view, changed his packages from letters to parcels. He then switched to smaller envelopes so he could classify his packages as letters, and he saved a fortune in postage. More importantly, he found that breakage didn't increase with the change. Aside from making sure he's choosing the best envelope, Phil is always on the lookout for the most cost-effective packing supplies. He's amazed that some sellers pay $0.20 for a single CD sleeve, only to find out later that they could have bought something just as suitable for half the price. The lesson? Even when it comes to buying something as simple as an envelope, scout around for the least expensive, best packaging you can find. Remember: Every penny counts.

Packing Your Items

It seems that every household has one: the person who can wrap a box so it really looks like a present. In our house, people can always tell the difference between a present that Deb wrapped and one that Brad wrapped. (We won't say any more than that.)

You want your package to be neat, clean, and solid all the way. Your customer should receive that box and know it was prepared with pride and care. Aside from appearance, your package has to adequately protect the item it contains. It's nearly impossible to have too much packing material. Imagine that someone is going to purposely damage what you're shipping, and you'll know exactly how carefully you need to package it. Seller John Wade, who sells books and paper ephemera, packs his items so they're almost impervious to damage. He's learned through his years as an eBay seller that a lot of people receive damaged stuff. So he double-boxes fragile items. That means he pads the item, places it in a box, pads the box, and seals it carefully in another, larger box.

Labeling is important, too. Address your label clearly and tape over the label after you affix it. That way, if the package gets drizzled on, the address won't smear. Speaking of weather, it's important to plan your packaging with an eye toward what your item is going to have to endure as it makes its way to its new home. This is even more crucial during the winter, but it's important year-round. You are usually shipping to individuals and not to businesses. Therefore, your package may sit on the other side of someone's front door for hours, and in all kinds of weather.

Professional Shippers

eBay sellers, Education Specialists, and Trading Assistants Harvey Levine and Marcia Cooper of Generalent believe it's important to provide great customer support, and that includes great shipping practices. Because they sell valuable items for other people, they actually have two customers: the ones who buy what they sell and the clients who trust them with the sale of their items. They told us that they "practically gift-wrap everything." They also frequently have their items professionally packaged and prepared for shipping. We think they are the exceptional seller, but there may well be occasions when you feel the item you're shipping requires special care. In those cases, it makes sense for you to have it professionally packaged and shipped out. Most shipping centers will also offer services for packaging. You can check your local phone book or ask your local librarian to refer you to businesses that offer this service in your area.

Presentation

Whether you do it yourself or pay a professional, your goal is to reward your customer with the safe delivery of a great-looking package. But it's not just appearance that matters. A great first impression results from lots of little things you do right to reward your customer. After all, the safe delivery of the item you sold is just the fulfillment of your responsibility as an eBay seller. Go a few steps beyond, and you'll reap the reward of a stream of happily satisfied customers.

It should go without saying, but be sure to include a packing slip with every item you ship. PayPal comes to the rescue once more here, by making it easy to print out a professional-looking packing slip. From the item page or your PayPal Account page, just click on the button that says Print Packing Slip (you saw that coming, right?). It amazes us how many shippers don't bother to take this simple but important step. A packing slip matters to many buyers. It has all the data they need in one place, including your name and contact information. We've even had buyers ask us to make sure to include a packing slip when sending out their items, so they have learned from experience that not all sellers do this.

While you're at it, why not personalize the packing slip with a handwritten "thank-you"? Or include a separate handwritten thank-you note (as discussed in chapter 14). Grandma really was right about this. It makes a terrific impression! You don't have to be eloquent or flowery. Just a cheery little note of thanks and best wishes will give your buyer a good feeling about dealing with you. You can also use this note to remind the buyer to "let you know she's received her package and is pleased with the merchandise by leaving a positive feedback comment." Of course, assure her that you'll also respond to her feedback with positive feedback for her, too. At the same time, remind your buyer that if there's any problem, she should contact you directly, and you'll try your best to resolve it. This can prevent a dissatisfied customer from jumping onto eBay and leaving you negative feedback before you get the chance to try to correct a mistake. Finally, some smart sellers even include a little freebie for good measure. We've gotten recipes, bookmarks, and even bags of seeds! This isn't mandatory, of course, but it sure can't hurt, and it always brings a smile.

How Much Should You Charge?

Here's our simple rule: Don't overcharge for shipping, but don't undercharge either.

As we mentioned in chapter 12, you can either specify a flat fee for postage in your auction, or you can include eBay's shipping calculator, in which case postage will be based on the shipping method chosen and where the item is being shipped. If you go the flat-fee route, it's quite possible that sometimes you'll wind up taking a loss on your shipping charges. That's fine as long as it doesn't happen too often. You'll probably make up for it with other packages. Don't forget to point out that you will offer a shipping discount if your buyer buys multiple items from you. (You can easily establish such a discount by going to My eBay>Preferences.) Most of your buyers will not do this, but the fact that you are agreeable to discounting in this way marks you as a fair businessperson. Whatever you do, don't make the mistake of forgetting to add shipping information altogether! That's easy to do. You don't want your customers to have to take the added step of asking you what postage will cost. Many won't bother and will simply move on to another seller.

Please remember, as we've said before, it's OK to include a fair handling fee; buyers expect to pay you for the time you spend and the materials you use to pack and ship what they buy. But again don't overcharge here. eBay buyers are very sensitive to gouging in this area. It's fine to keep the breakdown of these costs to yourself, rather than detailing them in a packing slip, or printing the postage out on a label. When you handle the calculation of shipping costs through eBay's shipping calculator, eBay adds your handling fee to the total, and doesn't break this fee out in any way.

Paying for Your Postage

How you pay for shipping depends, of course, on your shipper. Let's assume that you'll ship through the USPS. You have at least two options. You can just take your package(s) to the post office and wait in line like everyone else . Or you can pay for and then print your label right from your computer. (Buying postage through an online company such as Stamps.com is another option.)

We like printing out postage-paid labels right from our own computer. PayPal makes that simple. Just log on to PayPal, and from there you'll be taken to your Overview page. Locate the transaction for the item you need to ship, then click the Print Label option in the Action column. Enter weight information and the zip code for the address to which you're sending the item. Click on the correct option for the size of the package, and then choose the delivery option, such as Media Mail or Priority mail. You can print a postage-paid label right then and there. (The cost of the postage is then charged against your PayPal account.) Take your postage-paid package to the post office and just hand it to a clerk. (Or, better yet, hand it to your mail carrier.) But please don't wait in line—that just defeats the purpose of having paid for the postage at home!

Who's Your Carrier?

That's easy, the "Post Office." Many sellers love the USPS with its convenient, free boxes and tape for Priority Mail and its ubiquitous locations. But is it that simple? The main competitors to the USPS are United Parcel Service (UPS) and FedEx. If one shipper is more convenient to your location than the others, then that may be the one you choose to go with. For some oversized or awkwardly shaped items, one of the other carriers may actually offer you a more competitive price than the USPS. For example, UPS has a weight limit of 150 pounds while the USPS tops out at 70 pounds. You won't be shipping much that weighs over 70 pounds, but if you do, you'll need to know this. Also, UPS and FedEx include free delivery confirma-

EBAY'S SHIPPING CENTER

Now that you know how to create great packages and the supplies you'll need to do that, you can make the best use of eBay's shipping center. Located at http://pages.ebay.com/services/buyandsell/shipping.html, it provides information about shippers, including the USPS and UPS, and links to their sites as well. You can learn about eBay shipping calculators, tracking packages, printing shipping labels, buying insurance, and shipping—all paid for through your PayPal account. There's even a link for stamp collectors in case they happen to wander onto the site.

tion and insurance coverage up to $100 for each package at no extra charge. The USPS charges for both of these services. Most sellers find their own favorite carriers and stick with them. Others use a mix of shippers and choose the one that seems best for their circumstance.

What about Insurance?

Should you insure your items? Certainly, if you're sending out anything of significant value, you should. Too many times we've read listings that warn buyers that the seller will not be responsible for items damaged or lost in the mail. We never appreciate reading that. Besides, it isn't even true. If you send something to a buyer and it never arrives or it arrives broken, your buyer has a good claim to take back to eBay and/or PayPal to get reimbursed for the item he purchased. Why not make insurance optional in every case, but mandatory when shipping out items with a value of more than $100? Insurance is available from every major carrier. As you create your listing you can specify that insurance is either optional or required. If it's required, the amount you specify for that insurance is rolled up into your buyer's payment total. For guidance on what to charge, contact your shipper.

A Word about Timing

Once your buyer has paid for her item, she's expecting to get it ... yesterday! Maybe it's because she bought it through the Internet, or maybe it's just human nature to want something in your hands as soon as you've paid for it. If you only sell an occasional item, you should package it and send it out just as soon as you're sure you've been paid for it, as we told you in chapter 15. However, if you start selling a lot of items, your business may flow better if you choose to ship your items out a couple of times a week. That may help you balance your listing efforts with your shipping efforts and keep your business running smoothly. Either way, be sure to include this information in your listings and in all the e-mails you send to your buyers. As long as you're clear about your schedule and you follow up as you promise, your buyer should understand. If you will be delayed for more than three business days, be sure to send your buyer a note. She'll be wondering where her item is if you don't, and it's rude to keep your customer waiting without an explanation.

Send It Out Right. It Shows Them You Care

We've given you a solid start now on developing good packing and shipping practices. We hope that you will take away from this chapter one key point: that the package you ship is your best method for reaching out to your customers and touching them. As with other parts of the eBay selling process, you can learn a lot about how to do things right by noticing how other sellers do them. What effect does seeing and opening their packages have on you? Are you excited and satisfied? Or are you nervous that the item inside may not have survived the trip? Do you feel like a valued customer or the schnook who bought someone else's junk? Now you'll know which feeling you want your customer to have, whether you sell one item a year or 365 items a week. Now let's go take a look at feedback from the seller's point of view.

PowerSeller Paul Fletcher of Dealtree-auctions and his partner Gary Heath specialize in selling open-box returns and trade-ins for large retail stores. They are also Trading Assistants. Now they have two warehouses and fifty employees in two states, but once they were just starting out from Paul's garage. In 2001, they put their first listings up on eBay on a Friday night, popped open a couple of beers, and started watching their items sell! Then they realized that they had no packing supplies or shipping system in place. "It was scary!" Paul recalls. Their first attempt at shipping included a huge box of packing peanuts.

Unfortunately, the wind picked up, swept through the garage, and scattered the peanuts all over the neighborhood! Once again, they had no shipping supplies, but this time they also had no shortage of outraged neighbors. Considering the success they currently enjoy, they've certainly overcome their early lack of planning. Learn from them, and don't let your early efforts become the amusing story you'll tell for years to come.

Chapter 17

Feedback: Your Report Card for All the World to See

FEEDBACK, FEEDBACK, FEEDBACK: Somehow any discussion of eBay comes back to the term *feedback*. It's the underlying control center of the whole eBay system. Of course, buyers have to care about the feedback they receive, but it's the rare seller who will turn away a sale because a buyer's feedback rating is lacking. It's altogether different from a seller's point of view. As a seller, you'll be asking other people to risk their hard-earned money on a stranger. This prospective buyer will judge you based on your listings, your policies, maybe even your About Me page, but it will be your feedback that makes or breaks the deal. How many feedbacks have you earned and what percentage of those are positive? You know from your own experience as a buyer that this is where the balance tips on any potential eBay sale. No wonder sellers obsess over their feedback the way teenagers obsess over their skin! Your feedback is the face you show the world, and if you want to enjoy success as an eBay seller, it must be as blemish-free as possible.

A Seller's Feedback

As you already know, you'll need to build a feedback score even before you start to sell anything on eBay. As that score increases, you'll be able to sell more expensive and valuable items. Your confidence and experience level will grow, and you'll have a base of knowledge, policies, and practices that are proven by the direct results of your efforts. With every sale and purchase, the feedback you receive and the feedback you leave strengthen your position on eBay.

As a matter of fact, eBay itself bases your opportunities and rewards on your feedback score. In order for you to list items in a Fixed Price listing, for example, you must have at least ten feedbacks. To become a PowerSeller or to list on eBay Express, you must have achieved a feedback score of at least 100 with 98 percent of those comments being positive. So it's not just your fellow eBay users who base their opinions about you on your feedback. eBay does it, too!

Timing Is Everything

When you were strictly a buyer, timing your feedback comments to your trading partner was easy. You received your item, opened the package, and if everything was satisfactory, you were ready to leave feedback. If not, you put off your feedback comment until you'd had the chance to straighten things out with the seller, then you left your feedback accordingly. Remember, we already told you that positive feedback can still be the result of a disappointing purchase, when the seller handles the problem well and treats you right. So as long as you keep in mind that feedback is the last—the very last—part of any transaction, you are standing on solid ground.

Timing your feedback is not quite so obvious when you are the seller. Some sellers will tell you that they leave feedback as soon as the buyer pays. Others will tell you to hold your horses. Let's look at each side of this argument.

YOU'VE BEEN PAID, SO HAVE YOUR SAY

Jim Brown of Indianapolis just won your auction for a Euro Disney commemorative cap. He's dutifully gone to PayPal and paid for his item, almost as soon as he received the invoice. He followed all your stipulated rules for payment, included the correct shipping and handling fees, and you're ready to ship his cap to him. Some sellers say that does it. He's agreed to purchase your item, he's done everything by the book, and now he's earned his positive feedback score. Okay, very well, everything stated above is true. It may even seem simple to send off that positive feedback when you send off the package, and then you can call the whole transaction complete. Plenty of sellers operate just like this. Others say, "Not so fast."

IT AIN'T OVER TILL IT'S OVER

Other sellers argue that the transaction isn't complete until the buyer has received the item and the seller has been notified that everything is satisfactory. After all, just because the buyer has paid, and you know you're going to ship it promptly, that doesn't mean the transaction is over. Suppose the buyer is unhappy once he receives the item? Suppose the buyer claims he never received the cap? Suppose you've fallen into the hands of a crooked trading partner? How will you know until you've been notified by the buyer himself that everything's all right? You can only leave feedback once, so if you jump the gun and leave nice positive feedback, you can't go back and change it if the buyer proves to be a real problem. Until the very end, a seller can't be sure that her work is truly complete.

The most likely way for you to know that everything is fine will be when you receive a positive feedback comment from your buyer. Some buyers will send along an e-mail to let you know they're happy, but most of the buyers who use feedback will let the comment they leave there do the talking for them. That's why you included that friendly little note on the packing slip you popped into the package before you shipped it. On it, you assured your buyer that he would receive a positive feedback from you once you knew, through the feedback you received from him, that he was completely satisfied. So far, you've done everything you could to make sure your good conduct as a seller resulted in positive feedback for you.

The Statistics Are Against You

We favor the second approach to feedback from sellers to buyers. It's really to your benefit to protect yourself until you're certain everything is fine. You can leave feedback up to ninety days after the end of a listing, so although you may be eager to get the transaction completed, we advise you to wait until you've heard from your buyer before you leave a feedback comment for her. But the sad fact is that many, many, many eBay users never bother to leave feedback comments at all.

Academics study everything these days, including how eBay's feedback system works. According to several such studies, 40 to 50 percent of eBay buyers never leave feedback of any kind. You may just come across some who won't bother, no matter what you do. But these studies had some good news for us as well. More than 95 percent of the feedback that is left is positive. So what about all those people who don't leave feedback at all? What can you do about this?

Honestly, you can't do much of anything. You can only set the right example for your eBay buyers. If you make sure you always leave appropriate feedback, you are already doing everything you can to help keep the system healthy and vibrant. As a seller, do your best work, and then put it out there for all of eBay to judge. You may want to keep your sales in an active status for a few weeks, or until you've received feedback. Your My eBay page keeps you updated on the status of feedback that's due you. If you go to the All Selling link on the left, and then click on Selling, you will come to a screen that shows a summary of your recent transactions. The column with a star at the top is the one you can check to see if a buyer has left feedback for you. A bold star in the row for his transaction means he has; if the star is grayed out, he hasn't. If you don't receive feedback, you can send a friendly reminder, suggesting that you are looking forward to leaving a positive feedback comment, once you've heard that your buyer is happy, but beyond that, you've done all you can do.

The Feedback You Leave

The only thing you can do to control your feedback score and keep it strong is to tend to your eBay business carefully. When you're doing your best to conduct every transaction with honesty and consideration for your customer, you are bound to create a great feedback history. You don't have the power to make anyone leave you good feedback, and there's little you can do about it when someone leaves you disappointing feedback. At the same time, you can't allow yourself to get too bogged down with any one particular feedback exchange. Just keep your eyes on the next one, and the next one, and the next one. You'll be fine.

What you can control, however, is the feedback that you leave. If you work on that, you are actually helping the whole feedback system to thrive. First, let's remember that the feedback you leave for others speaks volumes about you personally. Yes, that feedback shows up on your trading partner's Member Profile page, but you know very well that anyone thinking about buying from you should also check the comments you leave for others. Make sure what you say has a respectful, professional tone and includes content that will make you proud you said it a month from now or six months from now. It will always be part of your history on eBay.

It's easy enough to know what to say when you've had a good experience with a buyer. Most likely, you'll come up with a few favorite comments that you'll use over and over again. You might point out the buyer's fast payment or friendly e-mails. You might commend the buyer as an eBay user worthy of fame, or you might just stick strictly to business. It's best not to use the same exact phrase time and again. Think about how it will look when someone sees an entire page of the feedback comments you've left. If you always say exactly the same thing, it really looks as if you can't be bothered treating your customers individually. At the same time, some repetition is to be expected. Large sellers who use automated systems tend to rotate several phrases repeatedly. That's understandable. Just keep in mind that you don't want anyone to feel "processed" when they get their feedback comment. They're looking forward to adding your feedback to their scores, just as you're looking forward to adding theirs to yours.

Responding to a Negative

Negative feedback is bound to happen. It's the same with all things brand new and shiny. They start out perfect, but at some point, everything you own gets a scratch, scrape, ding, or dent. We all know how that feels! It's nothing more than the simple act of living. So when you get that first negative comment, know that we understand: It hurts. It hurts even more when you don't think you deserved the comment. We'll try to help you keep some perspective, and we'll show you what to do to improve a bad situation once it's already occurred.

Most negative feedback comes from new users and those who don't really understand the feedback system and how it works. In fact, an eBay survey found that more than 50 percent of buyers do not try to communicate with sellers before leaving negative feedback! To help offset unnecessary negatives, eBay recently announced that new members (with a feedback score of less than 10) must complete a tutorial before leaving neutral or negative feedback. If nothing else, this tutorial acts as a warning sign on the eBay highway. It won't prevent a determined trading partner from leaving you a negative, but it will make an inexperienced user stop and think twice before proceeding to mar your history. Still, if someone is really determined to leave you a negative, you simply can't stop him.

What happens next is completely within your control, however, and it can go a long way toward showing others what kind of person you are and how you conduct your eBay life. First of all, if you decide to hold off submitting your feedback comment until you've received one, you are in a position to respond to a negative rating you receive with a negative of your own. Once this trading partner has given you a negative, there's not much more he can do. If you do leave a negative, keep it brief and all business. Don't be insulting, don't call anyone names, don't threaten, and don't show your anger. You'll gain a lot more by looking professional and in control than you will by satisfying your desire to call a jerk a jerk.

Some potential responses might include:

> Wish he'd told me directly about problem. I would have made it right.
> Never gave me a chance to correct my mistake. I would have.
> Claims item never received. Delivery confirmation shows delivery 3/15/06.

As you can see, the important thing here is to stick strictly to the facts and show that you would have willingly done everything you could to make the situation right, if only you'd been given a chance. Resist the temptation to get too defensive. It makes you look weak and desperate. And never say nasty, spiteful, or insulting things. It makes you look like a hothead, and people on eBay rightfully avoid doing business with hotheads.

For each feedback you receive, you are able to leave a brief comment in response. In the case of a negative, you can add to your own feedback page with a comment similar to the ones listed above. This won't wipe out the negative comment, but it will ameliorate it a bit, giving your side of the dispute. If you stick strictly to business and leave the distinct impression that your customers' satisfaction is your chief concern, people who read your feedback page will have respect for the manner in which you handled the situation. They may even go on to check the feedback history of the person who left you the feedback. It will be very easy for them to see if that person was a new user at the time of the incident or if he is generally a disgruntled eBay user. In that context, your negative comment will lead to sympathy and understanding among knowledgeable eBay users, not judgment and criticism.

Once again, life on eBay comes back to the lessons our elders taught us when we were young. You can't control the actions of the other guy, but you have complete control over your own actions. Just make sure that you conduct yourself in a manner that will make you feel proud of yourself in the future, when you look back at this. Now let's take a look at the other big worry in the lives of all eBay sellers: Where are you going to find more stuff to sell?

MY BEST eBAY SALE

Nick Boyd operates on eBay as tradernick. He's been successfully selling and building his eBay business for more than seven years. Nick specializes in coins and decorative collectibles. As a result of his efforts on eBay, Nick has also opened a bricks-and-mortar store in his Florida hometown. He employs four people and enjoys traveling around the country and the world in search of more items to sell. Nick has a feedback score of nearly 9,000 with a 100 percent positive rating! He told us about one of his favorite sales.

Nick bought a box of stuff at an estate sale. Among other things, he found inside a Prussian helmet from World War I. He knew it was old, but what he didn't know at the time of his purchase was that it was a helmet from one of the Kaiser's personal guards. By the time he finished his eBay sale, he'd earned $6,000 from that helmet alone. He still had all the other stuff in that box to go through, too!

Finding More Stuff to Sell

AT THIS POINT, YOU PROBABLY have a good idea of how you feel about selling on eBay. If you've been bitten by the eBay bug, you may just be thinking about starting your own eBay business. If that's what you have in mind, the rest of the book will help you. First, it's time to start thinking about where you'll get the inventory you'll need to keep your new venture moving along.

That's one thing we've learned from the scores of presentations and interviews we've done about buying and selling on eBay. People are predictable. Without fail, at least one person will ask the same question each time we host a seminar: "Where do I find products to sell on eBay?"

Perhaps, like you, they have already cleaned out their closets. Sometimes they have even gone on to sell a few things for their friends and neighbors. Now what? Eventually even the fattest pack rat starts running out of stuff to sell. How do you keep your business moving forward without selling your favorite Roseville vases, that valuable coin collection, or your kids' new iPods? No matter how good your customer service, feedback, or listing and marketing skills are, unless you have more products coming in, you don't have a business. Not for long, anyway. Without finding consistent and reliable new sources of merchandise, your business will soon come to a grinding halt.

A whole industry has sprung up to serve people looking to buy products for resale on eBay. Many folks may offer to sell you lists of wholesalers who presumably are dying to sell you products that you can then resell on eBay at a huge profit. Others may claim to have amassed and compiled lists of "secrets" from those in the know about just where to find those hidden pockets of products that no one else knows about! Let's get this clear: No eBay seller is ever going to give away his best supplier's name and address to his competitors. And everyone who sells on eBay is his competitor! What successful sellers may do, however, is share how they unearthed their super supplier in the first place. Actually, this works out better for you in the long run. It goes back to the old Chinese proverb: Give a man a fish, and you feed him for a day. Teach a man to fish, and you feed him for a lifetime.

In this chapter we'll give you the straight scoop on wholesalers, drop shippers, closeouts, thrift shops, garage sales, estate sales, and other product sources, because we know they're on your mind. We'll also mention other places for inspiration and leads you may not have thought of. In addition, we'll talk a lot about market research. That's because you must take the time to do your research before acquiring inventory, no matter how much of a sure thing those hot designer jeans may appear to be. Keep in mind that market research can also unearth fresh sourcing ideas that may not have occurred to you initially.

You Profit When You Buy

If there is any single secret to making a good sourcing decision, it's this little nugget of wisdom passed down to us by countless successful eBay sellers. Although no one has ever willingly told us where she buys her products for resale, many have told us that buying is the key to successful selling on eBay. If you buy your inventory at the right price, you'll always be able to sell it at a profit. This seems so simple, but finding the right product and then finding it at the right price are the most difficult parts of operating an eBay business. There's no way around it. The work is hard and the task is endless. Aren't you glad we're here to help?

How Do I Decide What to Sell?

Most of the sellers we know got their starts on eBay by selling things from around the house. They cleaned out closets, attics, basements, and garages. They regifted holiday and birthday disappointments. And they all recommended this as the way for any newcomer to get started selling on eBay.

Of course, the first advantage to selling these things is that they've already been paid for. You're not risking much, because even if you don't earn a lot of money, you still get to clean out your closets, and that's valuable, too! Another advantage of selling your own cast-offs is that you'll be selling something you own, so you'll probably know enough about it to describe it accurately and in plenty of detail. You will also have an easier time researching its value. If you do make a beginner's mistake and, as a result, earn less than you could have from your listing, you haven't lost much.

So just like many others who have gone before you, you too will probably start off by selling used items. Before you reach the back of that last closet, you'll need to ask yourself what you want from selling on eBay. The answer to that question will help you determine whether your sourcing efforts will go toward buying used items for resale or finding sources of new merchandise. Your sourcing tasks will be very different depending on which of these two options you choose.

You probably already have an inkling about which way you're going to go with this decision. Take a look at your life, and you'll see. It's not such a mystery. When you're deciding what to sell on eBay, consider what you already know about. Do you have a hobby? Are you an amateur enthusiast of some sort? Have you already spent a good number of years immersed in a particular area of interest or career? The answers to what you'll want to sell on eBay are as varied as the people who ask the question. Once you have a clear idea, you'll do your market research to see if you're thinking of selling something that other people come to eBay to buy. That's the final determining factor of what you'll sell.

Now that you've gotten some ideas, we need to tell you that sourcing your eBay business is just like housekeeping. It's never done. You'll find a great source of product that's selling well on eBay, and you'll be busy as can be making money and moving inventory. Just as you think you've got it made, you'll notice sales starting to falter. It seems that others on eBay have also discovered your great idea, and you've now got competition. Or you may be selling something fabulous, based on a current hot fad, like the latest diet or exercise craze. We all know what happens to great fads. So just as you're doing very well, and you're busier than ever moving your inventory out, you also have to be busy searching for that next great opportunity. You'll either love this challenge or it will drive you crazy. But the realities of it will go a long way toward helping you decide which type of eBay life is right for you.

Selling Used Items

If you're someone who spends every pleasant weekend morning scouring the yard sales, you probably already know you're going after used goods. Finding second-hand merchandise to sell on eBay isn't much of a mystery. Just check out garage and yard sales, estate sales, flea markets, and thrift shops. Maybe you'll sell truly old things, or maybe you'll specialize in gently used newer products. For example, PowerSeller Marguerite Swope has built a very comfortable business reselling gently used women's clothing. Of course, she'll sell other things when she finds them, but she sets out looking for items that fit her niche. Many of the sellers we know started out as yard sale scavengers or antiques dealers.

Before we go too much further, we want to alert you to a common misconception. Lots of people think that the older an item is, the more valuable it is, according to eBay Education Specialists Harvey Levine and Marcia Cooper. But often this isn't the case. "Enrico Caruso made records in the very beginning of the 1900s. RCA Victor gave out many of his records for free. People think they're very valuable, but they aren't worth anything," Harvey says. Like so many other things, this points up the need to do your research before deciding to buy something in bulk to sell on eBay.

GARAGE SALES, YARD SALES, AND THRIFT SHOPS

Of course you're familiar with these sources already. However, eBay's influence has filtered down to these local venues in both good and bad ways. The good part is that all the attention eBay gets in the media has encouraged people to clean out their closets and get yard sales going. So there's more stuff available. The bad part is that it's more challenging to find good items for resale through these channels, because so many other people are also looking for them. Sometimes the garage sale or yard sale sponsors have already cherry-picked the best items to list on eBay themselves!

There's no harm in checking out these opportunities, but please do everything you can to maximize your chances for success. For example, in the case of yard sales, you should strive to be among the first to arrive. If it's 7:00 on a Saturday morning, and you're not on your way, you're late already. Plus, in order to make this a consistent source of product, you have to commit to it every single weekend. In most parts of the country, yard sales are also a seasonal phenomenon. Consider what you will do to replace this inventory source from November through May when the yard sale season gives way to winter.

Scope out neighborhoods that are most likely to yield the kind of items that would do well on eBay. For instance, the more expensive neighborhoods in town may have the most valuable and gently used items among their yard sale inventory. Or consider neighborhoods with older populations, whose residents may be cleaning out a house in preparation for putting it on the market, and may offer just the kind of rare collectibles and other cool knick-knacks that sell well on eBay.

ESTATE SALES AND AUCTIONS

Not to sound crass, but estate sales generally mean someone has died and an entire household is being liquidated. On the plus side, you'll find many older items collectors may find desirable. The negative is that many dealers in collectibles attend estate sales. That doesn't mean they're buying items in order to resell them on eBay. They could own stores, for example. But it does mean that you've got some stiff competition for the good stuff. Many PowerSellers have told us of great finds they've gotten at estate sales, but they're for more experienced sellers. Those sellers clearly know their markets and can quickly assess not only the value of the items offered for sale, but also the likelihood that those items will be good for the eBay market.

The same advice holds true for live auctions. They can be a great source of used items, but you'll also be competing with experienced sellers. Get there early so you have plenty of time to check out the inventory before the sale starts. Then set your price limits and abide by them. You may ultimately have some luck with the mixed lots that usually turn up at the end of an auction. You never know what you might find in those boxes, and you can often scoop them up at bargain-basement prices.

SOURCING OPPORTUNITY? LOCAL VIDEO STORE GOES BUST

Not long ago, our local mom-and-pop video store went out of business. As a result, we had the chance to buy used DVDs of recent movies at $2.00 a pop. We're always on the lookout for things to sell on eBay, as all sellers should be, and these seemed like a great deal. Surely at $2.00 each we could make a decent profit reselling them on eBay. Right? Well, maybe—and maybe not. Fortunately, before we whipped out our wallets and bought the entire inventory, we went home and checked out some Completed Listings. We searched for some sample movies to see how listings for them fared. We found out that they were selling decently, but not for all that much money. In the case of the Reese Witherspoon film *Legally Blonde,* for example, copies had sold for as little as $.01, but on average, used copies sold for $2.00 to $3.00. (Those selling for a penny came with healthy shipping and handling charges.) Brand-new copies were only $5.00 or so. We were surprised at the low prices and the experience definitely illustrated the need, once again, to research before you buy.

Same place, different story. Our son Ethan (who worked at the store at the time) told us a guy who "had an online business" bought sixty used copies of the Will Smith movie *Hitch* at $5.00 each. At the time, the video had only been out for about two months. Curious, we again went to Completed Listings and found that he could probably get about $7.00 or so a copy. Those sellers who received the most money for the movie were advertising the DVDs as "used, but no visible scratches, case/cover in great condition!" (Good marketing, by the way, since they managed both to make the product sound like a good deal, but also covered themselves with the word "visible.") So in this case, the guy was onto something: Buying *Hitch* was a good idea. Ethan said later that this same fellow also bought some "old, obscure 'B' VHS movies" for $1.99 each. Presumably, he had a feel for what they'd sell for on eBay. Indeed, a movie like the 1970 Carrie Snodgrass/Richard Benjamin film *Diary of a Mad Housewife,* which is hard to find, can go for up to $40.00 or so. If he bought some of those, his time in that store was definitely well spent.

Sourcing New Items

Many sellers switch from secondhand goods to brand-new items early in their eBay careers. Many more sellers will turn to new items with the advent of eBay Express, which doesn't allow for used goods to be sold. Selling new items is even more challenging than selling used items, so you'll need to be especially careful that you're buying things that your research has shown can sell on eBay. You'll also need to be sure you're buying things that will bring a price high enough for you to earn a decent profit.

There are two schools of thought about how to choose which new items to list. One school says stick with what you know. Look at your own life and see where your heart is. If you like home furnishings, that may be the right area for you. Or if you love fashion, there you have it. The same is true for crafts, hobbies, and professional expertise. The reasoning behind this philosophy is that you'll be working in an area that you already know a lot about. You'll be able to spot bargains and good quality, because you'll be immersing yourself in something you already understand. The other school of thought holds that you should first find out what sells on eBay, and then search around for a source of that item at the lowest possible price. You may not know a lot about the item when you start, but you will know that you can make a profit on it. You'll get your education about the item as you deal with it and sell it. You'll have to decide which approach seems right to you. Regardless, when you're sourcing new items for resale on eBay, your goal is to get as close to the original source of that product as possible. Each set of hands that takes the item from the manufacturer to the final owner takes a cut. You want to position yourself as the direct link between the product's origin and your customer, and that's not an easy position to attain.

You will also need to keep your eyes open and tune your mind to spot a great opportunity when you see it. Your skills will sharpen with practice. It's much like the phenomenon you experience when you buy a new car. Until you make your decision, you may never see another one on the road, but as soon as you buy one, they're all over the place. They were always there, of course, but you just started noticing them. Great sourcing opportunities work the same way.

As you begin to look for sources of new items to sell on eBay, you'll need to step even further out of the eBay hobbyist suit and put on the eBay business suit.

When you're buying things to resell from yard sales, garage sales, end-of-season inventory, or store closeouts, you can easily operate as you would if you were buying things in bulk for any other reason. Maybe you have a couple dozen nieces and nephews, so it's not unusual for you to buy thirty of the same type of closeout toy. But, if you're going to be working with wholesalers, drop shippers, or manufacturers, you're going to need to have credentials, beyond just being an eccentric shopper.

First among these is a tax ID number. Most states have a sales tax, and if yours does too, you'll need this number to operate a business. In your state, the tax ID number may also be called a *resale certificate.* Either way, it's the document that allows you to collect sales tax from your customers. Even if you only ever sell on eBay, when someone who lives in your own state purchases an item from you, you'll owe the state a sales tax. Not only does getting a tax ID number allow you to deal with your state's taxes, it also registers you with the state as a regulated

COMMON BEGINNERS' MISTAKES

The panel of eBay experts who worked with us as consultants for this book wanted to make sure we told our readers to avoid these mistakes:

- Selling seasonal items, rather that starting out with items that will sell year-round. —Stephanie Inge, stephintexas
- Trying to sell everything to everybody. Just because there is a category for it, doesn't mean it will sell. —Drew Friedman, whitemountaintrading
- Not circling back in a few weeks to recheck the viability of a product. eBay is cyclical, so if your initial Completed Listings research suggests there isn't a market for a given item, set that item aside and wait a few weeks or a month. You may find it starts selling again at a good profit margin. —Stephen Ganus, eagleauctionsUSA
- Trying to sell the same things that everyone else is selling. Some items are in great supply and the market for them is thin—like Hummels. —Hendrik Sharples, hendrik.
- Not being thorough enough in their market research, and trying to sell something without knowing the market, the competition, and the correct category. —Stephanie Inge, stephintexas

and legitimate business. Many wholesalers or manufacturers will not even talk to you without this number.

Getting a tax ID number is simple. Start by going to your favorite search engine and doing a search for *tax ID number [your state]*. You'll quickly see what's involved in completing this process for your particular jurisdiction. If you're stumped, your local business librarian will gladly help you get everything you need in place to start the process. With your tax ID number at the ready, you can move on to serious product sourcing.

STORE CLOSEOUTS

We think closeouts, going-out-of-business sales, fire sales, and the like, represent a tremendous opportunity for sourcing products to sell on eBay. Small towns with mom-and-pop shops that have been around for a long time are a rich source indeed. We recently bought on eBay a NIB (New in Box) Kodak slide projector from 1972. The seller had bought out the inventory of an old photography studio/camera shop that had operated in his town for more than fifty years. As a result, he was able to offer wonderful vintage items, all in perfect condition. Once more, with feeling: Be prepared to do your research before shelling out wads of money for old inventory. (For more details behind this great find, see the My Best eBay Sale story at the end of this chapter.)

END-OF-SEASON INVENTORY

If you live in a smoke-free home and can keep items stored away from pets, basement smells, and cooking odors, consider buying items at the end of a season and saving them for resale when the next season comes along. We came across a closeout sale of beautiful stuffed Easter bunnies being sold at nearly 90 percent off one sunny July day. They would easily bring $10.00 each next March, and we could have gotten nearly a dozen at $1.50 each. You can't create your entire inventory this way, but you can certainly supplement what you sell when a bargain appears. Just make sure you have a good place to store the off-season items you purchase.

BIG DISCOUNT STORES

Just because you have ready access to one of the big discount stores, doesn't mean everyone else does. One of our seller friends found a great supply of software right at his local Sam's Club. Because he knew the product, he knew he could sell it for much more on eBay. He bought every last one of them and sold them to people who didn't have a Sam's Club nearby.

WHOLESALERS

Wholesalers, of course, sell products in bulk, which a buyer can then sell at prices closer to retail. However, margins being are what they are on eBay, making decent money by selling products bought from wholesalers won't be easy. This doesn't mean you will never find a great deal through a wholesaler ... it can still happen. Just remember that wholesalers need to make a profit too, and that means smaller profits for you. To locate reputable wholesalers, check out *The Light Bulk Wholesale Directory*, available through a company called Worldwide Brands (www.worldwide brands.com). Worldwide Brands (see Figure 18-1) has a team of researchers who screen the companies that are listed in its directories to ensure that they are reputable and will work with eBay sellers looking to place modest orders. Actually, World Wide Brands is the only drop ship and wholesale directory publisher certified by eBay.

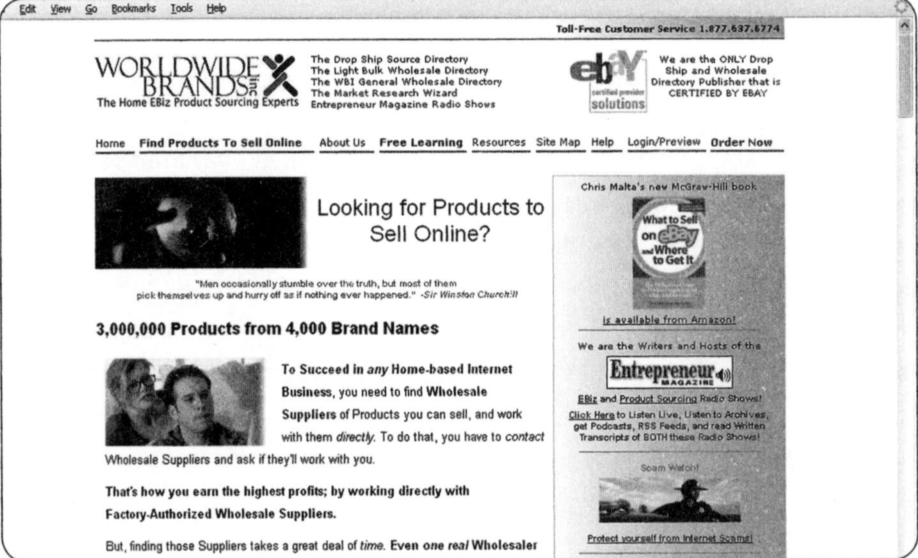

Figure 18-1: *Worldwide Brands has a team of researchers who prescreen companies before listing them in its directories.*

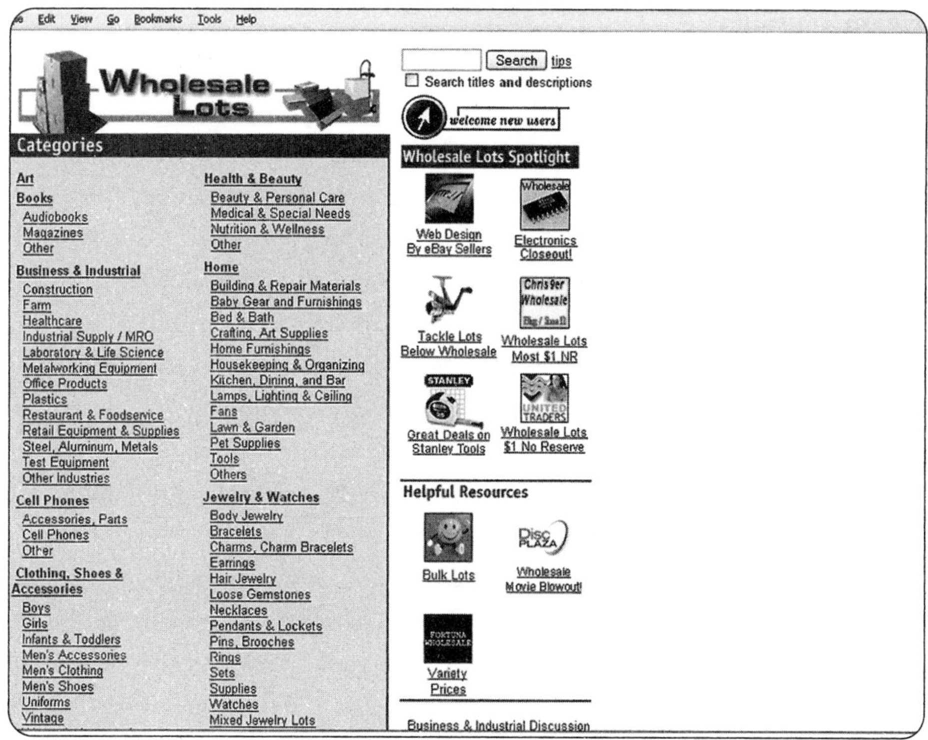

***Figure 18-2:** eBay's Wholesale Lots category makes sourcing products simple, but whether you can then resell the items for a good profit is another story.*

In addition, eBay has its own Wholesale Lots category. Click the Wholesale link at the end of the categories column on eBay's homepage, and a world of opportunity appears to open up before you (see Figure 18-2). You'll find categories for wholesalers selling everything from Art to Video Games. We bet many people who find this link imagine themselves to be smart and clever for uncovering this secret sourcing opportunity! But as you well know, every one of eBay's nearly 200 million members has access to what's right there on the site, especially if there's a link for it from the homepage. So finding true deals there isn't going to be that simple. Keep in mind that the people selling these wholesale lots are already on eBay, so they know how the game is played. You need to buy something at a low enough price to make a profit from it, and if it were that simple, many more wholesalers would be selling direct.

DROP SHIPPERS

On the surface, drop shippers appear to be a new eBay seller's dream. A drop shipper is in the business of buying, storing, and then shipping inventory that others sell. If you had an arrangement with a drop shipper to fulfill your orders for self-scooping litter boxes, for example, you'd create and post the auctions. (The drop shipper may have marketing materials that would help.) When your auction ends in a sale, you notify the drop shipper, who then ships your item to your buyer.

So the drop shipper has reduced your job to posting the auctions and collecting the money. He takes all the risk involved with buying, storing, and managing the inventory. You don't even have to bother with the shipping. Of course, you share your profit with him in return.

Reality check! Remember what you've been told about things that sound too good to be true? Here are some problems with drop shippers:

- You lose control. When you sell something that's in your possession, you complete the order yourself on your own terms. Looking at the drop shipper scenario, what if your supplier doesn't have the item on hand? Then it has to be backordered. This makes for a poor customer experience. In fact, it's not unusual to find neutral, and even negative feedback from buyers who were disappointed that a seller was unable to ship their items. That's why sellers such as Carlos Paris of elvibora don't like drop shippers. "I couldn't trust anybody else," he said. "I want the item in my warehouse where I can look at it, touch it, and feel it."
- Dependable drop shippers are not easy to find. Some are scammers, some won't do business with small sellers, and, as noted above, some are just not reliable.
- Too many other sellers also use them. PowerSeller Jack Walters told us the story of the time he went on eBay to shop for an electric razor. He found "scores of the same exact model, all in a row." While the sellers were different, they all had the same stock descriptions, even the same shipping terms (all dictated by the drop shipper). You can't stand out from your competition this way. Using drop shippers makes it difficult for you to separate yourself from the pack, which is a serious problem. "You have to have a unique selling proposition," says Jack.

We're not saying that you can't ever include a drop shipper in your eBay sourcing plans. Many big sellers do, but using a drop shipper isn't for the beginner. The sellers we know who use them successfully have been at this for years, know how to develop solid relationships with businesses, and understand all the ins and outs of their e-commerce operations. If you want to give drop shipping a try, we recommend that you consult the *Drop Ship Source Directory*, available through Worldwide Brands (www.worldwidebrands.com).

MANUFACTURERS

If working with wholesalers isn't usually cost-effective, and drop shippers are often not worth the trouble, then where does that leave you? As we mentioned earlier, we recommend that when you're looking for new items to sell on eBay you get as close as possible to the product source. And you can't get any closer than the manufacturers. At first, working with manufacturers will be difficult, because your business will be small, and you may not have the weight behind you to find and then strike deals with these companies. You may not be ready to buy items in the quantities required by many manufacturers. But as your eBay business grows and you yourself grow more sophisticated, that time will come. In the meantime, seek out the smaller manufacturers, and if there are any in your area, by all means try them first! Also, attend trade shows. They can provide excellent opportunities to meet with manufacturers face to face.

When approaching a new manufacturer, present yourself as an e-business owner. Don't walk right up and start talking about your eBay business. You may be proud of your eBay business, but as much as it pains us to say this, some manufacturers still have a prejudice against eBay, viewing the site as the "Internet yard sale." They may think that allowing you to sell their products new on eBay will devalue them. Let them get to know you as an honorable businessperson first.

Researching Reliable Sources

If you've determined that you're going to sell used items on eBay, your researching efforts will amount to keeping up with all the local sales and sources that you're already familiar with. It's a weekly trek that you probably already enjoy making. But if you're leaning toward selling new things, your main sourcing task will become research. At first you'll spend more time researching sources of products than anything else related to your eBay business. As a matter of fact, if your business really takes off, you'll probably hire your first part-time employee to do the listing and shipping so you can free yourself up for more extensive sourcing research. The job is just that important.

Many eBay sellers naturally turn to the Internet when looking for product sources. But type *eBay and sourcing products* or *eBay and wholesalers* or *eBay and distributors* into Google, and you'll retrieve an overwhelming array of companies, books, articles, and names. Many promise to provide *the* magic source of information that's available to you, and only you, oh wise master of the Google search engine. The presence of so many disparate information sources, including many that aren't worth the pixels, frustrates and honestly angers PowerSellers and other eBay experts. This is one reason why we like the directories from Worldwide Brands—the company's staff has done the legwork for you, calling all the companies listed in its directories, and fact-checking 'til the cows come home.

We are also fans of good old-fashioned research, and we encourage our readers to visit their local business librarian (or make contact through your library's Web site). Librarians are information specialists, and to an eBay entrepreneur, information is like gold dust. Librarians not only know how to make the most of search engines like Google, but they also have access to databases and other sources of information you may not even know exist. Take, for example, *Reference U.S.A.* Our local reference librarian explained that this is a database of twelve million U.S. companies. It can be used to find wholesalers and manufacturers, local and national associations, and many other types of businesses that can help you in your own eBay business. So get to know your local business and reference librarians. They are paid to help you!

CHECK YOUR RESEARCH

However you manage to uncover a great new potential source of product, you'll want to do some checking to make sure you're dealing with a real and reputable company. Here are some steps you can take to lower your risk of falling into the wrong hands.

- Make sure the company actually exists. Just because someone has a Web site doesn't mean he also has a real business. So do some further checking to confirm that any company you're considering has a real presence in the physical world. Any reputable company should be happy to put you in touch with a list of satisfied clients.

- Get a physical address for the building—don't be satisfied with a post office box. Even easier to acquire than a Web site is a P.O. box.
- Get a telephone number for the company and speak with a person there. Don't be satisfied leaving a message on voice mail and getting a call back. A reputable company has someone on staff during business hours to deal with customers in person.
- Find out if the company belongs to its trade association. If it doesn't, find out why. Not belonging isn't, in and of itself, a disqualifier, but you'll want to know why the company isn't part of its industry group.

So, once again, your eBay venture brings you back to research, research, and more research. You'll be looking for great sources of products. Next, you'll be researching those sources to make sure they really are great. Then, your research will continue with all the work you'll have to do in order to stay current with both the culture of eBay and the culture of the rest of the world. How else will you know what the next great trend is?

Researching Sales Trends

Whether you sell used or new items, you'll need to keep track of trends on eBay in order to make good sourcing decisions. In this way, sourcing research is a two-part process. You need to research the sources, sure, but you also need to know what items are actually selling on the site. Finding a great source of inexpensive products won't help you if no one on eBay wants to buy what you have to offer.

Searching Completed Listings is a great place to start, but it's not your only source for useful information about what products are worth buying. In chapter 13 we told you all about Terapeak, which can be a tremendous source of pricing information, but it's also great for information about what's actually selling on eBay.

Using research services is one important way to see what's hot, but there are other ways too. You'll find very useful information in more mundane places, including other areas of eBay itself as well as newspapers, magazines, and trade journals.

Magazines, Newspapers, and Trade Journals

As writers, we are always on the lookout for trends in popular culture, technology, and the other areas we write about. Trends help guide our decisions about what to write about and how to frame what we finally do write. In fact, a good exercise a writing professor once suggested to us is to go to a large newsstand and scan the headlines of the magazines there. That will give you a quick take on what's on people's minds (that is, if the editors behind those headlines are doing their jobs well). Newspapers are also good sources for trends. For example, a review in our local paper, the *Washington Post,* got us thinking about how many of the sports biographies about to be published center on sports stars and sportscasters from the 1950s and 1960s, such as Muhammad Ali, Roberto Clemente, and Howard Cosell. Of course, the market is flooded with memorabilia related to Ali, but apparently people are also quite interested in Roberto Clemente and Howard Cosell. An article about focus groups and how to sign up to participate in them really got our gears going. Hmmm, what topics are companies putting together focus groups about, and what might that suggest as far as our product sourcing is concerned?

Trade journals cover niches, from agriculture, apparel, and architecture to food and drink, gambling, media, personal care, and transportation. While everybody has ready access to magazines and newspapers, trade journals pretty much remain the province of those in their respective fields. That's precisely why you might find worthwhile product ideas by paging through some at a larger public library or at your closest college library.

You're a Person Who Needs People

What's on the minds of your friends and family? How are they dressed, what kinds of restaurants do they like, how are they decorating their homes, do they all seem to be buying more exotic pets? Be a snoop when you go out in public. Eavesdrop on conversations when you're on public transportation, at the mall, or in a restaurant. This is your market talking. Listen and learn from it!

Research Services

Okay, now let's look at research services. You already know that we're fans of Terapeak, so let's use that service as an example, although there are others. You'll find some more listed in the Resources section at the end of the book. You might think you already know a lot about what's hot on eBay from checking Completed Listings, but some of the information gathered by a third party can surprise you. Through Terapeak, for example, you can learn which products have sold in the greatest quantities over a specific time period, which categories are showing the highest growth in overall bids, and which have had the greatest success rate (listings resulting in a sale). For example, when we checked Terapeak for "hot" eBay categories we found the following items:

Lobby cards prior to 1940
Graded baseball cards from 1930–1939
Pool heaters and solar panels
Pre-1970 "Lesney" Matchbox cars
Laser pointers, specifically those with green beams

Once you have this kind of information, you can use it to help guide your sourcing expeditions. Just be sure to account for seasonality. For example, there may be a good reason why snowblowers are not among the hot categories between May and October. Data from a company such as Terapeak can also inform your decisions about how to price your items and even the day/time you should post your listing for maximum impact.

eBay Itself

There's a wealth of information on eBay, and we're no longer talking about Completed Listings. Also useful are eBay's Hot Items by Category List, lists of top search terms, the Merchandising Calendar, and eBay's marketplace reports.

The Hot Items by Category List identifies the categories and products that received the most bids on eBay for the previous month. You can find the most popular search terms on eBay, as well as the most watched items, through eBay Pulse, a daily snapshot of the action on the auction site. The Merchandising Calendar lists upcoming promotions on eBay's homepage. For example, as we write this, eBay is planning an Americana promotion. During this promotion the site will feature certain categories such as antiques and stamps. Finally, eBay Marketplace Research reports provide you with ninety days worth of data on completed items. Reviewing this data will give you a good idea of the demand for given products, at least over the past 90 days. Just as with data from a third party, you can use this information to guide your decisions about which items to sell, when to sell them, and how to price them.

All of these resources are simple to find. Click on the Site Map link at the top of most eBay pages and navigate to the Sell heading to find the resources mentioned here. Just keep in mind that all this information is just as easy for every one of your competitors to locate as it is for you to find. That means it will be hard for you to scoop anyone if you stick strictly to the information you can gather directly from eBay. Still, anything that revs your engines can help you uncover your next great sourcing idea.

Once you develop your sources and hone your skill at locating new ones, you may be ready to put more of a stake in the ground on eBay. By that we mean you may want to open your own eBay store. In the next chapter we'll look at eBay stores, and even consider your own store on the Web at large! See how far you've come?

JIM AND KELLI SHAW ARE POWERSELLERS who operate dream-adventures from their home on twenty acres of woods in the rural Midwest. They are self-proclaimed eBay addicts, and they love the life they've made for themselves. Not long ago, they found a great source of products when they noticed a small ad in their local paper for an auction to liquidate the contents of an old camera shop in town. They had noticed the run-down camera shop when they arrived in this small town several years earlier. They even speculated to each other about what it might look like inside. Still, it was in such bad condition, they wondered if anyone still operated the place.

When they saw the ad for the auction, they couldn't contain their curiosity, and they hoped to purchase some lighting and photo equipment for their eBay business. As it turns out, the original owner's son was liquidating everything from the store, which hadn't been renovated for about thirty years! Although the Shaws weren't able to find what they wanted for their own photography needs, they did find brand-new, never-opened boxes of slide projectors, movie cameras, Kodak and Duracell advertising displays, and boxes upon boxes of old projector and camera bulbs and fittings.

Because the auction was so poorly advertised, there were very few buyers and little competition. The couple spent $253 and completely filled their car with merchandise—twice! When we spoke with them, they'd sold only a small portion of the items they purchased that day, and they'd already recovered all the costs of acquiring the stock. They'll be selling these things on eBay for a long time to come. Not bad for a single day's work!

Ready for an eBay Store?

IN THE EARLY DAYS, eBay was strictly an auction site. But those days are long gone. Now eBay also runs the largest "mall" in the world, with nearly 500,000 stores worldwide under its roof! This mall only exists online, of course, and it's not at all like the one your teenage kids love to troll, but you can still find virtually everything you want there. eBay's mall is made up of stores run by eBay sellers, just like the sellers who post auctions.

Having your own eBay store puts a seller in a whole different league. A store can reflect your personality and showcase your inventory. Sure, opening an eBay store is a big step up from being just someone who lists items for sale on the eBay site, but it's also a simple way to become a real shopkeeper. Chances are, you'll know when you're ready to hang out a shingle and take this next step.

In this chapter we'll stroll into some eBay stores to see what they're like and whether opening one may be a good idea for you. We'll also venture out of the eBay mall entirely, onto the Web at large. There you'll find Web merchants of all sizes, standing side by side with the giants of the e-commerce world.

Inside an eBay Store

Before we consider whether you should open an eBay store, let's walk inside one to see what they're like. This exercise will help you decide whether you're ready to open your own store. Figure 19-1 shows the storefront of Hdglasses, operated by PowerSeller Gary Richardson of harleyglasses. Look around the store, and you'll see a very successful and professional eBay presentation. Of course, the layout of the store should be very familiar to you, as it includes eBay features and tools you've seen many times before. Along the top you'll see the usual features of any eBay page.

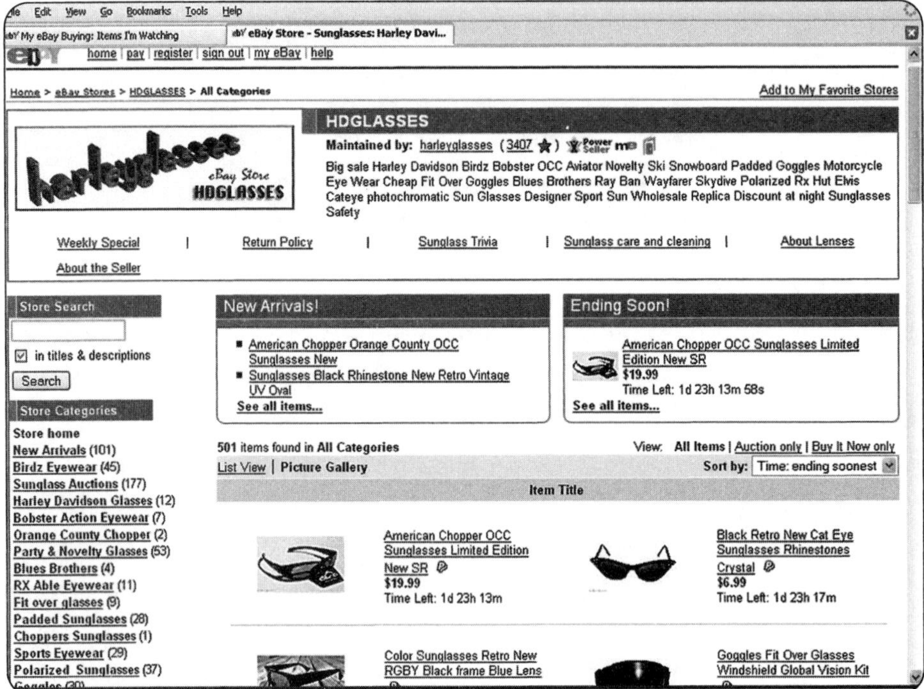

Figure 19-1: *Hdglasses' eBay store. This is a typical eBay store and illustrates how having your own store allows you to list more merchandise for a longer time period.*

At the very top of the page is the familiar eBay logo and toolbar. Below that is a box that includes the name of the store as well as the manager's description of it.

You'll also see sections to highlight the current specials being offered and listings that are very close to ending. Along the left-hand side is the store search box, where buyers can enter terms to search for items in this particular store only. The store categories are next. Buyers can use these to go up and down the aisles and check the shelves to find things that interest them. Also, please notice the number of items Gary keeps in stock. When we visited, he had more than 500 things for sale!

Should You Have an eBay Store?

So now that you've seen a great example of an eBay store, you may be in a better position to evaluate whether a store is right for you. The answer depends partly on how you view yourself as an eBay seller. Are you satisfied listing things on eBay once in a while, when the mood strikes you, or do you see yourself as someday having an eBay *business*? Do you enjoy eBay selling, and are you willing to do the work to make eBay a real contributor to your family income? Like so many aspects of eBay life, you'll get out of it what you put into your eBay store in terms of time and effort. At first, the time commitments will be great and the rewards, well, not so great. And the whole time you'll pay a monthly subscription fee. The fee will not stop just because you can't devote much time to your store that month.

Because of the time and savvy needed and the monthly fees you're charged, stores aren't for brand-new eBay sellers. At the same time, we're not suggesting that you have to be a captain of eBay industry to open a store, either. In addition to the fees and the constant work a store will require, you should also consider whether or not you're up to keeping it stocked. Do you have the inventory, and can you keep filling your pipeline with, say, fifty or more items that you can have in stock almost all the time? Most importantly, do you have enough time to devote to stocking and managing a store to justify the fees? And do you want to commit yourself to devoting this amount of time to your eBay business? Operating a store moves you up the scale of eBay sellers, and plenty of people operate happily for years on eBay enjoying success without one. But if you've decided you want to build a real eBay business, opening a store is a required step toward that goal.

The Advantages of Having Your Own eBay Store

There's a feeling of satisfaction that comes with having your own eBay store. Few of us can ever actually own a store of our own outside of eBay. It's just too expensive and risky. But when you create an eBay store, you've created your own shopping nook that's separate from eBay at large. You've got a store! Shoppers walk through your door and step out of eBay. Once they're in your store, you can display your items, design your look, and offer your own brand of customer attractions. While they're in your store, your competitors are no longer a click away, as they are when your wares just appear in search results.

An eBay store lets you better organize your merchandise, and showcase items of interest to buyers who've come from your regular auction listings—buyers, presumably, who already like your product line. Having a store gives you added credibility as an online merchant. As a storeowner you're no longer just someone who lists things for sale on eBay. You've put a real stake in the ground. You come across as more professional than before and better established.

With a store you can also list things for longer periods of time, and for less money than with regular listings. To many sellers, lower listing fees are the biggest boon stores offer. Storeowners can list items in "store inventory format" for $0.05 each for items priced $0.01–$24.99, or $0.10 for items priced $25.00 or higher, for a period of thirty days. After that, you can renew items for an additional thirty days. You also have the option of listing things as "good 'til cancelled," meaning that they'll automatically renew every thirty days, as long as your inventory holds out. So you don't have to concern yourself with relisting things that don't sell. That happens automatically. Because your store items have a longer shelf life than your eBay auctions do, search engines, which can take a few days to catch up to new Web items, are more likely to index them. This gives buyers more opportunities to find them.

eBay claims that 75 percent of its storeowners say having a store has increased their eBay sales. (Of course, how could it not, since having a store provides you with a whole new selling venue.) Parrothead88, a long-time eBay seller specializing in shipping supplies, has had an eBay store up for more than five years. Co-owner Michael Kolman told us they sell more through their store than they do through their auctions. You should also know it usually takes longer to sell items through an eBay store than it does through the main site.

eBay Store Fees

There are three levels of monthly subscriptions available for eBay stores: Basic, Featured, and Anchor. Your first step, of course, will be a Basic store, and that will probably satisfy your needs for a good long time. But just so you know what your options are, the table below provides a few of the differences among the three levels.

	Basic	Featured	Anchor
Monthly Subscription Fee	$15.95	$49.95	$499.95
Monthly Keyword Advertising Credit	None	$30.00	$100.00
Customer Support	6–6 PST	6–6 PST	24 hour
Custom Pages	5	10	15

Note: In the above table, *Monthly Keyword Advertising Credit* refers to the amount of money eBay will give you to buy keywords on its site for advertising purposes. When you buy an eBay keyword (say sunglasses), depending on how much you bid for that keyword, your ad will appear on search results pages when searchers enter your term in eBay's search box. The more you can budget, the greater the number of times your ad will appear. *Custom Pages* allow you to go beyond what's available through eBay's templates to create a unique homepage, incorporate your own colors for better branding of your store, and add things like sizing charts to facilitate sales.

There are many other differences among these levels. They pertain to the kind of eBay auction management software the subscription includes, the kind of data analysis eBay provides, and the amount and kind of advertising and e-mail marketing support you receive.

In addition to a monthly fee, you'll have to pay final value fees as follows:

Final Selling Price	Final Value fee
$0.01–$25.00	10% of the closing price
$25.01–$100.00	10% of the initial $25.00 ($2.50), plus 7% of the balance, up to $100.00
$100.01–$1,000.00	10% of the initial $25.00 ($2.50), plus 7% of the initial $25.01 to $100.00 ($5.25), plus 5% of the balance, up to $1,000.00
Over $1,000.00	10% of the initial $25.00 ($2.50), plus 7% of the initial $25.01 to $100.00 ($5.25), plus 5% of the next $100.01 to $1,000.00 ($45.00), plus 3% of the remaining closing value balance.

All these choices and fees can seem a bit imposing to the would-be storeowner. As with many of the options eBay gives you (for example, listing upgrades), we suggest you start small until you've learned the lay of the land, and then move on when you're more experienced. In the case of an eBay store, starting small means opening a Basic store. Finally, be sure to monitor store fees, as eBay has raised them considerably in the last two years.

How to Open an eBay Store

Just as it's easy to start listing things to sell on eBay, setting up an eBay store is also pretty simple. Not only that, any level of seller can open one. Here are eBay's modest requirements for opening a store. You only have to meet *one* of these requirements:

- A feedback score of 20 or higher, or
- You must be ID verified ($5.00 is all that takes), or
- You need a PayPal account in good standing

So you see there's little standing in your way, at least from eBay, if you decide you'd like to open a store on its site. Once you decide to open an eBay store of your own, here's what you need to do:

1. Create a name for your store
2. Write a description for it
3. Use eBay's templates to create a look for your store
4. Choose your subscription level

That's all there is to it. Now you're ready to stock your store and work on promoting it. For more information, click your way to http://pages.ebay.com/storefronts/start.html.

The steps you'll take will be somewhat familiar to you if you are already experienced in selling things on eBay (and, as we suggest, you should be before opening a store). One point to consider carefully, however, is how to select the name of your store. Sears, Wal-Mart, and Barnes & Noble are taken, so let's start from scratch.

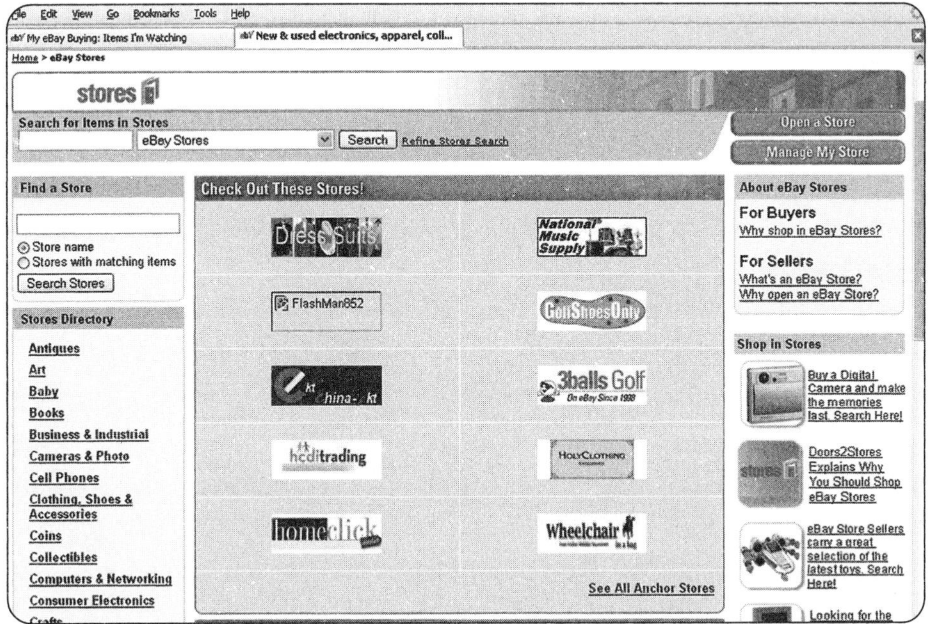

Figure 19-2: *Begin your exploration of eBay stores at this page of the eBay site.*

Like your member ID, your store name should be easy to remember; suggestive of what you sell, if possible; and not easily misspelled. If using your member ID would work well, that's great. If not, this is the perfect opportunity to come up with a great name for your store. There's no need for your store name and member ID to be identical. Why not check out some eBay stores that sell merchandise similar to yours, and see which names grab you and make you want to step inside and look around? Start at http://stores.ebay.com/ (see Figure 19-2).

Stocking Your Store

You've already seen that you can list store items in store inventory format for less money and for much longer periods of time than through regular auction listings or Fixed Price listings. So why wouldn't you have everything you sell be strictly in your eBay store? You'll always want to have things for sale on the regular eBay site, even while you maintain an active store. Your activity on the rest of eBay makes it more likely that shoppers will find your store inventory.

Store inventory items don't always show up in regular eBay searches. They'll only appear if fewer than thirty auction or Fixed Price listings of that exact product are available on the entire site. Then eBay will start adding a few store inventory items to search result pages. It is also not the default, when browsing, to include items listed in store inventory. Now, we'll show you how to have the best of both worlds: the longer-lasting, less expensive store inventory items, and the traffic-driving auction listings.

Here's an example. Suppose you've come across a great selection of flip-flops in various sizes and colors. Let's say, you've bought one hundred pairs of them. You can list a few of the most popular colors and sizes in regular auction listings. These get greater exposure in search results on eBay than store inventory items do. Then you can state right in your description that buyers can visit your store for additional sizes and colors.

If you sell primarily one-of-a-kind or more unusual items, such as those you locate at estate sales and live auctions, you may not need a store at all. But if you tend to buy items in bulk or lots, it makes sense to keep a good supply in your store and use some for auctions and Fixed Price listings to drive your customers to your greater inventory. Please don't use your store as a place to stock slow-moving merchandise. The listing fees may be cheaper than on the main site, but they can still add up quickly.

Managing Your Store

Managing your store will be a necessary but not complicated or unrewarding task. To do so, you'll just click the Seller, Manage Store link near the bottom of your storefront. It's almost as easy as revising a listing to change prices or add and delete inventory from your store. You have a lot of room here for experimentation, and eBay gives you the tools and data you need to do this as wisely as possible. For one thing you can list your merchandise under any of three hundred different categories. As a storeowner, you can receive "traffic reports" that show the route shoppers took to get to your store, such as the keywords that brought them there. With this data in hand, you can list and promote your items accordingly, by making sure you incorporate these keywords when you create your titles and descriptions.

Promoting Your Store

As you've seen, one of the best ways to promote your store is through your regular listings, which, of course, should continue even once your store is up and running. Your member ID, for example, will include an eBay store icon, which members can click on to go to your store's homepage. Also, because you're operating an *eBay* store, eBay will do a lot to drive customers right to your door. As you know, whenever someone searches the eBay site for something, search results appear, showing matching items. Items from eBay stores appear at the end of these searches, in their own category, if the search yields thirty or fewer items. Your store will also appear in eBay's Store Directory, a version of the mall directory at the entrance of many malls. You'll find it under the Specialty Sites heading on eBay's homepage.

USE YOUR AUCTIONS TO SELL MORE THROUGH YOUR STORE

Another way to use your listings and store merchandise together is to think about the accessories a person buying your items listed for auction might need, and then stock them in your store. For example, if you sell MP3 players, consider offering a line of earbuds, batteries, or carrying cases that you can keep on hand in your store. Be sure to include a mention of your store in your listings, so your customers can see what else you have for sale. That way you're driving more traffic to your store, and hopefully increasing your sales.

Even if you don't have matching accessories for the items you sell, this strategy can still work for you. When you're sourcing your auction items, think about what other things people who shop for those items may also like. If you sell cookware, consider offering unusual spices or sauces in your store. If you list home décor items for auction, imagine which candles or dried-flower arrangements might go well with your items and have them available in your store. You get the idea. This will help you—and your customers—think of your eBay business as a whole, rather than as a collection of stray items you've found here and there.

Your Own Web Store

An eBay store is a good way to get started as an online merchant, but you're still operating within the confines of eBay. eBay is the landlord to whom you pay rent, and the landlord who determines the general look and feel of your store. It's also the front door through which most buyers will reach you. Sure, you're still a seller with your own store, but you're an eBay storeowner first, not an independent online merchant. It won't feel exactly like your own outpost, because it won't be.

If you decide this is the life for you, you might want something completely independent of eBay. Even there you have choices. You can take a baby step away from Mother eBay and work through eBay's ProStores, or you can leave the eBay womb entirely. If you do, keep in mind that your promotional skills will be challenged. "It's on you this time," as eBay consultant Debbie Levitt advises her clients.

ProStores

ProStores is an eBay company that provides technology and services for operating stores out on the Web at large. eBay created ProStores, shown in Figure 19-3, because it recognized that many sellers wanted their own Web stores, independent of eBay, with their own Web addresses. So a ProStores store is different from an eBay store, and, indeed, some sellers operate both. When you're ready to move beyond eBay out onto the Web at large, take a good look at opening a ProStores store. As with most offerings from eBay, ProStores is easy to start using, and it might be just right as a first step toward getting your feet wet in the broader sea of e-commerce.

Here's some insider information for you to consider, though. The experienced sellers we've spoken with are not big fans of ProStores. They feel that while opening a ProStores store is simple enough, changing things around after that is not that simple. They also question why, when you have other options, you would want to pay eBay not only a monthly subscription fee for this service, but also a percentage of your sales. (We'll explore these fees shortly.) For example, when we asked a prominent PowerSeller recently if he would be opening a ProStores store, he said, "Not at this time—there are other eStore solutions that don't require a piece of my sales and a monthly fee."

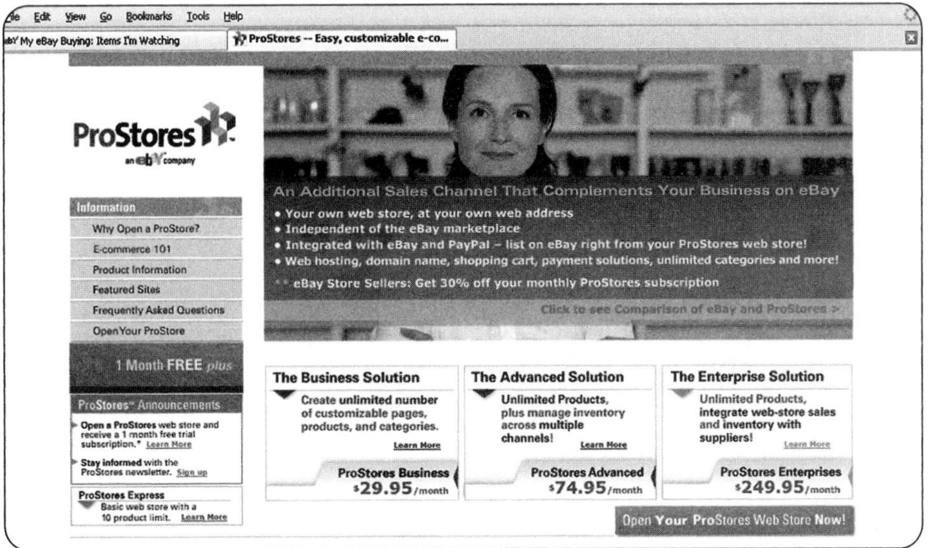

Figure 19-3: *From here you can begin exploring ProStores, a suite of services designed for sellers building their first Web stores off the eBay site.*

ProStores was very new when we researched it for this book, so we think you should check it out for yourself at http://www.prostores.com/. eBay is behind it, and, considering eBay's tremendous marketing muscle, that can also be a good thing. The only thing you risk at first is your time, since you can try ProStores for a month for free.

PROSTORES SUBSCRIPTION LEVELS

A ProStores store is intended to be the best of both worlds—the security and clout of eBay combined with the independence of your own Web store. However, some would say it's the worst of both, and the fees eBay charges have something to do with that.

As with eBay stores, there are different subscription levels for ProStores. You'll probably want to consider an Express Store, which costs $6.95 a month. However, you'll only get two pages to list products, and you can only list ten products in all. According to the ProStores' literature, you can create an Express Store in as little as thirty minutes.

With ProStores Business, at $29.95 a month, you can create an unlimited number of pages, and feature an unlimited number of products. The two higher

Figure 19-4: *The storefront from solidcolorneckties.com, a Web store built with software from ShopPal.*

levels are ProStores Advanced ($74.95 a month), and ProStores Enterprise ($249.95 a month), but neither of these options is a good choice for a beginner.

As we've noted, with ProStores you'll pay both a monthly subscription fee and a percentage of your sales. This ranges from 0.50 percent to 1.5 percent, depending on your subscription plan.

Your Very Own Little Place on the Web—Or What's eBay Got to Do with It?

It may be heresy to suggest this within the pages of an eBay book, but you don't have to work with eBay at all to create a store on the Web. Many PowerSellers we've spoken with see a lot of their future growth coming from non-eBay sales venues, and they aren't the least bit hesitant to say so. More than a few feel that having your own store—completely independent of eBay—is the only way you can match and surpass your eBay sales. Of course, they may have huge inventories and brands that they've painstakingly built up over years. Their experience also makes it easier for them to handle the learning curve that only grows as you move away from the eBay Mothership.

There are prominent companies, such as ChannelAdvisor (www.channel advisor.com) and Marketworks (www.marketworks.com), that will work with you to create and then manage your own Web store. These companies are also experienced at working with eBay stores, so if you have both operations they can handle everything. We'll warn you, though, that you're getting into the big leagues (read: dollars) with some of these companies, so research them carefully, and take your time before making a commitment.

Another option is to work with a smaller company that provides the software you need to build an independent Web store, but that leaves more of the day-to-day responsibilities—such as tracking inventory—to you. ShopPal (www.shoppal.com) is one of our favorites because it's simple and cost-effective. One of our PowerSeller friends, Mike Martyka, opened his store, solidcolorneckties.com, shown in Figure 19-4, with the help of this company's software and other services for only $200.00. He still has his eBay store, but ShopPal enabled him to have an independent Web store, too. His monthly ShopPal fee is just $19.95, with no additional percentage of his sales required.

So there you have it. In just a few chapters, you've gone from setting up a seller's account on eBay to thinking about opening your own Web store. That's quite a journey. As you look back on all you've learned and achieved, you're free to think about what you'd like to see happening next. Is this the life for you? If so, you may want to work toward becoming a PowerSeller yourself, or perhaps an eBay Trading Assistant. Let's move on now and take a look at the life of these eBay professionals in chapter 20.

POWERSELLER KEVIN BOYD of preferreddiscounts sells collectible pipe and cigar accessories. He also invented his own special case called the Pipe Guardian. This allows pipe and cigar smokers to take their favorite equipment with them and safely store their supplies while traveling or camping. He's also an eBay Education Specialist, and he's been a big help to us as we were researching this book. Here's a great story about how he blended his auction listings with his store inventory for a big boost in his holiday-season sales.

Collectible pipes are a huge market. Folks who love them may buy them just to decorate their mantles. Kevin visited the Chicago International Pipe Show and purchased a beautiful, collectible pipe created by a Polish pipe carver. It had the Marines emblem carved in 3-D, and Kevin found it "stunningly gorgeous." He listed the pipe as a Featured Plus listing.

He really wanted this pipe to go up at the beginning of the holiday shopping season. At the same time, he was stocking a lot of items in his store inventory. He knew that the Featured Plus listing, combined with the pipe itself, would drive a lot of traffic to his store. He was right.

He usually can expect about forty hits for his listings. For the pipe, he got more than six hundred! He sold the pipe to a Marine colonel, for somewhere between $500 and $600. But he also sold $1,500 worth of merchandise from his store inventory because buyers interested in that pipe with the Marines insignia also checked out his store offerings. His investment in a well-placed Featured Plus listing, plus a well-stocked store, led to a very prosperous holiday season for this eBay seller.

Chapter 20

Become a PowerSeller!

YOU COULDN'T POSSIBLY HAVE REACHED the last chapter of this book without noticing that we're big fans of eBay PowerSellers. We've mentioned them just a time or two already. But who wouldn't admire all that it takes to build a thriving business on eBay? Like any pioneer in a new land, the PowerSellers have used their wits, guts, determination, and dreams to forge a life of their own design. They've weathered the storms of e-commerce while at the same time building their own shelters. They've had to adapt. They've had to reevaluate. They've had to let some old plans die while they cultivated new ones. There are as many fascinating stories about how PowerSellers built their businesses as there are PowerSellers themselves.

The final result may now seem like a dream to you. A PowerSeller's life is the stuff dreams are made of. The freedom and control alone are at the core of the American Dream. Indeed, there are many trying to capitalize on that dream and profit from you, the dreamer. The Internet is filled with get-rich-quick schemes about earning a fortune on eBay. Well, those easy-steps-to-riches plans didn't work for Fred Flintstone or Ralph Kramden, and we're here to tell you, they won't work for you, either. We've come too far together for us to start lying to you now.

There is no easy way to make a fortune by selling on eBay. Being a PowerSeller can be the most rewarding and bone-crushing experience in your life. In that way, it's a lot like parenthood. It's so much more intense and demanding than anyone can imagine before it begins, and yet, you know once you're there, it's worth every moment.

The first thing we'll do as we explore the world of the PowerSeller is to take a good, hard look at the lifestyle. Then we'll do our best to discourage you from aspiring to PowerSeller status by spelling out all the realities, challenges, and responsibilities you'll face. Finally, we'll stand and look at the whole thing together, to see if you think the risk-to-reward ratio is right for you. Then we'll send you on your way down the road with some advice about where you'll get more information about how to make your dream come true, not quickly and easily, but smart and steady.

What Exactly Is a PowerSeller?

To qualify as a PowerSeller on eBay, you must be an active member for at least ninety days and have an average minimum of $1,000 in sales per month for three consecutive months. Your feedback score must be at least 100, with a positive rating of at least 98 percent. In addition to these basics, there are also a few more stipulations:

- You must uphold the eBay community values, including honesty, timeliness, and mutual respect. No shill bidding (you can't get a coworker or relative to bid just to artificially increase your item's price), flaming feedback that attacks people vindictively, or neglecting to ship what you've sold.
- Your eBay account must be in good financial standing. No owing the company any unpaid fees.
- You can't violate any "severe" policies within a sixty-day period. These include interfering with the transactions of others (by sending out those fake second-chance offers we told you about, for example) and malicious buying, such as buying an item just so you can leave nasty feedback.
- You also can't violate three or more of eBay's policies within sixty days. So you can't get caught keyword spamming, including links in your listings, or creating misleading titles more than three times within two months.

- You must also have maintained a minimum average of four monthly listings for the past three months.

For more information about the criteria for being a PowerSeller, or to take a look at more specific information, go to http://pages.ebay.com/services/buyandsell/powerseller/criteria.html.

Once you meet these criteria, you'll become a Bronze PowerSeller. You don't have to do anything to make that happen; eBay will automatically notify you when you qualify. We actually knew someone who became a PowerSeller without even realizing it! He made the discovery when he got the e-mail from eBay congratulating him on his achievement. He was *that* busy just selling things he cared about on the site! Of course, he paid much more attention once he realized what he'd done.

A Bronze PowerSeller is the basic level, but there are four other categories of PowerSellers as well. Here's a look at all the levels and the sales amounts required to reach each step up the PowerSeller ladder.

PowerSeller Designation	Average Monthly Sales
Bronze	$1,000
Silver	$3,000
Gold	$10,000
Platinum	$25,000
Titanium	$150,000

As you might imagine, there is a huge difference between the life of a Bronze-level PowerSeller and that of a Titanium PowerSeller. As a matter of fact, within the last couple of years, a new term has come into being on eBay: Top Seller. This refers to the Platinum- and Titanium-level sellers. The issues and challenges they face are significantly different from those of the lower-level PowerSellers. You'll find they often join together to address issues that arise in selling on eBay at such a high volume. One organization that supports PowerSellers and their interests is the Professional eBay Sellers Alliance (PeSA). Newcomers join this organization by invitation only, and come together to actively address concerns to eBay and to the third-party providers who offer products and services to large-scale sellers.

Once an eBay seller achieves PowerSeller status, not only does that seller achieve a certain standing as a professional on the site, but she also gains access to prioritized customer support from eBay itself, and she may be eligible for special eBay services such as health insurance. PowerSellers get up to $200 per quarter of free keyword ads on the site. They also receive special invitations to participate in eBay events; for example, they have their own registration area and lounge at eBay Live! PowerSellers can also network on PowerSeller-only discussion boards, and eBay recruits them to help design and test new eBay services and improvements.

Now that you have specifics about what it means to have become a PowerSeller, we'll take a look at what that life is really like. The numbers are important, but they don't tell the whole story of what it takes to live the life of a PowerSeller.

Ahhh, the Life of a PowerSeller! (Hey You, Get Back to Work!)

When you're working the usual nine-to-five grind, it's so tempting to dream of another life. Of course, you still have to earn money, but what if you could do it without that boss? Skip the commute? Forget about those annoying cubicle-mates? Escape from the whole day-to-day dreariness of ordinary, workaday life? Instead, you could get up, have your leisurely cup of coffee while you check your e-mail and see what sales were like overnight. Work at your own pace. Create a few listings. Package a few items for the post office. Send the kids off to school, and do all these things before you even get out of your pajamas. Ah, sounds like heaven, right? Okay, that's enough. Let's get real!

Yes, there are elements of the PowerSeller's life that truly are a dream come true. You can immerse yourself in the things you know and love. If you have a hobby or passion, you may just be able to find a way to make selling those things your day-to-day working life. A PowerSeller is free to live and work anywhere that suits her. If you've always dreamed of living in sunny climes, you can earn your living there as a PowerSeller. If you'd like to move out to the country, go ahead. As long as there's a post office nearby and a way to get high-speed Internet access, go right ahead. You can design your work life so that you can work when you choose to work, not when someone else says that you need to be productive. Night owls can work till the wee small hours of the morning and sleep in as late as they need to. Early birds can have the bulk of their workday done before the rest of us roll out of bed. You're free to decide when your family needs you or when you need to go run those errands. Finally, you'll probably really like your boss.

The Inevitable "But"

But, and we hope you knew there'd be a "but," working as a PowerSeller does not take the *work* out of your occupation. If there is only one lesson you take away from this chapter, make it this one. A PowerSeller owns his own business. That means he works harder as a PowerSeller than he's ever worked before. Think about it. Whether we're talking about your plumber or the local shopkeeper, nobody puts in more hours than the guy who operates his own business. When you're the boss, everything comes down to you, and that means you work as long as you have to in order to make your business a success. It's what you base your entire life on and how you support yourself and your family.

As the boss, you'll have to be strict with your most important employee. That means you have to make yourself work, even when you'd rather be doing something else. You'll also have to make yourself stop working. When your income is based directly on your own efforts, it's much harder to figure out when to close up shop. There will always be that one more e-mail or that one more item to list. It could mean the difference in your monthly earnings to do just one more thing before you quit for the day. If you're not careful, you can get so caught up in the work that your own dog starts to bark at you when you emerge from your workspace, and the kids ask your spouse who that strange person is. So time management is really a crucial issue.

You'll also have to handle all those little details that your employer has been taking care of for you up until now. For example, consider the small detail of health insurance. Add in that 401k plan, and the fact that there's no longer an employer to match your contributions. But aside from those bigger things, you'll also have to provide yourself with all the supplies you use. You'll keep your own records. You'll be the cleaning staff and the lunchroom attendant, too.

Oh, yeah, one more thing: You're now Tech Support, too. No more calling that maven down the hall to come and figure out whatever is wrong with your computer setup. That'd be you now. Add to that the pressure that you simply can't allow your computer to be down for any length of time. You need that computer to be doing its thing every single day. Any hour you miss at the computer is money you're not earning.

It can also be lonely at the top. You will spend most of your days sitting alone in your workspace. You'll miss the little impromptu chats in the hallway and by the water cooler, the guy with the corny jokes, the occasional birthday cake. You may think that won't matter to you, but the isolation of working from home gets to a lot of people. You'll have to figure out a way to introduce human company into your schedule, just so you won't feel like a hermit. Some suggestions include taking your laptop to the local coffee shop to do some e-mail correspondence among humans, spending a morning each week researching in the business section of the local library, or taking a class—either eBay-related or not. You'll know what seems right to you, but we're social creatures who need the company of others, so don't discount that aspect of life.

Okay, if you're still determined, be aware that you'll also have to keep learning at a pace you may not have thought about in years. You'll have to keep current on emerging technologies, so that you can take advantage of every new innovation that will make your life easier and your business more productive and profitable. You'll have to stay abreast of your sourcing efforts, always searching out that next great deal on the next great item to sell. You'll have to understand the Internet in ways you haven't even discovered yet. That means you'll have to learn about things like search engine optimization, so that your business will pop up as close to the top as possible in the search results from search engines like Google and MSN Search. You'll have to actively stay up to the minute on all of eBay's rules and changes. When you're selling in large volumes, the slightest mistake can be devastating.

eBay's Always Watching

Look back at the list of minor violations for which you'll lose your PowerSeller status. Let's consider just one, say, a misleading listing title. Now we know you wouldn't purposely create a misleading title, but what if you accidentally included information that was considered misleading. Suppose you, or an employee you recently trained, put a descriptor in the title that violated this rule. As a small seller, you could do that with an item and it wouldn't change the nature of your business. But as a PowerSeller, you may have created half a dozen listings that include this misleading title. Right there, you've violated the rule and you've jeopardized your PowerSeller status. It will take you at least sixty days to regain it, and, in that time, your competition is likely to gain some real advantage.

Then there's the issue of fees. When you sell from time to time, it's simple to keep track of those. But PowerSellers can easily start racking up fees that exceed the credit limit on the credit card they used to register with eBay. In no time, you're no longer holding an account that's in good financial standing with eBay. This might be a minor inconvenience or a troublesome issue for the casual seller, but for the PowerSeller, it can spell disaster and the loss of an entire business. So the rewards of being a PowerSeller are great, but so are the demands and risks. Only you can decide how you feel about the risk-to-reward ratio. And only you can decide if this is the right life for you.

Time for Some Good News

Now that we've given you a clear look at all the challenges you'll face on your path toward becoming a PowerSeller, let's take a look at some good news, too. First of all, you don't need to run down this road at a speed anyone else determines for you. If you decide you want to become a PowerSeller and devote yourself to selling full-time on eBay, you can do it at your own pace. Taking each step one at a time will help you overcome the intimidation you might feel at the thought of all that is ahead of you. If you keep your eBay sales a part-time effort, you can build your business while still keeping your regular day job. That minimizes your risk and gives you the security of employer-sponsored benefits. If and when you're ready to give up your job and devote yourself full time to being a PowerSeller, you'll know. You'll see that you are consistently earning enough money to provide for your family while still investing in your business and making it grow. Nothing says that you have to start selling today and set a deadline for yourself about what's going to happen next.

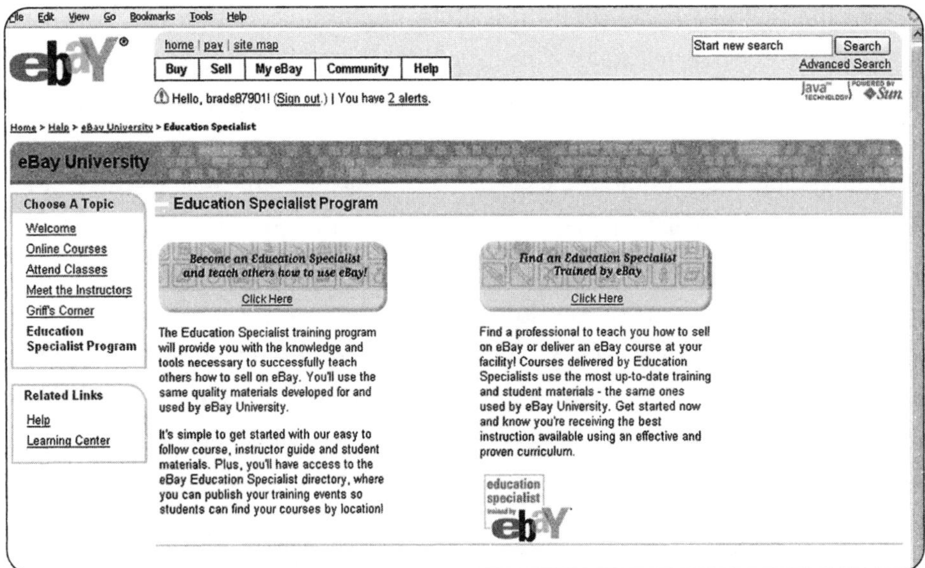

Figure 20-1: *From this page you can enroll in eBay's Education Specialist program or find an Education Specialist in your area.*

You also don't really need to travel the path toward PowerSeller status alone. There are great resources available to you now. You'll find books on the subject, such as *eBay PowerSeller Secrets* and *eBay PowerSeller Million Dollar Ideas,* from two authors we've seen in our bathroom mirror many times. You can also take classes from eBay Education Specialists close to your own hometown or through eBay University. These instructors are often PowerSellers themselves who offer classes and advice for people who are hoping to follow in their footsteps. Or consider hiring an eBay consultant to help you get started. This may be the same person as your eBay Education Specialist, or you might find another consultant nearby. You can easily locate an eBay-trained Education Specialist through eBay's Education Specialist Program Directory, shown in Figure 20-1. Simply go to http://www.poweru.net/ebay/student/searchIndex.asp.

Do your research carefully to make sure this person shares your philosophy about selling and understands the vision of the business you're trying to build. Investing in some professional help early on can save you time, money, and aggravation as you make your way along the learning curve. When PowerSeller Kevin Boyd decided to make his eBay business his full-time job, he turned to an eBay

University instructor. Today he is not only a PowerSeller, but also an Education Specialist himself. Another alternative to formal education can provide you with real-time, hands-on experience. Consider becoming an apprentice to a local PowerSeller. If you volunteer to help with listing, packaging, and record keeping, that veteran of the eBay marketplace may be more than happy to give you an inside look at the business.

Make yourself known on eBay's discussion boards and in eBay's groups. You'll find a whole community of people who are also working toward the same goal as you, so join them. It's amazing how giving and supportive these people are when it comes to sharing what they've already learned. True, no one is going to tell you where he's sourcing his latest great find. But you'd be surprised about how generous your peers will be when it comes to handling the day-to-day issues you're all facing together. It will help you to know you're not the only one facing these challenges, and the practical challenges all seem less intimidating when you're dealing with them together.

You're a Business Owner Now, So Start Thinking Like One

From the time you decide to build a business on eBay rather than to just sell for fun, you've become a businessperson. Thanks to eBay, it's never been easier to start your own business. So once you've made that decision, remember that now that you're a businessperson, you need to think like one. Fortunately, your monetary investment in the early stages is nothing compared to the investment you'll be making in time and energy.

As far as technology is concerned, you probably already have everything you need to get started. If you have a well-functioning computer and a high-speed Internet connection, you're ready to go. Most PowerSellers we spoke with started off with whatever equipment they already had and added new technology only when they needed it. The tasks involved in selling on eBay are not that challenging in terms of computer power. Whatever you use to shop on eBay probably has the speed and power you'll need to do your listings and deal with your e-mail challenges.

Although the hardware you have in place is probably sufficient, as soon as you decide to shoot for PowerSeller status, you'll need to reconsider your software needs. First of all will be the auction management software you'll choose. Now you may think we're getting way ahead of ourselves here, but please heed this warning. The time to decide about your auction management software is when you're just starting out. Sure, you don't actually need it this month when you may be listing only five or ten items, but you're thinking like a businessperson now, remember? What is life going to be like for you in three months, or six, when you're listing far more items each week? You'll be busier than ever. Do you really want to be doing the research to choose your program, installing it, learning all its workings, and retrofitting all your current records to fit it when you're already busier than you've

BECOMING A TRADING ASSISTANT

Once you've become proficient at selling on eBay, you'll see that a lot of other people would love to have you sell things for them. Even better, they'll be happy to pay you for your services. Trading Assistants earn about 35 percent of the FVF for each item sold, including all eBay fees and shipping costs. You may really love the work, but we've spoken to plenty of people who are intimidated by the thought of selling on eBay, and who wouldn't want to consider learning how to do it. They represent a business opportunity that may be just right for you.

To become an eBay Trading Assistant, you have to have sold at least ten items over the last three months. You must have a feedback score of one hundred or more and your feedback rating must be at least 97 percent positive. Your eBay account must be in good standing. Once you've achieved these numbers, eBay offers a good many resources to help you run your business as a Trading Assistant. For example, you'll have access to marketing tools such as customizable flyers and press releases. You will be eligible to be listed in eBay's Trading Assistant directory, and eBay charges nothing for you to take this additional step.

As a Trading Assistant, you can introduce yourself to local businesses and antique dealers, offering your services to them should they decide they'd like to try moving some inventory on eBay. For more information about the Trading Assistant program click on the Site Map and then the link for the Trading Assistant program, which appears under the Selling Resources heading.

ever been before? Of course you don't. So even if you haven't yet grown into it, get your auction management software up and running as soon as possible. You'll be glad you did.

As long as we're planning ahead, put all your systems in place with an eye toward your future needs. You have no way of knowing right now where that future will take you, and certainly you'll have to adapt your operation countless times before you've reached your goal, but do all your planning with your feet planted in the here and now and your eye looking toward the next level. To make it clear what you'll need, we'll look at your operation in terms of what it takes to complete each task.

Photography

If you haven't already done it, now is the time to invest in that digital camera. This point really is not negotiable. In addition to the camera, you'll also need a photography area. We told you about much of this in chapter 12, but once you've committed to selling as a business, you absolutely have to have an area that you can leave set up and ready for taking pictures quickly and easily. It will slow your operations to an unsustainable pace if you have to set up and take down your photography equipment every time you need to take photos.

Inventory Storage

When you were just selling the occasional item, it didn't matter where you kept it, but now it does. As you know, in order to sustain your business, you have to have enough inventory coming in to keep the orders going out. That means you need to have a storage area where you can keep everything in the meantime. It also means that you can't just stick this stuff in the hallway or stack it up in the corner of your bedroom. You won't be living a happy life if every time you need to go from the kitchen to the bathroom you have to make your way through a maze of boxes. Not only is it depressing, but it's also no way to keep things organized and running smoothly.

Set aside an area to store your inventory that won't be subject to cooking smells, basement odors, or potential damage from pets. Cliff Ennico, host of the Public Broadcasting Service's *Money Hunt,* recommends that you use some duct tape to outline the borders of your inventory storage area right on the floor. Then when you claim that area as a business expense on your taxes, you can clearly prove that this is how you're using the space.

Shipping

As long as you're planning for inventory storage, see if you can't also create your shipping area nearby. Just as your photography efforts require a designated place that you can leave set up and established, so does your shipping operation. If you can put it near your inventory storage area, you'll be saving time and steps between pulling the item you've sold from storage and packing it for shipment. We've sat in on meetings of PowerSellers to hear conversations about whether having your shipping operations three feet (.91m) away from your order-fulfillment table or five feet (1.5m) away makes a significant difference in the amount of time and effort an employee can save in packing orders for shipment. You don't have to think on those levels just yet, but consider the wisdom of making all your systems as convenient as possible for your business. This further means establishing the boundaries that keep your scissors, markers, tape, and packing supplies at your shipping station and not off in someone's room while he finishes his homework. (You know who we mean, buddy.)

Design a Business Plan

The task of developing a business plan is beyond the scope of this book, but you will need to have one in order to know what you must do along the way as you reach each of your goals. You'll want to know where you're headed six months from now, a year from now, and five years from now. How will you know how to get there if you don't know where you're going? Luckily, you don't have to face this task alone. Again, there are plenty of great books on the market about planning a business, and you already know we think your local business librarian should be among your new best friends, but we've got some other advice for you, too.

Marguerite Swope, PowerSeller and eBay Education Specialist, told us that when she first got started she visited her local Small Business Development Center (SBDC). There are more than sixty of these centers around the country. They often have office space at universities. According to Marguerite, they get funding from the state to provide free consultations to new small businesses. "I went to them to set up everything for my taxes," she said. These centers also offer Web-based consulting if there isn't one close by.

Having a business plan will help you clearly see the interim steps you have to take to make your way toward a successful business. Once you've met the necessary requirements, your next step might be to become a Trading Assistant. That way, you can keep building your feedback rating and supplement your sourcing efforts with items your clients bring your way.

You may someday decide you'd like to start teaching as an eBay Education Specialist. That can help your business by gaining you publicity and a local reputation. Students tend to become emissaries for your eBay proficiency, and they may hire you for personal consulting services. You'll also gain exposure as the community at large begins to think of you as the eBay expert. You can learn more about the program at http://pages.ebay.com/esp/. Of course, a supplemental income stream helps, too! So, you see, you have quite a few options open to you, and a business plan will help you focus on your next steps.

Make an Appointment with Your Accountant

If you already have an accountant, now is the time to arrange a meeting. If you don't have an accountant, find one by asking trusted friends for referrals. Talk to him about what you'll need to do to set up your records and files for tax purposes. Tax laws are so complex, and they vary so much from state to state, that only someone who is well versed in your particular needs should be giving you tax advice. There are a few things we know you'll need to do. As we've already mentioned, you'll need to get a federal tax ID number. You'll need this for recording your earnings with the Internal Revenue Service, but you'll also need it if you want to do business with manufacturers. They don't sell to individuals, so you need to have a business, and all businesses need this tax ID. You'll also have to register your business with the proper local governing bodies. For us, that's the county government, but your accountant will know what you have to do in your particular area.

Finally, your accountant will help you establish your record-keeping system and help you decide which accounting software would best fit your needs. Not only will you be operating a business, which means your tax issues will change, but you'll be operating a business from your own home. Working with a professional accountant will ensure that you're complying with all the necessary tax laws, and it will also help you gain all the tax advantages you can from your new status.

It's Been a Great Ride. Now Fasten Your Seat Belts and Off You Go!

Well, we've certainly enjoyed our trip together. To think when you hopped on board, you were just starting out by exploring the idea of buying on eBay. Now you're contemplating a life as one of eBay's PowerSellers. We hope you've enjoyed the trip and feel empowered by all you've learned and done. We're here to tell you that if you are considering a PowerSeller's life, you should fasten your seat belt! You're in for the ride of your life. You'll find more creativity, frustration, reward, challenge, and growth just around the bend than you can possibly imagine right now. You'll be amazed by who you are a year from now, and you'll hardly recognize yourself in five! As our parting gift to you, we've included a couple of appendices. Appendix A gives you a glimpse into the world of selling cars on eBay, and Appendix B is a quick guide to resources we find useful. There's also a glossary. We may not actually meet along life's highway, but we hope to bump into you someday on eBay!

MY BEST eBAY SALE

STEPHEN GANUS, THE POWERSELLER who operates eagleauctionsUSA, told us about his favorite sale. It actually amounts to a series of favorites. Stephen generally specializes in satellite radio equipment, electronics, and a variety of consignments he takes in as a Trading Assistant, but his favorite sale came from a most unlikely source.

"I call this auction 'Train Wreck,'" he told us. Stephen attended a going-out-of-business auction where he found eight big boxes of old model trains. The boxes included Lionel trains, American Flyers, and a variety of other brands, too. There were also pieces of track, transformers, switches, and other odds and ends. Stephen paid $75 for all eight boxes.

From all these tidbits, Stephen put together pieces of this and bunches of that and listed it as "Train Wreck" with about thirty-five separate items included in one listing. He took forty-eight photos to feature the items, and ran a seven-day auction. At the end of the listing, he'd received over a thousand hits and more than thirty bids. The Train Wreck sold for more than $100.

Best of all, that was only one auction listing from this collection of stuff. By the time he was done, Stephen had put up twenty-seven auctions, and he'd earned more than $2,000 from his initial outlay of $75. That's not a bad bit of work. See what we mean when we tell you the rewards are great, even if the work is hard?

Appendix A

Selling Vehicles on eBay

IN CHAPTER 10 WE EXPLORED buying vehicles and real estate on eBay. We told you then how huge eBay Motors is, accounting for more money changing hands than any other eBay category. eBay's Real Estate area, however, is quite modest. So we think it's unlikely you'll be selling property on eBay anytime soon, but you may want to try selling a car, van, or other type of vehicle one day. Please keep in mind that selling big-ticket items on eBay is a subject worthy of its own book. In this guide for beginners, we just wanted to introduce you to some of the things you'll have to consider if you decide you want to sell something so pricey.

To learn more about how to sell vehicles on eBay, we spoke with PowerSellers and Trading Assistants Harvey Levine and Marcia Cooper, who have a lot of experience selling cars on eBay for other people. They have some great stories to share about the cars they've sold over the years. The first car they sold was a 1969 Camaro that belonged to the former manager of the band U2. Since then, they have sold all kinds of cars, but they see collector cars as their specialty. They once sold a 1970 Dodge Charger for almost $84,000. Aside from the jaw-dropping price, what was unusual there was that the car didn't have a transmission or an engine. That coup taught Harvey and Marcia all about the value of certain car bodies to collectors!

Here are a few of lessons we can all learn from Harvey and Marcia when it comes to selling cars on eBay:

1. Be sure you know the value of what you're listing. That means looking at other eBay listings and researching the *Kelley Blue Book* Web site and other Internet sources for information on what your vehicle is worth on the open market. It may also mean having a mechanic check out the car from a prospective buyer's viewpoint, to see what repairs it needs. Armed with these specifics, you can price your car competitively.
2. Write a very detailed, honest description. With a vehicle, or any big-ticket item for that matter, it's crucial to be as detailed as possible in your description. This is not the time to leave out anything, especially a mention of the car's flaws! Include lots of pictures of the vehicle from all angles, inside and out, including photos of any flaws. If you do this, you shouldn't have any problems. Harvey and Marcia tell us that they have never had a car returned, nor has anyone ever said, "It's not what you described."
3. Qualifying buyers will take some extra work. This probably isn't the time to take a chance on someone who is brand-new to eBay, or who has a mediocre feedback record. You must also be 100 percent comfortable with the method of payment your prospective buyer will use. Realize he will probably want to come pick up the car in person, so be prepared for that. Or he may want to have it trucked to his location. He may also want to have his own mechanic check out the car (wouldn't you?). Chapter 10 has more information on these topics, as does the eBay Motors area on eBay.

Here's one more thing about selling cars and other high-priced items: If you aspire to be a PowerSeller, you'll get there much faster by selling such items. You need gross sales of $1,000 a month to reach the bottom rung of the PowerSeller ladder. That's not that difficult if you sell cars. This is why people who sell cars on eBay may have relatively low feedback scores yet be Titanium-level PowerSellers. Harvey and Marcia tell us they are not "huge PowerSellers," but their focus on big-ticket items puts them in the top 5 percent in terms of sales.

Appendix B

Our Favorite Resources for eBay Buyers and Sellers

IT'S SEEMS ALMOST QUAINT these days for a book to include a Resources list, because anyone who has access to the Internet can get up-to-date information on any topic any time they want it. But there's also a lot of noise you have to wade through online, and getting to the good stuff can take some time. So in the interest of getting you up to speed as quickly as possible, we're presenting the sources we regularly use to stay updated on everything eBay-related. We also include some services that you may want to consider if you do decide to start your own eBay business. Of course, Google your heart out when there's a specific topic you're researching. Just watch out for all that noise.

AuctionBytes—http://auctionbytes.com. AuctionBytes is one of our favorite sources for the latest auction news as well as helpful how-to articles. While the site emphasizes eBay, it also covers other auction sites, such as Yahoo! Auctions and Overstock.com. You can search by keyword through its substantial article archives. Be sure to subscribe to NewsFlash, its free newsletter that's e-mailed to subscribers three to four times a week. There are active discussion boards here, too.

Auction Software Review—http://www.auctionsoftwarereview.com/. When you're ready to automate how you list and manage your auctions, it's wise to review the many options available to you. This newsletter is the best place to start that review.

The Bookologist—Resources for Online Booksellers (newsletter) http://www.bookologist.com/cab. An incredible source of information for those selling books online. It includes details on where to buy books for resale, and where and how to research everything related to books, such as author's signatures, first editions, and rare books. There's also information about how to price books, and even how to ship them.

eBay Site Map—www.eBay.com. This is indispensable. We use it every day, sometimes several times a day. It provides easy access to the information that's on the vast eBay site. To reach it, just click on the link for it at the top of most eBay pages.

eBay Stores Discussion Board—http://forums.ebay.com/db2/forum.jspa?forumID=21. eBay's discussion boards and groups vary in how useful they are, but hands-down this is a good one. If you're thinking of opening a store, you have to check it out.

Endicia Internet Postage—http://www.endicia.com/. Endicia is one of several companies offering postage you can print directly from your PC. Stamps.com (http://stamps.com/) is another. Aside from postage, these companies also allow you to print electronic delivery confirmation and insure your packages. They charge a small monthly fee, but offer a free trial so you can assess how useful their services are.

***Entrepreneur's* eBay Startup Guides**—Periodically, *Entrepreneur* magazine publishes these special issues devoted to all aspects of running an eBay business. It's available on newsstands, or check the entrepreneur.com Web site.

HammerTap—http://www.hammertap.com/. We've mentioned Terapeak a lot in this book, but it's not the only source for eBay data that can help you with pricing and sourcing strategies. HammerTap, a division of Bright Builders, a company that helps businesses develop an Internet presence, is another very good source. The jewel in its crown is its DeepAnalysis product, which helps you determine where to start your pricing.

Negative/Neutral Feedback Tool—http://www.toolhaus.org. This is one of several brilliant eBay tools from a small company called Toolhaus.org. It's only natural when you check someone's feedback comments to want to zero in on those that are neutral or negative. Unfortunately, in the case of sellers with a lot of feedback, you could have to scroll through many pages of comments before reaching those that are less than positive. That's why we love this software tool. To use it, you go to the company's Web site, where you merely enter an eBay member's user ID. You're immediately presented with all the negative and neutral feedback comments she has received (or left, if you click the Left By button). This can save you lots of scrolling time. One reason a similar capability isn't available right on the eBay site is that the company doesn't want members to focus unduly on neutrals and negatives. We have more faith in you than that, and think you're smart enough to place the information in context.

Seller Sourcebook (blog)—http://www.sellersourcebook.com/. Not only can the Seller Sourcebook help you create great auctions at reasonable prices, but it can also keep you updated on the latest news from eBay. We subscribe to its blog and suggest that you do as well if you're serious about selling on eBay. First you'll need to create an account, and then just sign up to receive notices when new articles are posted to the Seller Sourcebook blog. You'll receive regular e-mail messages with links to articles of interest to eBay sellers, including news items, tips and tricks to boost your eBay selling, and details on promotions and new features.

Small Business Development Centers—Operated by the U.S. Small Business

Association (SBA), these centers exist to help prospective (and current) small business owners by providing counseling, training, and technical assistance. Specifically, they can offer you pointers on drawing up a business plan, obtaining financing, and marketing your business. There are sixty-three centers throughout the United States (at least one per state). We've checked, and they do work with people looking into starting an eBay business, so we advise you get in touch with the closest one before you get too far along. The SBA also provides counseling services through SCORE (Service Corps of Retired Executives), and you can obtain these services in person or over the phone.

***TREND HUNTER* Magazine**—www.trendhunter.com. This free online magazine features articles on the newest pop-culture trends, often before you may have heard of them. A recent issue, for example, had articles on the comeback that mustaches are making; a taxi service geared to women, called Pink Ladies; and "comfy" sweaters that are big now thanks to Bolivia's new president, Evo Morales (who favors these to shirts and ties). *TREND HUNTER* is certain to provide inspiration and a wealth of ideas for sourcing products and even tweaking your listings.

Glossary

About Me page: A Web page that eBay provides each member for the purpose of telling other members about her background, interests, and qualifications (if she is a seller). Creating an About Me page is especially important for sellers as a way to give buyers background information that doesn't fit within the item description area of an auction or other type of listing.

Ad Format: A type of listing used by sellers of property, or certain items and services on eBay. These are actually more like classified ads, in that they serve as mere advertisements, intended to generate leads. To pursue a transaction, a buyer must independently contact the seller.

Answer Center: The section of eBay's Community area where members help other members who have questions on any topic related to eBay selling or buying.

auction listing: The most familiar and popular type of eBay item listing, whereby a seller sets an opening price and lets bidders determine what the item sells for.

auction management program: Software that enables you to automate (handle more quickly and efficiently) many of the functions associated with eBay selling, such as listing, responding to e-mail and posting feedback, tracking inventory, and generating sales reports. When deciding on an auction management program, be sure to research your needs thoroughly through sites such as Auction Software Review (http://www.auctionsoftwarereview.com/).

Best Offer: When a seller specifies that he will accept a best offer for an item, bidders may e-mail offers lower than the auction price. Sellers are not obligated to accept a Best Offer. You should expect to pay about 10 percent less than the price listed, although there's nothing prohibiting you from making any type of offer you'd like.

bidder search: A type of Advanced Search, which is used to view all the items a bidder has bid on during the previous thirty days.

bid retraction: When a bidder cancels his bid for an item. Bids are "binding" and eBay will only permit you to cancel a bid under certain circumstances. For example, if you make a mistake when you enter your bid, or the seller has significantly changed the item description since you placed your bid. Be sure to bid carefully, because eBay investigates each bid retraction. The company will suspend your account if they feel you have abused this feature. In any case, the number of bid retractions you've made within the previous six months becomes part of your member profile.

Blackthorne Basic: A software application from eBay for automating many of the processes related to creating, posting, and managing listings; it also makes it easier to handle e-mail communications and feedback. The software is desktop-based (that is, you download it to your desktop, as opposed to using it through an Internet site). It's designed for sellers who post twenty-five or more listings a month, and costs $9.99 a month. You can try it for free for thirty days.

Blackthorne Pro: The more advanced version of Blackthorne Basic, designed for higher-volume sellers. Blackthorne Pro has all of Basic's features, but also can handle inventory management, multiple users, the generation of monthly profit-and-loss reports, and a greater variety of listing designs. It costs $24.99 a month, and, as with Basic, a thirty-day free trial is available.

Buy It Now: A type of listing that gives buyers willing to pay the Buy it Now price you've set the opportunity to purchase your item immediately, without having to wait for your auction to end. If no one is willing to pay your Buy It Now price, the auction proceeds as would any other auction. A Buy It Now auction is distinguished by the Buy It Now icon that appears next to the price.

BuySAFE: A company that provides a bonding service for sellers seeking to assure buyers that they are legitimate and trustworthy trading partners. BuySAFE sellers have undergone a thorough background check.

categories: The manner by which eBay organizes the items for sale on its site. One way to locate an item is to browse through the categories. A faster way to find what you're seeking is by searching via the search box.

Completed Listings: eBay listings that have ended within the previous fifteen days, which you can search. By searching Completed Listings, you can get a feel for what a given item might sell for, and what the overall demand for an item may be. To start a Completed Listings search, click on Advanced Search.

discussion boards: The section of eBay's Community area where members can exchange ideas, information, and observations with other members. There are a wide variety of distinct discussion boards, covering just about any eBay topic you can think of, including many popular item categories, such as antiques, dolls, and pottery.

drop-off store: A business that will list and sell items on eBay for you, usually for a percentage of the price realized. Drop-off stores are springing up faster than dandelions in the spring, as they offer an alternative to those who would rather not go through the time and trouble of learning how to sell items on eBay for themselves.

Dutch auction: An auction in which a seller offers a quantity of identical items for sale. Buyers specify how many items they'd liken to buy and how much they are willing to pay. The term *Dutch auction* has pretty much been replaced by *Multiple Item auction.*

eBay Education Specialist: An experienced seller who has completed formal training in how to teach others to sell on eBay. The eBay Education Specialist directory at www.poweru.net/ebay/student/searchIndex.asp lists classes being held by these instructors, as well as their contact information and areas of expertise.

eBay Express: A separate part of eBay, whereby sellers who meet certain criteria can sell fixed-price items. In this way, buyers can be assured that they are buying from sellers who have met certain standards, and they can buy products immediately rather than have to wait for an auction to end. eBay Express is set up more like a traditional Internet retailer, such as barnesandnoble.com.

eBay Live: eBay's once-a-year confab that's a combination party, trade show, and conference, attracting thousands of eBay members. The location varies from year to year.

eBay Motors: An eBay specialty site for the sale of motor vehicles of all types, as well as parts. eBay Motors has many of its own rules and regulations.

eBay stores: Individual areas within eBay, established and run by one eBay member, and featuring only that member's items.

eBay University: eBay's own university (http://pages.ebay.com/university/index.html). eBay University instructors travel from city to city, teaching the basics of buying and selling on eBay. The university also offers courses on more advanced selling techniques. The cost of these courses is reasonable ($59 for a full day of instruction, plus a take-home workbook), so check eBay's site to see when the university will be near you. As an alternative, for $19.95 eBay

University courses are also available online and on CD-ROM. Remember, you'll be getting the official company line (only) when taking eBay University courses, so be sure to supplement what you learn there with your own research.

escrow service: A company that acts as an intermediary between buyer and seller to ensure that an item meets the buyer's expectations. The service will collect, hold, and release payments only when instructed to do so. It's clearly advisable to use an escrow service for large purchases.

feedback: The method by which eBay trading partners rate each other after a completed transaction. Three ratings are possible: positive, neutral, or negative. It's very important to review a prospective trading partner's feedback rating and comments before entering into a transaction.

feedback manipulation: The practice by which buyers or sellers manipulate their feedback scores to appear better established, more experienced, or even more trustworthy to the eBay community. A seller might do this, for example, by selling very inexpensive items, say, a downloadable e-book for $.01. His auction may state that he'll leave buyer feedback upon being paid, thus encouraging buyers to leave feedback as well. eBay frowns upon this practice because it diminishes the reliability of the feedback system.

feedback score: The at-a-glance number that rates an eBay member's performance, as determined by his trading partners. The score consists of all the ratings individual users have given a member. Each positive rating adds a +1 to a feedback score, a neutral doesn't add or subtract anything, and a negative subtracts one (–1).

final value fee: The additional fee you pay to eBay when a listing is successful, that is, it ends with a winning bidder. The amount of this fee is contingent on the amount the winning bidder has agreed to pay for your item.

Fixed Price: This type of listing enables buyers to purchase your item at a set price, and that price only, without having to bid on your item. Sellers must have a minimum feedback score of 10, or be ID verified, in order to list an item in this format.

groups: A part of eBay's Community area, where members can exchange information, files, graphics, and the like, relating to specific topics. Groups are a bit more focused than discussion boards, somewhat more professional in tone, and are of two types: public and private. Public groups, are of course, open to any eBay member, whereas private groups will only accept members whom the group leader has accepted for membership, or who have been invited to join. An example of a private group is the Professional eBay Sellers Alliance (PESA).

HTML (Hypertext Mark-Up Language): The programming language that underlies Internet Web pages. Because HTML is much less complex than other programming languages, you can easily learn basic HTML commands. Knowing a little HTML enables you to enhance your auction descriptions by adding colors and varying the point size and positioning of your text. When you're writing descriptions for your auctions, you can use eBay's built-in HTML editor.

ID verify: The process you can go through (for a $5 fee) to prove your identity, and therefore provide greater assurance to your trading partners that you are who you say you are and that you can be trusted.

insertion fee: The amount eBay charges you to list a given item. This amount generally depends on the minimum price you set for the item when you list it.

listing upgrades: Extra options available to sellers when they're creating listings. These are available for an added fee, and include things such as boldface, highlighting, added pictures, and special placement (for example, on eBay's homepage). The price for upgrades can quickly add up, and whether an option is worth it depends on what you're selling and the price you hope to get for it.

Member ID: The unique name you use to buy and sell on eBay. Also known as a User ID.

member profile: Your eBay rating, consisting of your feedback score (number of individual trading partners you've had) and the level (for example, 99%) of *positive* feedback you've received. Your member profile is the face you show the eBay world. Savvy trading partners will check it before deciding whether or not to do business with you.

merchandise calendar: Where eBay shows you what its homepage will promote over the next few months. The promotion is often geared to a holiday on the horizon (for instance, Father's Day). By knowing what promotions are planned, sellers can anticipate the inventory they might want to look for, and start planning how they will create appropriate auctions. As with so many things on eBay, you'll have a lot of competition, so you may want to feature products on the periphery. For example, for Mother's Day you could sell crafts or picture frames, rather than jewelry or perfume (http://pages.ebay.com/sellercentral/calendar.html).

mutual feedback withdrawal: The process by which a buyer and seller can agree to have a negative feedback number removed from each one's feedback score. While the number is removed (so your score returns to what it was beforehand) the comment remains as part of your permanent eBay record.

My eBay page: Your own area on the eBay site, from which you can monitor and organize all your buying and selling activity. Your My eBay page also contains links to other personal preferences, such as your Favorite Sellers and Searches, as well as links to your account details.

New Old Stock (NOS): One of the many colorful acronyms that are prevalent on eBay. Sellers refer to something as NOS when they purchase old inventory (say, baseball cards from 1965) that had been tucked away somewhere, and therefore appears in "new" condition today. The stock is technically "old" but it's available for sale for the first time and appears new.

PayPal: An eBay company that allows trading partners to securely pay for eBay (and other Internet and offline vendor) purchases via credit or debit card. PayPal is how the majority of buyers pay for eBay purchases, which is why sellers should accept it. PayPal is free for buyers, but there are fees for sellers. Separate PayPal registration is required. See www.paypal.com for more information.

PayPal Buyer Protection: A buyer protection program sellers must qualify for by having at least 50 feedbacks, a 98 percent positive feedback record, and by meeting other criteria. Sellers who offer this protection provide up to $1,000 in purchase protection on qualifying listings. If the phrase *PayPal Buyer Protection* appears in the Seller Information box, then the seller participates in this program.

phishing: When someone uses fake, but real-looking Web sites, or similar means, to steal personal information. For example, someone may send you an e-mail that appears to be from AOL, asking you to confirm your social security number. The e-mail may contain a link that takes you to a site that looks like AOL's. You enter personal information, as directed, only to discover later on that the data went to a scam artist, looking to steal your identity. The term *phishing* comes from *fishing,* suggesting that bait is tossed out in the hope some fool will "bite."

PowerSeller: An eBay seller who has reached a level of gross sales of at least $1,000 for the previous three months, and an overall feedback rating of at least 100, of which 98 percent or better is positive. PowerSellers have a distinctive icon as part of their user IDs. Note that not every seller who reaches this sales level chooses to be a part of the PowerSeller program.

ProStores: The name for an eBay-branded service by which you can set up your own Internet store. In return for providing the templates and other software tools needed to set up and operate their stores, ProStore sellers pay eBay a percentage of their monthly sales.

proxy bidding: The method by which eBay's computers place automatic bids for you up to the maximum bid you first specified. Proxy bids are placed as new bidders compete for an item; eBay will only bid enough for you to maintain your high bidder position.

QuickBooks: An accounting software program, favored by many eBay sellers for managing their basic accounting needs, including recording invoices and receipts, paying bills, creating financial reports, and writing checks. QuickBooks is also useful for keeping tax records. Intuit, Inc., produces QuickBooks. Although it's promoted as easy to use, there's actually a pretty fair learning curve. For help, you can turn to one of the many books on the market or work with your accountant.

reserve: The minimum price a seller will accept for an item. Setting a reserve protects a seller from selling an item for less than she feels it's worth; this is a strategy used by some Trading Assistants as well, to ensure that an item sells for at least what the owner wants for it. However, the presence of a reserve may discourage some buyers from placing bids, since often the reserve price is not revealed within a listing.

second chance offer: An offer sellers may extend to losing bidders under certain circumstances; for example, if the seller has identical items for sale, or if the winning bidder doesn't pay for the item he's won. Unfortunately, some unscrupulous "sellers " use second chance offers to defraud other eBay members, so you must carefully evaluate and verify such offers.

seller search: When you search eBay for a particular seller. To get to the Web page where you can do this, click on Advanced Search, which appears along the top of most eBay pages.

Sellers Sourcebook: A company that provides inexpensive services for eBay sellers, including image hosting and auction templates. Their Web address is www.sellersourcebook.com.

Selling Manager: eBay's Internet-based selling tool for automating the creation of listings, tracking sales information, and handling buyer communications. Selling Manager is designed to be used with Turbo Lister (see below). A monthly subscription costs $4.99.

Selling Manager Pro: A more sophisticated version of Selling Manager, geared to high-volume sellers, and available for $15.99 a month.

shill bidding: When a seller submits a fake bid, or enlists others to do so, to inflate the price of an item. eBay, of course, frowns on this activity (see http://pages.ebay.com/help/policies/seller-shill-bidding.html) and suggests that family members and coworkers not even bid on each other's items to avoid the appearance of shill bidding. This seems unreasonable. As long as you intend to honor your bid, you can bid on a friend's auction, or even your sister's. But you'd better mean it! In a variation of shill bidding, some "sellers" create auctions for items that don't even exist, to scoop up "winning bids" from unsuspecting buyers. Obviously, once the money is collected, the sellers are never heard from again. This is one more reason to check out your prospective trading partners very carefully.

shipping calculator: A free calculator you can add to your listings that buyers may use to determine their shipping costs, based on their zip codes and the shipping method chosen. You may also specify that the handling fee you set is automatically added to these charges.

Site Map: Here's one of eBay's best-kept secrets. From eBay's Site Map, you have one-click access to many of eBay's most important areas. You can reach the Site Map from almost any eBay screen (the link is right along the top, next to Home, Pay, Register, and Services). Click the link, and you'll see many of eBay's areas displayed there as hyperlinks. Everything falls under one of only a few major headings (Browse, Search, Sell, My Community, and Services). Use the Site Map regularly, and you're likely to stay ahead of your eBay competition.

Skype: Software that lets Internet users make free computer-to-computer calls. eBay owns the company that provides Skype, so it's likely that one day eBay members will be able to Skype each other (yes, it's a verb, too) easily, right through the eBay site.

sniping programs: Web-based services that automatically submit buyers' bids in the last few seconds of an auction, enabling "snipers" to win out over other bidders. To use such sites, you simply enter the auction number for the item you want to snipe. The program takes over, entering your bid so late in the auction that other buyers don't have time to react (unless they're also using sniping software that happens to be quicker on the draw than yours). While some of these programs are free to use, most charge a nominal fee, usually per snipe. One such program is BidNip (http://bidnip.com/), the program we happen to use. Be careful: Sniping programs can give you a sense of invincibility, and you may find yourself participating in more auctions than you would otherwise.

spoof e-mail: A fake e-mail, purportedly from a reliable person or company, which is intended to separate you from your money. An example would be when a "seller" sends you an e-mail with a second chance offer, but doesn't have the item in question. To ensure that an eBay-related e-mail is legitimate, check to make sure it appears in the My Messages section of your My eBay page.

SquareTrade: A company specializing in verifying the safety of online transactions. SquareTrade also provides a dispute resolution service.

Standard Purchase Protection program: The free eBay program that protects buyers by reimbursing them up to $200 (minus a $25 processing fee), if an item isn't received or is "significantly not as described" in the listing.

tax ID number (also known as a resale certificate): A sales tax ID number that allows you to legitimately sell in your state. You must go through your state government to obtain one. For further information, just type "Tax ID Number [your state]" into Google, and the link you need should appear within one of the first few citations. The forms you must complete may even be online. Your library's business librarian can also provide the information you need in minutes.

Trading Assistants: Seasoned eBay sellers who make their services available to others who would like to sell items on eBay, but prefer to let someone else do the work for them. Trading Assistants (http://pages.ebay.com/help/confidence/know-seller-trading-assistant.html) must meet some basic requirements (feedback ratings of at least 100, for example). Their fee is usually a percentage of your item's selling price. While eBay helps promote Trading Assistants by including a searchable directory of them on its site, it doesn't endorse or approve them, so be sure to check out prospective Trading Assistants thoroughly by reviewing their member profiles and checking with past customers.

Turbo Lister: A free software program, available from eBay, that makes it simpler to create and upload listings in quantity. With Turbo Lister you can create your listings offline (when you're not on the eBay site) and upload them at your convenience.

User Agreement: The agreement you agree to abide by when you register for eBay. It spells out the terms under which you may buy and sell on eBay.

user ID: The name that you use on the eBay site, and which you create during the registration process. Also known as your username or member ID.

username: Another way to refer to your eBay user ID or member ID.

Want It Now: An eBay service that enables you to post an ad on the eBay site, describing an item you'd like to buy. This is a relatively new service, and we suggest you use it sparingly. Be prepared to wade through off-target responses.

Index

C

D

E

F

G

H

I

J

K

L

M

N

O

P

Q

R

S

T

U

V

W